The Net

Sherif Hetata

Translated from the Arabic
by the author

Zed Books Ltd.

The Net was first published in Arabic under the title
al-Shabaka, in 1982; it was first published in English by
Zed Books Ltd., 57 Caledonian Road, London N1 9BU, UK,
and 171 First Avenue, Atlantic Highlands,
New Jersey 07716, USA, in 1986.

Cover designed by Henry Iles.

British Library Cataloguing in Publication Data

Hatátah. Šaríf
  The net.
  I. Title
  892'.736[F]   PJ7832.A757

ISBN 0-86232-533-1
ISBN 0-86232-534-X Pbk

The Net

Part I

Khalil Mansour Khalil

"Do you deny having murdered Ruth Harrison on the morning of the 17 August 1980?" The President's voice came from somewhere far above on the elevated rostrum. It seemed to arise from deep down inside him, to echo hollowly in the huge courtroom. His lips were immobile, his face expressionless. The spear-headed bars of the box where I sat brandished a threat. But I had become a bird flying in a calm blue sky.

"Yes, I do. What I have described is exactly what happened."

"Are there other details you wish to mention to the court?"

I watch their eyes look out through metal rimmed spectacles, and the play of electric light on the lenses, see the lawyers' dark robes flutter restlessly and then become motionless.

"The Court must be told everything. How else can it judge this case?"

Where have I seen that mouth before? In the concentration camp? Everything is strangely lucid, in slow motion, precise. No, not in the concentration camp . . . but where? Ah, now I remember. A mouth like a trap, with lips that disappeared each time the cane was lifted ready to fall on my body. Headmaster, missionary, and British spy who led the morning prayer, and in the evening read passages from the Bible.

The dry hollow tones from above brought me back to the present. "How did you first become acquainted with Ruth Harrison?"

I can see her wide open eyes staring at me from the pillow.

I closed the door of her room and returned to where I had been sitting near the window. I could feel Gaafar's stare going through me, like dark, icy liquid. I didn't need much imagination to know what would happen now. I could see them coming, in a grey van, crowding through the door, slipping the handcuffs around my wrists, hear the quick, cold clicks as the teeth sank into their grooves, closing the steel tightly over flesh and bone. They were new handcuffs, imported recently, very different from the clumsy British ones from which I used to slip my hands so easily. Yes, I knew to the most minute detail what would happen once Gaafar had put down the receiver. Yet it was I who looked up the number in the little blue diary she gave me. She had noted down all the numbers I might need, including that of the "Emergency Police".

Just one bullet. I kept turning the idea over in my mind. I stood up. My feet led me through the corridor back to her room. Her once rebellious hair lay over the pillow and the scarlet stain continued to seep from beneath her pallor. My fingers touched the smooth surface of her arm, then jerked back as though stung by a lingering warmth. The shock brought me back to reality. I am seized by a strange sense of having at last escaped her, of becoming myself once more.

"The court is waiting for an answer. How did you come to know Ruth Harrison?"

Perhaps it is best to start with that evening when the telephone rang in my house. It was a summer evening, fresh and innocent, with a scent of flowers. The white-washed walls of the house stood silently at the edge of the open fields. Many houses had sprung up in the Cairo suburb of Dar El Salam and it was no different from them, except that we had transformed the roof top into a terrace with chairs, an umbrella, and earthenware pots planted with orange and purple flowers.

Amina had moved into this house when she left her parents. We had married less than a year after I was released from prison, and settled in the same house. We couldn't afford a more expensive home, nor the money to furnish it. We both worked nearby in Helwan, so that the small, three-roomed house, the peaceful open fields and the modest rental, together constituted a satisfying combination.

I remember that summer evening very well. I was seated at my desk examining the contract we were planning to sign with the French pharmaceutical concern, Larochelle. Amina was away, visiting a friend in Minia. The lamp shed a circle of light on the desk, leaving the rest of the room in darkness. From the cup placed before me rose the aroma of coffee mingled with spices.

I remembered that when I went to his office that morning he had not invited me to have the usual cup of coffee. A trifle, yet it reflected his streak of meanness. I sat in front of his desk, my eyes travelling over the photographs on the wall. The Chairman surrounded by a circle of smiling faces as he shook the hand of some foreign visitor. The Chairman talking to the Minister at the inauguration of the new plant. The Chairman giving a speech to the workers on the anniversary of "Corrective Revolution Day".

The desk separating us looked bigger than ever before. The conference table, forlorn and neglected, was pushed against the wall at the far end of the room. A characterless, formless room; an empty space in which chairs, tables, shelves, cupboards, a desk, a photo-copying machine, papers and files, and two telephones had been placed for the use of its occupant.

He seemed quite at home in this charmless and rather dusty medio-crity. He was a man with a powerful voice which, when raised, could make the window panes in his room vibrate. He was also very tall. The loud voice he reserved for lesser employees. His tallness was concentrated in the lower limbs, so that seated behind his desk he looked short.

I bided my time, waiting for him to finish with the papers he was examining with deep concentration, as though he had forgotten my presence. His eyes were small and when he raised them they were never still, but darted rapid glances around the room. The movements of his hands and lips indicated the contained anxiety he was wont to relieve by unexpected bursts of laughter or anger. He had a small flattened head and an elongated face, and when he smiled his lips drew back to reveal two rows of large, yellow teeth. Sometimes in my dreams he would take on the form of a horse sitting behind the huge desk. Now and again he would lean back and drum with his fore hoofs on the wooden surface, while I sat staring bemusedly at a pair of flaring nostrils and bloodshot eyes.

At last he lifted his head and said: "This report you have written about the contract with Larochelle. I want you to amend it."

"Amend it? why?"

"The conclusions you have reached are not all to the interest of the company. For example, most of the pharmaceutical products listed for joint production can be a source of substantial profits."

His glance kept moving round the room, his eyes like little animals sensing a trap; they always seemed to be in search of something. He had inherited three pharmacies in Gharbieh Province from his father, and had later added a factory in Cairo, and an import-export office for chemicals and drugs. After the nationalizations of 1961 he joined the public sector where he settled down to wait for the storm to blow over, for he had soon realized that Nasser had overlooked something important. In the absence of a real popular alliance, the nationalized sector could become an instrument only in the hands of the new capitalist class.

"I am not opposed to our company making profits, on the contrary. Nor do I object to an agreement with Larochelle which would include production of those new drugs for which we lack the necessary expertise. My objections are limited to the joint production of drugs already on the company list, and which we can continue to produce without help from anyone. If Larochelle comes in here it can only be at our expense, and at the expense of the national drug industry in general."

The previous month he had visited Larochelle's plant in France. He came back with rosy cheeks, an expensive Rolex wristwatch, and a purple necktie, signed Jacques Fath. His conversation shifted to new subjects. Instead of dwelling on the seductiveness of women from Mansourah, and the beneficial effects of hashish smoking on the brain and of regular prayers on the soul, he now discoursed with authority on the beauty of Paris, its streets, its numerous restaurants, the sexual arts of French women, and the flavours of French wines.

His rasping voice cut through my chain of thoughts.

"Am I to infer, therefore, that you refuse to make changes in your report?"

"I have expressed what I think is in the best interests of the company and, therefore, I see no reason to amend it. What difference does my opinion make, since in any case I am not the one who makes the decisions? If you wish to sign this contract as it stands my report should be no obstacle. All you need is the agreement of the Board of Directors and that should not be difficult to get. But you cannot force me to say what I do not believe to be true."

I had been speaking calmly, but lurking inside me was a desire not to antagonize the man. It was useless trying to swim against the current; things were very different these days. Yet what exactly was I afraid of? It was most unlikely that I would lose my job. Besides, did it really matter? At least I would be rid of the feeling of worthlessness, almost smallness, which often assailed me. But then, I would have to start looking for work again, and there was no guarantee that if I did find a new job it would be any different from the present one.

He pressed the bell and a moment later one of the messengers appeared and stood motionless, waiting for his orders.

"A cup of coffee and a packet of Kent cigarettes."

He had omitted to ask me whether I would like coffee. I knew it was intentional. I hesitated for a moment — it was such a trifling thing, I could have let it pass. But suddenly I felt it was the most important thing that had happened between us that morning. It was as though he was saying to me: "You are just an employee working under my orders. You are a nobody and I can afford to ignore you."

I addressed the messenger across the room: "Ali, please bring me a cup of coffee with just a strain of sugar."

I could hear his fingers tapping on the desk. The messenger stood by the door without moving, as though he had sensed that something was going on. He threw the Chairman a questioning glance but receiving no response went out, closing the door silently behind him. I caught a gleam of anger in the bloodshot eyes as they rested on my face for a moment, before resuming their fretful movement.

"If you are only concerned with the interests of the company why did you publish that article about patents in *Gama-heer?*"

Now we had arrived at the crux of the matter. As long as everything went on behind closed doors he had no reason to worry. But once they came out into the open it could be dangerous. If people found out what was happening they might start to do something about it. As I kept silent he resumed: "Would it not be better if you paid more attention to your own affairs instead of worrying about such matters. There is no reason for you to go looking for trouble. You probably do not know that the Minister is considering the possibility of referring you for prosecution. This is confidential and I should not be speaking to you about it. But I owe it to you, since you are one of the employees of the company."

I wondered whether what he said about my being prosecuted was true. My mouth went dry, and I stretched out a hand to the glass of water on the desk, took a few sips and put it back.

I could feel his glance flitting over my face. Friendly advice and small wary eyes had pursued me ever since my student days. The man was dressed in a black uniform and pieces of metal shone on his shoulder. He lifted the telephone receiver and spoke into it pronouncing his words with a quiet emphasis: "Let him go this time. Then we shall see."

I walked out into the summer night. I love summer nights . . . the scent of flowers, the stars . . . I went to close the shutters, then the telephone rang. I had no desire to talk to anyone but it continued to peal insistently as though whoever was calling knew that there was someone at home. As I put the receiver to my ear a woman's voice spoke: "Hello. Is that the house of Khalil Mansour Khalil?" She spoke Arabic with a foreign accent.

"Yes. Who is speaking please?"

"Oh. My name is Ruth Harrison."

The judge sitting on the right of the President reminded me of Nahas Pasha. The benevolent features, the marked squint, and the large mouth with a toothbrush moustache. The only thing missing was the fez. His right eye stared fixedly at me while the left wandered off somewhere in space. Whenever I spoke he would lean forward over the massive wooden table as though trying to catch every word. Sometimes he gave almost imperceptible shakes of his head which I interpreted as signs of approbation, compensating at least partially for the attitude of cold neutrality and boredom which the President had maintained from the beginning. The changing light of day shed moving shadows over the rigid faces looking down upon me from above like the statues of antiquity. On the granite hill hung the temple of Ramses, and below it flowed white sails in an afternoon sun.

That summer night was laden with the scent of Jasmine. The Arabic spoken with an American accent took me by surprise. I missed the first few words, but after a moment picked up what she was saying: "I tried to phone you at the beginning of the year, but no one answered. Then I left for the United States and returned only last week. One of my friends suggested that when I came to Cairo I should meet you. I lecture in the International Institute for Third World Countries, which opened an office in Cairo a year ago. My area of interest is research related to the trade union movement."

I remained silent as her words flowed over the telephone wires. She stopped abruptly and asked: "Hello . . . Is my Arabic understandable?"

"Yes, it's very clear" I said, and almost added "and your voice is beautiful." She went on: "My friend told me that you are involved in studies on the trade union movement and have also engaged in a certain amount of trade union activity. Please correct me if I'm wrong."

"No your information is accurate. But I am not a specialist in the area."

"I will be in Cairo for some time. I would like to meet you. Is that possible?"

"Excuse me, but could you please tell me the name of the friend who spoke to you about me?"

"Oh . . . of course. Professor Aida Ragab. We were living in the same house for some time."

I thought quickly, trying to recall a face that fitted the name of Aida Ragab, but failed.

"I think I have heard the name before but I'm afraid that I am not able to remember who the lady is."

I heard a faint scratching noise in the receiver followed by silence. Perhaps she was embarrassed by my answer, or thought I was trying to avoid meeting her. Why had she chosen me of all people? She could easily get whatever information she might need from official sources. On the other hand perhaps she had learnt about my previous activities and wanted to hear a different point of view. I could meet her just once. That voice!! It moved with such richness up and down the scale. Besides she had made an effort to reach me, and it was so rare to find someone interested in people like myself nowadays. I said: "Hello." She answered quickly, "Hello."

"What is it that you want of me exactly?"

"I would like to ask you a number of questions about the trade union movement in Egypt. I am interested in the period from the end of the Second World War to the eve of the July Revolution. I am preparing a thesis on the subject, but I am still in the initial phase, gathering facts and information, and sifting out the different points of view concerning the development of the movement."

"I will try to answer your questions. When shall we meet?"

"I think it is for you to suggest a convenient time. After all it is I who stand to benefit."

"Not at all. I am looking forward to our exchange and to the pleasure of meeting you. Would next Thursday at six be convenient?"

"Yes . . . Where can we meet?"

"We can meet here at my house, if you like."

She didn't answer immediately, then said: "May I suggest instead that we meet at my place, if it is no trouble to you. I still find it difficult to locate places in Cairo. Besides I will have to carry the things I might need with me, whereas at home everything is at hand."

"If you wish. Then it's agreed. Next Thursday at six. I wish you a good night."

I heard her laugh in a voice full of amusement. "Don't you want to know my address?"

I laughed back and answered quickly, "Excuse my forgetfulness. Where do you live?"

"My flat is on Nile Bank Road. Number 141. Ninth Floor, Flat 54."

"I know the road, so it will be easy to find your flat."

"Then I look forward to seeing you on Thursday. Thank you very much. Good night."

There was a click as she replaced the receiver. I sat there, resting my head against the back of the chair, my legs stretched out, still holding the receiver in my hand. Aida Ragab, Aida Ragab. Suddenly I remembered. That must have become her name after she married. In those days her name was Aida Rashid, and Aida has a sister called Tahani whom I knew very well. How could I have forgotten Tahani Rashid?

I collected the papers scattered over my desk, put them away, and turned off the light. I undressed quickly, slipped between the fresh, white sheets, and stretched out my legs in voluptuous anticipation of the few hours sleep which lay ahead of me. I was aching with fatigue after the hours spent sitting at my desk. But inside was a feeling of deep satisfaction. I had gone through the contract word by word, and carefully worked out a limited number of changes meant to go half way towards meeting the Chairman's requirements. There was no sense in adopting a rigid stand. This damned contract was not going to change the course of history! After all, I had to earn a living . . . The warm tones of her voice still echoed in my ears like distant music.

I remembered how it was Amina's voice that first drew my attention to her. I was seated in the suburban train on my way to Helwan. My eyes were closed and a winter sun warmed my face, penetrating my eyelids with an orange glow.

I opened my eyes each time we approached a station, to watch the dense crowds rush over the platform, surge through the doors in a struggling mass of bodies, until they had filled every inch of space in the carriage. They would remain motionless until the train neared the next station, then something like a high tension current of movement would pass through the human mass in preparation for the coming battle.

I heard her speaking to someone. The ring in her voice caught my ear. It radiated with pure optimism, a full and spontaneous joy. Yet beneath it I sensed a seriousness which every now and then was swept aside by small avalanches of delighted laughter. Her voice came to me from somewhere nearby. I kept my eyes closed, enjoying its freshness, letting myself be carried along on its flow, until someone stepped on my foot. I turned round and found myself gazing into two black eyes. Their look was steadfast, almost taunting, and I quickly dropped my eyes as though I had been caught in a shameful act, for I still felt intimidated when faced by a woman. After a while I looked around for her again, but she had disappeared in the crowd. Gone with her was a sudden sensation of "coming alive" that her voice had awakened within me. Once again I was assailed by an obscure feeling of sadness as though I was just hovering on the edge of life — a barely perceptible sadness, a dismal half light, like dusk, and so elusive that at each moment it seemed to be there and yet not there inside me, a dream aborted or a still-born hope. From the moment I walked out of the huge wooden portico into the street, only when I was deeply absorbed in something, could I forget.

But now my life entered a new phase. Every day I took the morning train like thousands of others, rushed with them over the platform to catch it in the nick of time, sat at a desk, read files, drank coffee and gradually slipped into the daily, unchanging routine. At the end of the day I would hurry back home with the jostling crowds, eager to take refuge in my room.

I was now an employee. Nothing distinguished me from the others except perhaps for a tiny flame which continued to burn inside. Through the window of the train I watched the houses go by, and wondered whether this was all.

At moments a sudden panic took hold of me. I would jump out of the train before it came to a stop, and rush out of the station, fleeing from a net I could almost see closing around me. The city harried me with short bayonets fixed to automatic rifles, with bottles of Vat 69 and off-shore banks, with the roar of endless traffic and the glare of blinding lights, with the beat of disco music and the muezzin's call to prayer in the quietest hour of night, with sewer water in the back streets, and gas fumes in my eyes. I could see my city falling apart, its entrails bursting with people, its arteries blocked with cars. And there I was pushing my way through the crowded streets, a stranger searching for the things I had once known and could recognize, for the ring of truth in a voice which would lighten my heart.

The train raced from one station to another. I stood, hemmed in by a mass of bodies. A woman's voice rang out pure and vibrant, over the clatter and thud of wheels. I had been hoping to hear her voice again ever since that morning when I had first heard it. Something within me came to life. My eyes travelled slowly over the people crowded on the seats, and thronging the aisles. I found myself contemplating two black eyes that returned my look with a serene confidence. This time I tried not to lose sight of her, but every now and then my increasingly insistent looks were interrupted by the head, the arm or the movement of some passenger. Her hair was rich, falling in dense waves to the shoulders. I kept saying to myself: "don't run away from this encounter." As the train drew near to Helwan I saw her edge slowly towards the door. She was tall and slender, her black hair shone in the sunlight flickering through the windows.

I pushed my way through in her wake, oblivious to the voices muttering in protest. She walked slowly down the platform by the side of her companion, her long limbs moving gracefully, her waist narrowed abruptly above the fullness of her hips. I contemplated her with the emotion of someone embarking on a wonderful experience. My heart beat strongly. I felt fearful, bold, determined and hesitant all at once. My pace quickened when I came up to her, I said: "Good morning", in a firm voice.

She turned her head towards me, but before she had time to answer I continued: "Please excuse me. My name is Khalil Mansour, I work in the Thebes Pharmaceutical Company. I have seen both of you in the train before, and assume you work in Helwan. Do you mind if I accompany you part of the way so we can talk?"

She examined me with a long steady look. Everything around seemed to recede and disappear, except her eyes with their expression of unhurried contemplation, as though I was being carefully weighed; her full lips pouted slightly as she framed the words: "No, of course not. My name is Amina Tewfik," and waving her hand towards her companion, she added. "And this is my friend Aleya Moustapha."

I nodded my head in greeting and was silent, searching for words to continue the conversation. She came to my rescue with a question: "How long have you been working in Helwan?"

"Since last August."

"I saw you in the train only once."

Cautious but confident in herself, I thought. Just once, and she had not forgotten. My heart was beating quietly now.

"The train is always so crowded. Besides, maybe we take it at different hours. I also saw you only once."

I could see she had not missed my point. A quick smile lit up her face. She reacted with a calm, yet immediate spontaneity. "Do you remember when that was?"

"Yes. Four and a half months ago. Your voice attracted my attention. You were standing in the aisle talking to Miss Aleya Moustapha."

She looked pleased, but turned the conversation away from herself by remarking: "My friend is married, and has two children."

"She looks like a young university student," I said.

Their laughter rang out over the monotonous sound of hurrying feet. On one of the balconies I glimpsed rows of flowers, their colours vivid under the morning sun.

My mind flew over desert sands. There was an artesian well but its water came up hot, so we dug a reservoir two metres deep, forty metres long and twenty-five metres wide, using a plough drawn by oxen, and shovels. We used to leave the water to cool in the reservoir at night, and run it out through a canal to irrigate the reclaimed land during the day. Around the sides we embedded aquatic plants, and at the end of the day's work sat there looking at the wide expanses of sand, the setting sun, and the colourful flowers.

The vibrant ring of her voice cut through my wanderings: "What are you thinking about?"

I shrugged my shoulders and said: "The flowers," pointing to the balcony.

She eyed me curiously. When we arrived in front of a high wall with a big gate guarded by men in blue uniforms, she turned to me and said: "This is where we work. It's called the International Modern Furniture Company." There was a hint of irony in the way she pronounced the name. "I am head of the designing section and Aleya is responsible for plan execution."

"Then this is where we part?"

"Yes."

I hesitated, reluctant to continue on my way. My heart had started thumping again. If I said nothing, this could be the end. The thought made me bolder than usual: "How can we meet again?"

She answered slowly, as though turning something over in her mind. "We take this train every morning at half-past seven from Dar El Salam."

We shook hands quickly, and they passed through the big gate, disappearing behind the wall. For a moment I felt I was on the verge of losing something very precious. My feet remained rooted to the ground. A few passers-by threw curious glances at me, as I stood there. So I moved along mingling with the early morning crowd.

We started to meet every day at the station of Dar El Salam. Usually she came alone. Whatever barriers there might have been between us quickly broke down and we talked freely. She had been married to a doctor of medicine, but before the first year of their marriage was over, they divorced. He wanted her to resign from work and devote all her time to the home. Since then she had refused to marry again. After the divorce she went to live with her parents, but with a deep need to be alone, she rented a small house in Dar El Salam. There she spent most of her free time, reading, painting, or receiving friends. There had been little room in her life for relations with men. Once a certain intimacy developed, they started to interfere in her life, tried to take decisions for her; she was now turned thirty. I watched the corners of her mouth lift in a smile as she said: "Men do not like intelligent, independent women. Lack of self-confidence seems to be a male characteristic."

She ended her sentence with a burst of laughter. A couple of passengers stared at us as though we had been caught kissing in public, but she did not seem to notice anything. "I have a small studio in my house, but my work does not leave me enough time for painting. I've done nothing really worthwhile."

I looked forward to these meetings with a growing eagerness. I used to take the train from Bab El Louk to Dar El Salam, waking up at dawn in order to be on time and ensure that she wouldn't have to wait for me. The moment I saw her walking over the platform towards me everything seemed to take on different colours. With her I opened up to life again, to the green of the fields, the dark glow of the Nile under a setting sun, the flavour of liquorice sherbet, or a meal of brown beans shared with her during the luncheon hour. Now nothing was the same as before. My ears detected a hidden music in the calls of street vendors, the flutter of birds, the turning of wheels. We stood in the train, our bodies touching, oblivious to the waves of people surging around us, as though on an island. Or we sat, looking out of the window at the children playing in a yard, donkey carts covered with neat piles of vegetables, the sun shining out of a blue sky.

It was a summer evening, full of the fragrance of flowers. Our footsteps echoed on the station platform, abandoned by the habitual crowds of waiting people. At the bottom of the steps a group of children were playing hopscotch, jumping over the squares and rectangles and circles chalked in white. Heaps of water melons piled on the pavements mysteriously, dark green under the street lights. The evening crowds bustled around the shops making last minute purchases before dinner.

We traversed a narrow street between two rows of houses. The night air was filled with the throaty hiss of kerosene stoves burning in the kitchens. We stopped in front of a low wooden gate; she pushed it

14

open and we continued over a short, narrow path and then up a few stone steps, their white surface shining in the dark. I heard the subdued wheeze of the bolt ending in a soft thud, as she shot it back. To guide my steps I put a hand on her shoulder, felt it warm beneath the fine material of her dress. She pressed a switch and the lights revealed a hall, bookshelves rising to the ceiling, two armchairs, a sofa and a table. The walls were white and the furniture stained a dark, mahogany brown. The room was alive with flaming pinks, oranges and crimsons in the chair covers, the curtains, and the handwoven rugs. On the wall, opposite the front door was a painting of a woman, weaving a carpet.

Amina pointed to one of the armchairs, stood motionless. in the centre of the room for a moment, and then turning asked abruptly, "Do you want to eat? I have some yoghourt, white cheese, eggs, bread and tea."

"What about you?"

"Yes, I think I'll have something too."

"Then I'll join you."

"While I prepare the meal, you can lie on the sofa and rest."

She disappeared in the interior of the house, and soon returned with a tray which she placed on the low table between us. Her movements were quick, slightly tense, as though she was doing something for which she had no patience. I felt she was making an effort to please me. She went away again and came back after some time with a plate of toasted sandwiches, then while I held the ladder for her, she extracted a jar of lemon pickles and an earthenware pot of honey from a cupboard near the kitchen ceiling. She seemed happy and at ease in my presence despite the late hour.

It was the first time since I was set free that I didn't feel a stranger in somebody else's house. My body seemed to relax of its own accord in the armchair as I sat listening to the rich tones of her voice: "Next time you must come during the day so that I can show you the studio I have set up on the roof. I would have liked to devote myself entirely to painting. But my circumstances do not permit me to do it yet. There are things I want to express on a canvas, but instead I am wasting my time designing furniture. It's true I get some pleasure out of it, since I can create useful and sometimes beautiful things. But this is not really my domain. I feel I have a talent for painting and if I work hard should be able to do something really outstanding. Perhaps if I had more courage I would abandon my work in the factory. Several times I was on the point of taking the plunge, but each time I retreated at the last moment. How can I live without a job? That's the real problem."

There was a hint of sadness in her voice. At moments like this she seemed to forget where she was, as though transported to another world. She made a visible effort to return, and once more the sparkle returned to her eyes. She turned to me and said: "Tell me more about yourself."

"It's past three in the morning. Time for me to go. We'll continue our conversation some other time."

She looked into my eyes. Her voice had a quality of deep restfulness about it. "Why do you want to leave? It's a long way home. Here we are close to your office, so why not stay the night? We'll have breakfast in the garden and then take the train."

I felt intimidated, not by her invitation, but because she always seemed to be one step ahead of me, always able to transcend formalities and go straight to the core of things. I kept silent for a moment then said slowly: "Why not? I like being with you."

"Then why don't you express what you feel."

"People aren't used to that."

"Who cares about people?! I decide for myself what to do, and what not to do, at least in matters which concern me." She rested her head on the back of the chair for a while then added in a quiet voice: "There's another bed in my room. You can sleep on that."

"I can sleep here on the sofa, instead of inconveniencing you."

She gave me a quizzical look.

"As you wish. The bed is much more comfortable and I've sprayed my room to chase away mosquitos. It's time to get some sleep, otherwise we won't wake up in the morning."

She put out the lights. I could hear her undress in the dark, and then lie on the bed. My eyes remained wide open. I could not dispel the vision of her hair, her lips, her powerful body. Hot, sharp needles of desire flowed through me. I heard her whisper. "Are you still awake?"

"Yes."

"What are you thinking?"

"Nothing of importance. I suppose it's just that I'm not used to the bed, or perhaps . . ."

"Perhaps what?"

"Perhaps, if I were closer to you . . ."

My heart was beating strongly. It seemed a long time before she answered.

16

"I also would like to be close to you. But promise not to touch me. I am not ready for you. Maybe later . . ."

Suddenly I felt her warm body slip into the bed by my side. She drew my head on to her shoulder, and put her arm around me. I heard her say in a low voice: "Now you can sleep."

Amina Tewfik

I hesitated for a long time before deciding to attend his trial. I was pulled in different directions. I felt that if I attended I would never be able to regain that control over myself which had permitted me to endure the most difficult circumstances, never be able to be myself again. But in the end I realized the need to stand by his side. I could not let him down now. He had harmed and hurt me very deeply. I no longer loved him. But I could not forget that once he had given me a lot, and done many worthwhile things.

Nowadays, when I think over all that happened between us, I have a growing tendency to dwell on the things which attracted me to him. He treated me really as his equal, not just as a woman, as other men I had known before him had done. His hatred of oppression did not diminish. He had weaknesses, which I began to notice as the days went by. I knew what went on in his mind, and very often I could predict how he would act. Real love however does not permit one to divide up a person. I saw him as a whole, as a man worthy of my affection. For Khalil Mansour Khalil had qualities that made a woman like myself admire and love him very much.

I know they want to use me as a witness against him, to play on my feelings, on a possible desire for vengeance, or a jealousy. The prosecutor and the SSSPS have tried repeatedly to influence me with promises and threats. They don't understand that it's useless. I cannot deny that sometimes the idea of vengeance has occurred to me. But after thinking things over I decided that all I could do was to stand up for the truth. And the truth in this case is that Khalil Mansour Khalil did not kill Ruth Harrison.

17

A long silence lay heavily over the court room. The bodies of the judges seemed to shrink behind the huge table, as though they were taking refuge on the high rostrum. The glitter of the electric lights in their spectacles seemed to wane. I stood in front of them, upright. Only the movements of my fingers betrayed the tautness of mind and body holding me up. My voice rang out clearly in the court room. I looked into his eyes and once more lived the journey of our life.

They want to know why I married Khalil Mansour Khalil, what he did after we married, and why later I decided to leave him? Difficult questions, not because I haven't thought of them, but because to answer them I must disclose a world of thoughts and emotions I have kept concealed.

That night he slept in my arms like someone who feels that at last he is in safe hands. I stayed awake until the morning. I, too, felt calm and at peace with myself, listening to the regular sound of his breathing as he slept. I felt I had given him rest from a conflict which was shaking his depths. When I saw him in the train there was a sadness about him, a shadow that floated on his face. He sat near the window and my eyes observed him without haste. His lids were closed but I felt the eyes beneath were wide awake. Suddenly he opened his eyes, turned and looked me straight in the face. I found myself gazing into the clear water of a mountain lake, then he turned away.

The days and months went by but I did not forget. Then one morning I saw him standing in the aisle amidst the usual crowds that take the train. He got down at the same station, and followed us over the platform, down the steps and into the road. I was with my friend Aleya. It was a sunny winter day, and the clover in the fields was a bluey green. The imminent encounter with this man made my heart beat in a strange way. The caution of past years seemed to melt away in the warmth of his looks as they rested on my face. As we crossed the road, and mounted the opposite pavement I felt his glance travel over my back. A moment later he was by my side. He said "Good morning. Do you mind if I accompany you part of the way?" And by the time we got to the plant we had agreed to meet again. It all seemed to happen so easily.

We met every morning at the Dar El Salam station, took the train to Helwan, and then walked to the plant where I worked. We met again during the luncheon hour, and ate together in the fields, or in a small eating-place.

I had a few friends at the time but we met only occasionally. With

Khalil, however, from the beginning, things were different. He came into my life like a summer breeze. He had none of the "masculine" characteristics which made me fear men, so with him I dropped my defences and allowed myself to be invaded. He respected my freedom and my desire to remain in control of my life, and seemed to have a "feminine side" which permitted him to understand those things in a woman which men find difficult, to realize the rare happiness she can experience in an equal relationship.

I gave free rein to my emotions and fell in love with him. Of course there were differences between us, but we overcame them together. I never felt any aggression in Khalil. When he took me into his arms it was a new experience, a mutual giving of ourselves to each other, a flow of warmth, and love and pleasure.

I watched the tense lines of deprivation in his face melt away, his movements lose their edge. He now had a ready laugh, and his moments of sadness grew rare. My love for him grew so strong that at moments it frightened me, for I have always wanted to remain free. But also I lost the feeling of loneliness which had never left me since I was a child. It was as if he brought back to me a lost part of myself.

We married about six months after our first meeting. I remember that day very well. It was raining, and a strong wind whistled between the buildings. The sky was full of grey clouds. We went to the *Maazoun* of the district where Khalil lived. He brought a friend of his, Farouk El Maghrabi, as his witness, and I chose one of my colleagues from the plant. I was shivering. There was a draught from under the door. Or perhaps it was the spectre of marriage looming before me once more — and the narrow eyes of the *Maazoun*. He never looked at me, even once, as if I was an unclean thing to be avoided, and he pronounced the words of the marriage ceremony with the haste of someone anxious to be through with an unpleasant task. At one point I heard him enquire about the dowry, what would be the down payment, and how much would be deferred. I felt deeply insulted at being priced on the marriage market like any other commodity. We had agreed on a nominal sum in order to reduce his fee to a minimum. But when Farouk butted in and said "One pound" I was furious, and never forgave him.

After the ceremony we went to a coffee house. The front was made of glass, and we sat inside looking at the people as they moved through the streets. Farouk tried to cheer us up by telling us the latest jokes. I can still remember one of them, "The President went to visit the Zoological Gardens after they had been renewed. When he arrived in front

19

of a hillock where the monkeys lived, they insisted on having a picture taken with him. On the following day the picture was on the front page of all the dailies and underneath was written: "The President visiting the monkeys during his tour of the Zoological Gardens yesterday. His Excellency is in the front row, third from the right."

Those are my memories of the day on which Khalil and I were married. Somehow I felt that the extreme simplicity of the marriage ceremony was more the result of his financial straits than of his conviction that this was the right way to do things. He seemed nervous, I kept telling myself that this was natural, since our marriage was an important decision in his life. I brushed these fleeting impressions aside and abandoned myself to the more joyful aspects of that day.

We laughed, patted one another on the back with affection, and then took leave of our two companions in a flurry of hugs, kisses, and warm wishes for a long life of conjugal bliss. I accompanied Khalil to his room in Boulac El Dakrour. His belongings were ready, and we carried them down into the street under the stare of the doorkeeper, who kept throwing suspicious looks in my direction. Khalil went to look for a taxi, while I stood guarding the bags. He returned after about half an hour, and the taxi driver took us to what was now our home in Dar El Salam. We unloaded the bags in front of the small gate, and there ensued a long argument between Khalil and the man who insisted on being paid what was virtually double the normal fare.

We put the bags in the bedroom. I lit a stove in the living room and unhooked the telephone. We prepared a meal of grilled meat, sesame salad, a bottle of wine, and some fruit. After the meal we sat talking, about our childhood, the songs of Fairouz, love and other things, as though postponing the moment of physical contact. Gradually the warmth and joy of being together overcame whatever dreariness the morning had left in our hearts. Khalil put his arm around me. A few moments later we undressed, slipped under soft woollen covers and I gave myself with passion to the man I loved.

Thus began our married life. We were close to one another most of the time. Our general outlook on life was the same in many ways, although each of us had arrived at it by a different path. He through his militant politics, and I as a result of my upbringing. I was brought up to respect knowledge and work, and to despise people who strutted about like peacocks just because they had money. My father's parents were peasants, whereas my mother belonged to a middle-class urban family. Her marriage to my father had been the culmination of a

20

romantic love affair, and she had obstinately refused all other suitors. This was very rare then and showed her force of character. But I grew up in the contradictory situation created by the differences between my parents. During the summer holidays I used to move from the small house of mud bricks and straw in my father's village Kafr Al Taheen, to the spacious white stone house in Heliopolis where my maternal grandfather lived. When my relatives from Kafr Al Taheen used to visit our home, they wore long dark *gallabeyas*, and smelt of burnt cotton sticks and fenugreek. Their cracked heels protruded from under the long flowing garments, and the lines on their faces were deeply ploughed. When I noticed our neighbours looking them up and down, I used to feel ashamed and hide inside the house. But it was different when my mother's relatives came to see us. The men wore smart suits, and the women beautiful dresses. I would hop around like a rabbit, and run in and out of the house all the time, so that the boys and girls who collected around would get a chance to ask me who our visitors were.

My father quickly taught me that the worth of a man or a woman was not in the land they owned, nor in jewellery and clothes. He respected my mother deeply because she had refused her rich suitors and chosen him. Their relationship remained tender and warm throughout, and when she died he soon followed her, as though intent on remaining by her side.

Thus I learnt that the worth of people has little to do with what they own. Khalil's values were like mine. In his case, however, they were the product of rational thought. But he was fond of art, and most importantly he never tried to impose his way of thinking in our life.

When I am alone in the evening my mind sometimes goes back to our days of married life. Then I feel very fortunate. For it was only at the end that he hurt me so deeply. Few women have known the relationship we shared for some time. And now he's in trouble I cannot forget.

Yes, I really loved him, with a deep and powerful emotion. But he did not realize that what I gave him was not easy to find. The flaw in his personality was difficult to define. In his young days he was used to getting everything he wanted. So that later, when deprived or frustrated, he was tempted to seek the easy way out. The prison walls, the iron bars, the ambitions which had not materialized, precipitated his crisis, especially in moments of fear or strife. So when this woman came along he surrendered without a fight. There are so many of his kind now, so many Khalil Mansour Khalils dazzled by blue eyes, dazzled by the lights. But at least he had one merit. A past that never completely died. Whereas those who posture on the stage these days have nothing.

When I spoke of this to the Court, the President stopped me. He said I was raising political issues which had nothing to do with this trial. But how can I avoid the things which deeply influenced our life? For, all that Khalil did was to go along with the changes initiated by others, by those in power.

The first month of our married life went by swiftly. Nothing marred our happiness. We were really partners, sharing the responsibilities and pleasure of life. Sometimes a deep instinct told me that somewhere a thin worm was gnawing away inside him, that a dark line was embedded in the tissue of our life. He would sit still and silent in a corner for hours. If I asked him what was wrong he would suddenly exhibit a desire for activity, talk about wasted time, turn over the pages of a book, become absorbed in one of his files, or climb a ladder and start cleaning our library shelves. If I tried to question him more he would discover that he had an urgent appointment which he had almost forgotten. He would change his clothes rapidly, and rush out without telling me when he intended to be back.

At moments like that I would see that he was erecting a barrier between us. There was a sadness in his face which I could neither describe, nor understand. He seemed to become an empty, inert thing with no hint of any internal struggle, or anger, or pain. Yet I was sure that what I felt was merely an impression, and that something I could not detect brought on these moods.

I hate to feel helpless. And when Khalil entered into one of his states all my attempts to help him seemed to be in vain.

Sometimes I was furious with him, for despite all my love and care, he did not respond in any way. I felt he was acting like a weakling by allowing himself to succumb to these attacks of what must have been almost total despair. I had to make an effort to avoid being overwhelmed by his moods.

I began to realise that he was allowing himself to drift, just like any other employee, instead of trying to do something with his life. But at this time I started giving more time to painting. I used to spend long hours in the studio after returning home. Usually it was close on midnight by the time I came downstairs. I would find him sunk in an easy chair staring at nothing, or languidly turning the pages of some book, or following one of those stupid foreign serials which have invaded our TV. Love continued to give warmth to our relationship, and to keep us together. But love is not enough to fill the life of a man like Khalil.

Three months after we married I became pregnant with our only child, a boy called Esam. But I had decided not to give up so easily. To get him to talk frankly it was necessary to corner him in a discussion. The month of May flew by quickly carrying away with it the Khamaseen winds. I suggested we take three days holiday in Alexandria. At this time of the year it would be warm and not yet overrun by swarms of holiday-makers, and if we travelled by the fast diesel train it would take less than three hours.

He welcomed the idea, and started to prepare for our trip with the excitement of a child. His eyes began to sparkle again, and he could hardly keep still in the house. Every now and then he had a new suggestion about how we should spend our time. We decided to go to Sidi Kreer on the outskirts of Alexandria. We arrived about eleven in the morning, had our bags carried up to the room, put on our bathing suits and ran out as fast as we could. The wide expanse of sea and sand was empty except for a few boys fishing. We lay on the beach under a cloudless sky. The warm rays of the sun went through me, so that soon I felt my body tingling with life. I abandoned myself to the pure air, to the drops of cool spray carried by the wind, to the taste of salt on my lips, to Khalil's face and his eyes slowly probing inside me. I took him in my arms, felt his lips under mine. He leaned over me and said: "I love the unspoken words in your eyes."

That night I recognized the man I loved. His heart was open, his mind sharp. I remember how suddenly the words started to pour out "Surely I was not made to sign papers written by others, to live like a worm in a hole. Something has happened to me, I feel paralysed, without confidence in myself, in my ability to achieve the things I desire. I wake up in the night, shivering with fear, see the stars looking down at me through iron bars, hear the lash of a whip landing on a naked back, clench my teeth to avoid crying out, live with the taste of blood in my mouth, and the feeling of being hunted down. When I sit at the breakfast table, put my fingers around a cup of tea, talk about ordinary things and look into your eyes, my fears are allayed. I feel secure again, strong, capable of facing anything. But then very often I open the morning paper, and read about a new law 'regulating democracy' which permits the police to arrest anyone on suspicion, or I notice eyes following me as I walk through the streets, waiting for me on the platform of the station, moving stealthily around my house. I keep running into black uniforms with brass buttons, police cars creeping up a road, automatic rifles flaunting their stunted bayonets in the sun, a man standing at the corner of our street carefully avoiding my eyes as I pass. When the door bell rings at night, visions of prison return to my mind, and at times when I'm listening to some responsible official or other I sense a threat disguised as friendly advice. In the past I never knuckled under, but perhaps my resistance was gradually weakening all the time, until the day came when they opened the prison doors and I walked out, with a bag in my hand and visions in my mind. I stood under the warm sun, lifted my face and looked at the trees, the clouds, the sky. A young woman stood at one of the windows. She wore a black shawl and her skin was white. When she saw me looking at her she left the window. Suddenly I realized it was useless to wait any longer. I stood, undecided. I was lonely. Five years in prison, and here I was, free at last, but alone. Perhaps at that very moment the construction I had built up inside me began slowly to crumble."

I said: "That's not true. You exaggerate. You feel a sense of guilt because you're not engaged in anything. But things take time. Now, at least, we're together."

"Yes that's true. You've already done a lot of good to me. But self-confidence is not something that comes from others. It's not an injection or a pill. You are strong. You know what you want and where you are going. I'm sure you'll get there. I'm always comparing myself with you, and maybe your strength accentuates my weakness."

"I don't understand why you should feel like that. You have a lot to be proud of in your past, and the future can be even better. I have not really done anything yet."

"But you will. I know it. The past is important, but it's not enough. It's not something one can live on, no matter how wonderful."

"Hold me in your arms Khalil. I love you."

Khalil Mansour Khalil

The days and weeks followed one another uneventfully. I settled down to work, slipped into my slot, and even started to climb the administrative ladder without the delay normally faced by a new employee, especially with a past like mine. Only six months had elapsed since I obtained the letter of appointment, and I had already become Director of the Research section, probably as a result of the staff shortage created by the increasing number of professionals working abroad.

I now had a spacious private office, a secretary who wore a white veil around her hair, but painted her lips and nails bright red, and a messenger boy who sprang to his feet and saluted each time I passed through the door of my room. I drank my coffee in a special cup, and found the newspapers neatly folded on my desk each morning.

I married Amina on the 5 February 1973. On the 3 October the Egyptian army crossed the Suez Canal, and destroyed the Barliev line with high pressure hoses. We lived through a period of great enthusiasm, but it didn't last. A few weeks after this military feat, the policy of surrender labelled "Peace" was inaugurated. Kissinger kept coming and going, newspaper headlines started to repeat the terms "Shuttle Diplomacy" and the "Step by Step Approach", and there was talk of negotiations over a separation between the armies 102 kilometres from Cairo. Kissinger's cold eyes stared out at me from the front page as I sipped my morning tea, and his ambiguous declarations were reported extensively in all the newspapers.

Amina was like fresh water to a wilting plant. I threw myself into the experience of everyday life, as though trying to make up for the years of deprivation as quickly as possible. I devoured the books we bought on our weekly tours of the bookshops and stalls, walked for hours on the open shores of the Nile, breathed in the smell of dew-wetted earth, plucked the delicate stalks of swaying jasmine, abandoned myself to the warmth of the sun, and to the smooth firmness of her woman's body. With her I rediscovered the pleasure of normal life, of food, and wine, and sex.

We were inseparable. At night I slept in her arms, and in the morning woke to find them still wound around me. I savoured a rare happiness, and yet somewhere in the depths of the harmony was a discordant note, an instrument out of tune, or a tiny wound which sometimes throbbed. And beneath the smooth surface of my happiness an obscure feeling of frustration sometimes made me withdraw into a gloomy silence. I had a world of my own which she did not know. It could shrink in fear, or grow with hope.

My father had been a landowner. I was born in a big country house surrounded by gardens, and stables for buffaloes and horses. At night the villagers could see its lights shining in the distance like stars. I went to bed between sheets smelling of soap, and in winter covered myself with blankets of sheep's wool. We used silver knives and forks and ate from silver bowls. Then one day I found myself sleeping on a bare prison floor, watching the bugs climb up the walls. I learnt to bear the lash of the whip, the oozing pus from my wounds, the lighted tip of a cigarette at my anus. I spent the nights looking through iron bars at the houses, imagining the kitchen cosy and warm, meat stew on the stove and a woman's naked body wrapped in a shawl.

Then one day I walked out of the gate. For the first time in years I stretched my legs as I walked. The sun shed its light on the oranges piled in pyramids on wooden stalls. My hand held tightly to my cotton bag as though afraid to lose it, and my eyes searched the crowds standing in front of the door, or bustling through the streets. I studied the features, the clothes, the bend of the shoulders, the feet as they paced over the pavements. I listened intently to the chattering voices, waiting for someone to cry out my name. I went round and round in circles, goaded by hope, obstinacy, or a blind despair. I was looking for my father who had died when I was still in the desert, or for my mother who had been buried the day after I was born. I was looking for a friend who might have remembered that this was the moment when I would be free. And after a while I hoped for a chance encounter with someone I had met before. But above all I was hoping to find Tahani, for she had promised to be waiting at the door.

That morning I looked for her everywhere. My eyes moved over every inch of the square, scoured the windows and the balconies, the cars and the carts, the shops and the stalls. But she was nowhere. The hours passed, and the sun rose high in the sky before I realized it was useless to wait. So I walked down the road, lost once more, forgotten and alone.

Our house was big and our furniture of rosewood; our tapestries were rich and in winter we wore Kashmiri wool. And yet I had always been lonely, always yearned for a mother's embrace, her praise when I did well at school. I was the son of a motherless home. It's easy for people to point their fingers at me and criticize. But a human being left alone stumbles and breaks.

Those who make it alone are gods — to be worshipped, adored — but they are in another category; the exceptions.

Amina was one of the gods. She was born to rise above the common lot, to climb the mountain and look at our world from the highest plateau. And when a man falls in love with such a woman he must climb with her, see the colours of spring explode, and the river flow on a moonlit night, look down on the beauty below.

My love for Amina was my path back to life. She was very different to Tahani Rashid, the companion of my younger days. There was a rare power in her, and an uncompromising attitude in the face of weakness or lies. And when I fell in love with her she left me no choice. I had to climb at her pace, or fall back below.

She was not responsible for what happened to me in the course of time. She belonged to that breed of people who are intent on sowing new seed, and cannot bear to mark time. Perhaps she should not have married a man like me, a prey to conflicting desires. These are things I gradually began to realize.

But in the early days of our marriage everything seemed bright, except for the distant feeling of dissatisfaction from time to time. I had become an insignificant cog, just another employee examining files, noting some remarks, or signing what other people had compiled, then returning home at the end of the day with a vague feeling of rebellion I could not define.

But one morning fate decided to intervene. There was a quiet knock on the door. I lifted my eyes from the papers before me to find a man standing silently in front of my desk. His white teeth shone in a black face. The blue overall he wore was clean and well-ironed and fitted around the lines of his supple body. He said, "Good morning, I am Saïd Abou Karam, head of the Trade Union Committee."

"Oh, welcome. Please sit down. Yes, here, away from the door. It's very cold today isn't it?"

"Yes very."

"Can I offer you a hot drink? You have a choice of coffee, tea, aniseed or cinnamon."

He laughed merrily as though amused by the way I had rattled out the names. "Cinnamon, please."

I don't remember all the things we talked about that morning. But I do remember that every now and again he would stare at me intently, as though trying to figure out what kind of person I was. After we had finished a few words of polite conversation and were drinking our

27

cinnamon he lowered his head for a long moment as though lost in thought and then suddenly asked: "Have you decided to abandon all militant activity?"

I was taken aback by his question. I looked past his shoulder at some spot on the wall and said: "My work is important for the company, don't you think?"

He kept silent as though my rather banal answer merited no response, but his eyes still confronted me. I broke the silence with a counter question, "Why do you ask?"

"Your experience is badly needed."

"There is not much I can do as an individual."

"That means you are prepared to participate in some organized activity?"

"I did not say that."

"Perhaps you don't know me well enough to discuss such matters?"

"No, it's not that. I have done what I can. Now it's other people's turn."

"You've decided to remain a spectator, is that it? You are a retired socialist?"

My irritation was growing. What gave him the right to speak like that?

"Why not tell me instead what you are doing?"

"I have already told you. I am head of the trade union organization in the company."

"Of course, you are one of the people carefully hand picked by the authorities."

There was a quick expression of hurt on his face, like a quick thought that had come and gone. A smile hovered around the corners of his mouth, then retreated.

"I prefer to ignore that remark. Instead I have a proposition to make to you. I am just a worker and have no political affiliations. Nevertheless, I know that if we don't put our efforts together we are liable to lose the few rights we have gained. That's why I give so much time to the trade union organization and to the Federation of Chemical Workers."

"What are you driving at exactly?"

"You cannot present yourself for trade union elections even though you're an obligatory member. The authorities will veto your candidature. But the trade union has the right to form an Advisory Council. Its function will be to study projects or ideas which can help strengthen and extend our activities. Would you agree to become a member of this body?"

There was something reassuring about his face, and his direct manner. But could I trust him so easily? It might be a trap. The shadow of the past still lay over me — a police van at dawn, a rough hand dragging me from under the warm covers — for the first time in long years I no longer slept on a rough mat on the cold bare floor but in her arms pressed against her body.

"I want nothing to do with your trade union activities. I might perhaps resume a study I undertook in the past about the development of the trade union movement. I may need some information from you later. That's, of course, if you agree."

He got up from his chair and turned to face me. His movements were steady, with a calm quickness about them, as though everything was the result of conscious reflection. We shook hands and he said: "Peace be with you Mr Khalil."

That is how my first meeting with Saïd Abou Karam ended, but somehow I suspected that it would not be the last. The weeks went by without any sign from him. I began to feel curious, and slightly exasperated. Yet was it not natural that he should keep away? I had made it clear that I wanted nothing to do with the trade union committee. Why, then, did I feel exasperated? Apparently he did not consider me worthy of further attention, I was a person of little use, to be shelved and forgotten. But who was Saïd Abou Karam anyway? A trade unionist who devoted some efforts to finding solutions for a few minor worker's problems? Most trade unionists these days were yellow and not to be trusted. But I was different — a militant with political experience. I had been hunted down — imprisoned! People respected me. But how long could I go on like this, living on the margin, confined to my office and my desk, poring over the files they brought me each morning, serving the interests of people with whom I had nothing in common? Saïd was, at least, trying to do something, to fight back against those who were selling the country by auction.

I lifted the telephone and called my secretary. She walked in, ample hips swaying in a tight-fitting dress, head swathed in the usual veil, eyes chastely fixed to the floor.

I pointed to a chair.

"Sit down, Eenas, I need some information about a man called Saïd Abou Karam. What do you know about him?"

Her features became slightly rigid and her eyes narrowed with caution.

29

"Saïd Abou Karam? I don't know him personally, but I've heard his name mentioned several times."

"What have you heard?"

"That he's a troublemaker."

"A troublemaker?! In what way?"

"They say he's always attacking the authorities in the company." She hesitated a moment, then added, "That he's a communist."

"A communist!"

I took advantage of the moment of silence which ensued to ponder over what I should say, and decided on a frontal offensive.

"Isn't that what people also say about me?"

This time she hesitated for a long while before answering. Her eyes kept circling the room looking for a way out.

"Yes, but they know that you have turned over a new leaf."

I felt the blood rush to my head. My heart fluttered as though it was on the verge of coming to a halt.

Her soft white face exuded the corrupt innocence of someone who, having given Allah his due, can now stoop to anything with a clear conscience. I ignored her remark and asked: "Why do they say he is a communist?"

"Because he does not fast in the month of Ramadan, and is never seen praying with the others."

"But there are a lot of people like that!"

"Anyhow that's what the Director of Administration, and the people in the Security Section say about him."

"And what do you think?"

"Every Muslim should fast and pray."

"I mean what do you think about Saïd?"

"Opinions about him differ, and I keep away from what's going on."

I knew that her relations with the head of the Security Unit were very intimate. They had probably chosen her as my secretary so that she could report what I was doing. One of these days I would have to get rid of her. There were times when I realized that she had searched my desk. She would remain seated in her room until I called her instead of coming in with the mail, and I would sense something changed in my papers. I looked her straight in the eyes for a moment and said, "Thank you. You may go."

She would certainly tell her lover about my questions. What did it matter? The proverb says: "If you're afraid of ghosts you're sure to meet one." I hated her eyes. Something furtive and lying about them. Perhaps there had been a time when she was just an innocent young girl, leaning out of her window lost in daydreams. But nowadays they left no one alone. It was better to get rid of her. I needed to rid myself of many things. Maybe then I would feel lighter, prepared to take a plunge. I should try to meet Saïd again. Yes, it's true. The world seems peopled with ghosts if one fears them.

Saïd Abou Karam

When I went to court as a witness in Khalil Mansour Khalil's trial they fired questions at me, as though I was in some way responsible for the death of Ruth Harrison. It was really a strange atmosphere. I kept calm and answered all their questions cautiously, lest I say anything which might harm him. To help him as much as I could it was necessary that I be given the chance to reveal my version of his story. They started by asking me things about myself. I explained that my name had always been Saïd Abou Karam since the day I was born. I had been employed as a worker supervisor in the tabletting section of the Thebes Pharmaceutical Company when Khalil arrived. I was born in the province of Aswan, but my parents migrated to Cairo six months later. After primary school I joined a vocational training institute where I learned to work on a lathe. After finishing my training I started to work in Helwan where I moved from one factory to the other, since as a result of my trade union activities the administrative and security authorities kept exerting pressure on me. I finally managed to get a stable job in the Thebes Pharmaceutical Company thanks to a relative of mine who worked as a cook for the Chairman of the Board. But I was fired because the company authorities considered me the prime instigator of a strike.

The trouble began with the negotiations to transform our company into a subsidiary of a French concern called Larochelle. The workers knew that such an agreement would result in nationalization of production and that about two hundred of them would be fired, so they went on strike.

A year earlier Khalil Mansour Khalil had been appointed in the company and we became close friends. I remember that when the workers discovered that he was in our midst a wave of rumours went round the plant. Almost everyone had heard of him. He made no bones about his views. True, he did not volunteer to say anything, but whenever anybody asked him where he stood, he would answer: "Since 1956 I have been a communist."

In the trade union committee we discussed whether or not we should contact him. Apart from myself, all the others were in favour of keeping their distance, some because of the atmosphere in which we were living, and the fear that any relations with him would lead to an accusation of the kind which had become very common at the time like: "the trade union committee has fallen into the clutches of the 'atheists and saboteurs'." Quite a number of members were completely opposed to his ideas, while a third group believed that trade unions should have nothing to do with politics and had better keep away from people with any kind of political leanings.

However, I saw things differently. I had no political affiliations at the time, nor was I interested in what was going on outside the trade union movement, yet it appeared to me that Khalil Mansour Khalil could not be against the interests of the workers. We might disagree with him on certain issues but the political ideas he was said to defend could only lead him to stand up for those who laboured to earn a living.

Maybe I was also a little curious. This man who had spent a good part of his life in a prison cell because of his ideas, what kind of a person could he be? Corrupt? A paid hireling? Anything was possible. At least he was interested in things outside his personal life, and sufficiently interested to go to jail for them. Besides, why was it that the same people who kicked up the greatest fuss about his appointment in the company, were the same who fought the workers without mercy, or were even just plain rascals and thieves?

I thought the matter over at length before deciding to visit him. As chairman of the trade union committee my position was sensitive. I knew there were spies watching me. I had been in trouble before.

So one morning after he arrived I went and knocked on his door. I heard him say "Come in." He was sitting at his desk, going through some papers. His desk was simple, full of ball pens of different colours and sizes, rulers, scotch tape, erasers, paper and a stapler. Both his in-tray and out-tray were empty. The wall behind carried a huge bar chart on which were registered figures for production, as well as the stages reached by new projects and research activities. The routine photograph of the President of the Republic was missing.

He stood up, shook hands and beckoned me to a chair. Then he asked me if I would like to have a hot drink, naming what was available on the premises carefully, as though trying to make sure he would not forget. He spoke in a quiet voice and had a way of breaking up some of his words. A smile lit up his face every now and then but at one moment a sudden sadness took its place. I sensed an inner tension, stretched to the extreme.

As the days went by we became increasingly intimate. In an atmosphere where division and competition held sway, fuelled by those in charge, our friendship was a rare thing. We became the object of curious glances and whispering, for from the beginning he did not hesitate to invite me to his house, despite the fact that I was only a worker supervisor, whereas he belonged to the higher technical staff. I met his wife Amina Tewfik; she resembled him in many ways. There was the same inner tension, but later I discovered that unlike Khalil she had a remarkable inner strength. This contrast between them often puzzled me. What was it that had made her more able to support the pressures of life? She was like a pebble, ground to smoothness and resilience.

The President of the Court insists on calling me a sophist. I don't know what that means but it seems to imply his dislike of the fact that I have tried to educate myself. I can't see what's wrong with that. He despises workers and wants people like me to remain cogs in a machine, turning and turning until we rust and crumble.

When I think about the trial I realize that I didn't really know very much about it. But somehow I feel that Ruth Harrison's relationship with Khalil was not that simple. These days there are a lot of Ruth Harrisons around. A poisonous cloud has invaded our life, and unless we dispel it quickly who knows what it will leave in its wake?

I am just a simple worker and I say things as I see them. I don't think I can ever forget Khalil Mansour Khalil. He helped me to see more clearly: one day he said: "You know Saïd, although things have sometimes gone the wrong way I still believe that the future lies in socialism."

Everyone knew that Khalil Mansour Khalil has been a militant socialist for quite some time. True, he had ceased to be active since his release from prison, but he had never crossed to the other side, nor become a mouthpiece of the system.

Anyway, sometime before I decided to visit him I had an idea. Why not constitute an advisory body to assist our trade union. I discussed the proposal with my colleagues and after they had agreed we started to think of who could join.

But when I talked the matter over with Khalil that morning, he refused to participate. From the way he listened, I could see that he was interested. He looked alert, his eyes shone. But then I sensed a deep caution. He started to ask me all sorts of questions and to express his doubts. And at one point he was even rude. I was on the point of leaving but then I remembered that he had suffered and that such a reaction was understandable.

We failed to reach any agreement. He said he might get in touch with me at some future date to seek information for a study he was doing on the trade union movement. As I descended the stairs and crossed the courtyard, different things flitted through my mind. I had been at ease in his presence. His direct looks gave me confidence; but at the same time I didn't like the way he hesitated about giving us a helping hand. Why was he so afraid of engaging in some activity? It wouldn't be the end of the world for him!

My colleagues made fun of me and said: "Now you have seen for yourself what these revolutionaries are like. A lot of high sounding phrases, but when it comes to doing something then the job, the office, the painted secretary are all that really matter."

A couple of months after our first encounter, I was leaning over one of the machines, trying to repair a fault, when I heard someone call out: "Saïd, Saïd, the Director of Research is looking for you." I turned to find Khalil approaching with the wary steps of someone who finds himself in a strange place. When he saw me his face lit up with a hesitant smile, as though unsure of his reception. I shook hands with him warmly, pulled up a chair and suggested that he drink a cup of coffee while I tried to find what was wrong with the machine. When I returned he was absorbed in conversation with one of the workers. He explained to me that he had come to continue the talk we had started in his office.

Thus we resumed our relations. He joined the Advisory Council as soon as it was established. The moment this became known, a new wave of rumours about the "communist" who had started making contacts with the workers, went round the factory. And since I was also accused of being a communist, the wave of rumours was gradually built up into a systematic campaign by the administration, and the

Security Unit agents. As a result the discussions in the trade union committee about Khalil started all over again. But the majority insisted on our not giving way. We agreed to space out the meetings of the Advisory Council in order to avoid the impression that it was particularly active. Gradually things quietened down except for an occasional muttering here and there to keep the issue alive. Some weeks later, however, Khalil told me that a few days after he joined the Advisory Council the chairman called him to his office, and offered him some advice about the inadvisability of mixing with the workers. He had refused to accept any interference in his affairs and explained that according to the labour law amended in 1963 he was an obligatory member of the trade union, and his dues were deducted from his monthly salary. It was, therefore, his right to participate in any trade union activity he saw fit. The juridical authorities would intervene if they felt he was infringing the law.

I appreciated his firm stand. Sometimes we met after work and walked to where Amina worked. At the beginning when people saw us together they looked slightly surprised, and sometimes disapproving. I often had dinner in Khalil's house. We would chat for hours. If it got very late I stayed the night and left early in the morning since at that time I lived alone.

In those days I could see he was happy. He was always active and enthusiastic as though discovering things anew.

I remember very clearly the first meeting of the Advisory Council we attended together. The atmosphere was rather reserved. Nobody laughed, or joked, or talked about what had happened since the last meeting. The other members avoided looking at him directly. They seemed a little too conscious of his presence, watching him out of the corner of their eye, and listening with silent attention whenever he spoke, but near the end of the meeting things began to ease up, and they started to chat and tell stories.

I liked the way he behaved. He was neither too familiar, nor did he maintain a distant silence, or show off. He was just right. From time to time he intervened in the discussion, and when he made a proposal one could see he had thought it over. What I liked the most about him was that he didn't try to be clever. When one of the stooges tried to draw him into a discussion about the prices of our finished products, he steered clear of the controversy by explaining that he didn't know enough about it.

I noticed that he remembered each one's name, listened most of the time, and avoided criticism. Before the end of the session I suggested that the Council examine an issue which had caused a lot of anxiety among the workers: the negotiations said to be underway between our company and Larochelle for the joint production of a large number of drugs. Larochelle would be paid 15% royalties on the wholesale price in exchange for expertise in production techniques and processes. It would also be the sole source for the provision of chemicals, excipients, machinery and spare parts.

Apparently the agreement was only a beginning, and later a merger was envisaged in which the Thebes Pharmaceutical Company would become a subsidiary of Larochelle. At this stage Larochelle would invest a sum equivalent to 49% of total capital and the company would enjoy the special customs and tax exemptions accorded to foreign investments.

There was discussion during which Khalil kept silent. To express views on this sensitive issue might put him in an awkward position, so he preferred to say nothing. I decided to ask him a direct question and see how he would react.

"Mr Khalil: what do you think about these negotiations?"

He stared at the table for a long moment, then lifted his head and looked directly at me before saying, "It's too early for me to say anything."

"But surely, as Director of the Research Section you are interested in the various aspects of joint production agreements?"

He looked at me in some bewilderment, as though wondering why I had sprung this difficult question on him so soon. He kept clasping and unclasping his fingers.

"That's true, but I haven't had a chance to study this particular agreement. Under certain conditions joint production agreements can be beneficial if they permit us to enter into areas where we have not ventured so far."

At this stage, a worker from Damietta, Mostapha Ramadan, intervened.

"Then what you need is a chance to study the details of the agreement?"

"Yes."

"Then Mr Khalil can we ask you to do it? Your experience will help us to see more clearly, and to understand both the positive and the negative aspects of the proposal."

Once more I saw a look of bewilderment traverse his face. No doubt he realized that if he started to poke his nose into this area he might get into trouble. Yet at the same time he knew that if the project with Larochelle was signed, the majority of the workers and employees stood to lose quite a lot.

I decided to come to his rescue.

"Let's give Mr Khalil a chance to think the matter over. He has a lot of work, and it might be difficult for him to undertake a detailed study of the proposals. I have another suggestion: a more general review of the benefits and disadvantages of joint production agreements with multinational concerns. This will make it easier for us to form an opinion. We can limit ourselves for the time being to the first stage of the proposal and later on move over to the merger that Larochelle is proposing. But we should be ready with a study as soon as possible to avoid being taken unawares. I am prepared to study the effects of an eventual merger once I get hold of a copy of the document. If we agree to these steps, we can break up now."

There was a general chorus of assent. Someone opened the door, and the chairs scraped. Khalil hurried out without waiting for me. I could see him walking rapidly across the courtyard, his thin body merging into the half-light, his shoulders slightly bent. Were they drooping more than usual, or was it my imagination? Perhaps it was better if I did not try to catch up with him. Sometimes one needs to be alone. Or would he feel happier if he had company? He had seemed disturbed when I dragged him into the discussion about the new proposal. But we had to know where he would stand. I shrugged my shoulders, sighed and slipped through the outer gate. I heard the guard say, "Good night comrade," and felt better. After all there were moments in life that weren't so bad. My thoughts rushed ahead of me to my two rooms high up, close to the sky. There were days when I needed affection, someone to care for me. But where was the girl who would accept my way of life? Since I had moved into this district I never knew what tomorrow might bring: the loss of my job, or my dwelling and perhaps a few nights spent in some police station? It was better not to occupy myself with thoughts of this kind. Alone I was free to do what I liked. Everything one did had some value. It could be value added to one's pocket or value added to one's life. Each had its compensations and each had its price.

Amina Tewfik

I was listening to the evening news when I heard the key turn in the latch. Khalil burst in without closing the door, pulled me out of my chair, and kissed me. I pushed him away gently. He had a faintly mysterious smile, as though he was hiding some secret and had not yet decided whether or not to tell me. He said: "I'll make some tea, and open a packet of biscuits. I've had nothing to eat since I left the house."

When he came back, he poured out two glasses of tea, and started to tell me about his meeting with Saïd Abou Karam. As he sat opposite me I could see he was much more relaxed. The lines on his face had disappeared, and he no longer broke off and stared gloomily into space.

Our relations with Saïd developed rapidly and he began to spend much of his free time with us. He often visited me in my studio, and would sit for hours without moving. I could feel him watching what I did with an almost frightening concentration. His nostrils seemed to quiver with the excitement of some impending discovery. When I rested he asked me questions about my work, and sometimes started a discussion about one of the paintings.

As the days went by I noticed that he had an instinctive sensitivity to line and colour. He expressed his opinions with spontaneity and saw things to which others remained blind. But sometimes he completely missed what I was hoping he would find. If I made fun of him he would give me a look of reproach mingled with surprise. His culture was still limited, and perhaps partly for that reason he was free of the kind of complexities which sometimes made Khalil lose sight of the essential. He absorbed knowledge quickly, then assimilated it quietly. I felt closer to him in some ways, as though we had both grown up in an environment which left no room for hiding one's heart behind intricate barricades.

When I offered to make a portrait of him, his visits to my studio grew more frequent. He welcomed the idea as though I was doing him a favour, and that made me very grateful to him. Khalil appreciated my talent, but he assessed my work with the careful yardstick of a person who knew what he was talking about, rather than the emotional and sensual appreciation of Saïd.

Around that time I became pregnant with Esam, and this began to hinder my movements. Saïd and Khalil co-operated in making up for my reduced activity. It was reassuring to see these two men working side by side in the kitchen, Khalil dressed in an old white laboratory coat, and Saïd in faded blue overalls. There they stood cutting rings of onion, and wiping the tears from their eyes. I would catch their quiet voices talking or arguing about some point as though it was the most crucial thing in life. They were different, but shared in a desire to rethink many things often taken for granted.

One afternoon, while I was trying to snatch a few moments rest after lunch, Khalil's voice came to me from the living room a little higher than usual. I strained my ears to try and follow the discussion, but the door was closed and I couldn't hear much. I opened the door a little and lay down again. I heard Khalil ask: "Why insist that I express my view?".

"Since you're in agreement with the stand taken by the majority of workers, why not come out into the open?"

"What use will it be if I do that?"

"To my mind, there are several good reasons. You are the director of research in the company, and your opinion carries special weight. Nobody will be able to say that only people with no expert knowledge on the subject are opposed to the agreement. In addition, the workers will feel that even in high positions there are people prepared to take a stand with them. To use the political terms you taught me, since you're no longer an active member of the party we can consider you one of our allies from the middle class."

I heard Saïd's laugh ring out relieving some of the mounting tension. I got up and slipped out of the bedroom. As soon as Saïd saw me, he said: "Here's Amina, let's ask her what she thinks. You tell her . . ."

I interrupted him.

"I heard your discussion. You know Khalil, I find it difficult to understand how you can hide what you really think. People will be asking you all the time, so why not come out openly right from the start?"

His face grew pale, and his fingers fumbled in his pockets for a cigarette. Whenever he smoked I knew something was wrong. He extracted a lone, crumpled cigarette, went to the kitchen and returned drawing on it with a nervous haste.

I said: "You haven't told me what you think."

"I think that nobody in his normal state of mind commits suicide. I made a study of the contract, wrote a detailed report, and gave a copy to Saïd so that his trade union committee could use it in the campaign. The position I hold permits me to give them help in different ways. But if I lose it what good will it do either to me or them? With the multinationals at our throat, this is neither the first nor the last battle we'll have to fight."

Saïd intervened abruptly. "In short you want to do a balancing act and keep your options open."

"Maybe; who's going to save me if I get into trouble? You? the trade union committee? The socialists with their eyes pinned on the higher levels, running around in circles?"

"You are being unfair. People do what they can to help."

"No, things have changed. And you have to know that, if you're going to do something about it."

"You are using good arguments to defend a bad cause. The truth is that you don't want to wet your feet."

"If that's so why not accept the fact, and learn to take from me what I am prepared to give."

There was a long gloomy silence. Khalil stared fixedly in front of him. After a short time Saïd got up abruptly said "Good night" and went out. I felt exhausted and incapable of doing anything, so I went back to bed. Khalil put out the lights and remained seated in the dark. Time passed slowly and after what seemed an eternity he came into the bedroom and undressed, making as little noise as possible. I felt him slip under the covers carefully as though anxious not to disturb me, and turn over on his side with his back to me. I whispered softly, "Khalil, are you angry with me?"

"Why should I be angry? Did you not express what you believe to be right?"

"Saïd was of the same opinion."

"You and Saïd always agree."

"That's not true. We don't always agree".

"Both of you are reacting with your feelings. You as an artist, and he because of his limited experience."

"What about you?"

He remained silent.

"Why don't you answer."

"We will continue the discussion tomorrow. Good night Amina."

But there was no discussion the next day, nor did we broach the subject again. I felt he was avoiding me. He even ceased to put his arms around me when we went to bed. Once again he was erecting a barrier between us. I tried to break through to him; at night I huddled close up to him, but he pretended to be asleep. Each morning I woke up early and prepared his breakfast. At table I chatted about this and that, commented on the news, or talked about my work. But all my attempts were useless. He hid behind a wall of silence, answering with a few words meant to close the subject. I was discouraged and hurt. Was that the treatment I deserved? Could he not tolerate me expressing a different point of view from his? I realized it had become a matter of pride with him, as though we were casting doubts on his courage, knowing full well that he had faced much more difficult circumstances.

Saïd stopped dropping in. Nobody enquired about him, and Khalil withdrew more and more. I could see he was lonely, and I wondered what I could do for him. Not having been in prison myself perhaps I didn't understand what he was going through, nor could I tell what he needed most.

One evening several weeks after the discussion with Khalil the telephone rang. He was out, and I was busy putting the final touches to a canvas. I didn't feel like answering but it continued to ring. When I picked up the receiver I heard Saïd's voice, "Hello, Amina? Good evening. How are you?"

"Not so bad. And you?"

"Everything's fine thank you."

"It's been some time since we last saw you. Why have you stopped coming?"

"I've been busy. Besides I thought it was better to keep away for a while after my last discussion with Khalil."

"No. You should have come. He might think you don't want to see him any more."

There was a brief silence before he said, "I didn't realize that. I will drop by soon. But meanwhile there's been a new development. You remember he wrote a report about the proposed agreement with Larochelle, and then followed it up with an article in *El Gamaheer*?"

"Yes."

"Well, it seems the chairman told him that the Minister has decided to open an inquiry with him for infringement of the law on state secrets."

"He said nothing to me about it."

"I'll try to come to your place soon. My regards to Khalil. Tell him I preferred not to call by his office after the meeting he had with the chairman. Good night Amina."

The day after his call I received a cable from one of my friends in Minia asking me to spend two or three days with her, as she needed my help badly. I made a few quick arrangements in the house, prepared my bag, and said goodbye to Khalil. At eight o'clock in the evening I was seated in the train headed for Upper Egypt, wondering whether it had been wise for me to leave Khalil alone at what seemed to be a difficult turning in his life. But even with the most fertile imagination in the world, it would still have been impossible for me to remotely anticipate the events which started to unfold that night, and which still seem like a dream.

Khalil Mansour Khalil

The taxi stopped in front of a building with the number 141 in white on blue enamel. I paid the driver and walked in between the dark marble pillars, which held up the giant construction. The doorkeeper, a huge man with ebony skin and a snow white turban threw me a quick glance, registered my features, and stored them in his mind. I said: "Good evening. Where is Mrs Ruth Harrison's flat?" He answered in a barely audible voice. "Ninth floor Flat 54, to the right as you come out of the lift." He continued to observe me, my clothes, my hair, and all the details he had been trained to note. The door of the lift opened automatically, and the red and green lights winked at me as I slipped inside. I walked out at the ninth floor, felt the door close behind me and the huge shadow slide down to carry on its task with quiet efficiency. A small brass plate with her name shone brightly on the polished surface of the thick wooden door. I pressed the bell, but heard nothing. As I stood waiting something seemed to cross my face like an invisible feather, or an unseen finger of light, then the door opened and I found myself looking at a man in a white jacket and black trousers, with a head of thick woolly hair. He said: "Please come in. Mrs Harrison is expecting you."

I followed him along a corridor with closed doors on either side between which hung paintings. I realized that he hadn't asked for my name, but I said nothing. Something in the general atmosphere stimulated my curiosity, created a sense of anticipation but also of apprehension. I felt myself transported into another world. The man crossed over a spacious room to an open window, bent over slightly and said something in a low voice. I looked around. A single table lamp shed dark shadows in the corners, shining eerily on metal surfaces. Through the open window I glimpsed the lights crossing over University Bridge, then clustering in the houses on the opposite side of the Nile. To the left rose the tall minaret of a mosque. I heard a woman's voice say, "Ah, you've shown him in. Good." She stood up and her hair shone in the moonlight. She said: "Please excuse the dim lights. I was resting after a long day." She put out her hand and suddenly the room came to life, bathed in white light. I was standing in the centre of the room, looking into an oval face surrounded by glowing chestnut hair. I was struck by her youthfulness. She looked like a university student. Her hand came out to meet mine and its fingers clasped mine firmly, with a warmth, almost an eagerness, as though she was greeting an old friend after long years of separation.

"I'm glad that you were able to come. My friend Aida Ragab admires you a lot. I hope you have been able to place her by now." She pointed to a low sofa. "Please sit down, or perhaps you would prefer the terrace? The night is beautiful."

"I've walked a lot today and this sofa looks very inviting."

She smiled. I could see her eyes now, like liquid honey in the light. Her mouth was full, with a hint of sensuality, her features finely chiselled.

She sat down opposite me as though presenting herself to be examined, and after a moment said: "Now tell me frankly, what have you found?"

I gave a short, rather embarrassed laugh, "A very beautiful person."

Her face lit up for a moment, then she became serious, almost gloomy. "Please don't say the usual things. Aida told me you are different."

I felt awkward, lowered my eyes and said nothing. The silence lasted for some time.

I heard her say: "I don't know how much time you can spare to help me with the research I spoke to you about. But before we begin talking about that, what can I offer you? Tea, or fruit juice? Or perhaps you would like a drink?"

I was on the point of asking for whisky but thought better of it and said: "A fresh lemon squash will quench my thirst."

"I'm going to have a whisky. It might relieve some of the fatigue of the day."

She pressed a bell by her side. The dark man in the white jacket appeared in a smaller doorway on one side of the room.

"Please bring a jug of fresh lemon squash, I'll have a whisky with a little more water than usual." She looked at me and said, "Or would you like to change your mind?"

"No thank you. I prefer lemon squash."

"I don't smoke, but if you wish to smoke please do. You will find cigars and cigarettes on the table next to you. And now perhaps I should explain things to you a little more. As I have already mentioned the aim of my research is to study the development of the trade union movement in Egypt during the period from the signature of the 1936 treaty with the British up to the revolution of 1952. It will be my thesis for a doctoral degree. Aida Ragab referred me to your book published in 1970. I found it very useful and informative. But there are aspects of the subject that require further elucidation, and I want to ask you a series of questions. I will be using a tape recorder for the sake of accuracy. It also saves me a lot of time since I have an excellent secretary who types everything out from the tapes. I correct it and delete anything which seems superfluous or irrelevant. Then I show it to whoever I have interviewed for checking. I have interviewed a number of other people, but I prefer not to show you their answers. I want to avoid influencing you in any way."

I gave a negligent movement of the hand in refutation of such a possibility. She said quickly: "Please don't misunderstand what I meant by your being influenced. If you know what the others have said you might sometimes instinctively respond to their views. At this stage I want to avoid polemics or discussion, and just find out what different people think, otherwise I might get lost in issues which are not mine, and find myself being led away from the line I want to follow. If I need your opinion on some issue I will ask you a direct question."

I gave a nod of assent. But I felt a little uneasy — as though she was using me. I wondered whom she had already interviewed. Why should I be placed on the same level as people I didn't even know? Perhaps it was only the pique of a man confronted with a beautiful woman! Besides, this taping business . . .

She interrupted my train of thought.

"I lack experience in this kind of work, and this is not helped by the fact that I'm not in my own country. Sometimes I really get lost. But I don't have enough time to experiment at this stage, so I'll stick to the method I've followed so far. Maybe later you can help me in other ways apart from merely answering my questions. I already feel I'm taking advantage of you and giving nothing in return."

I shrugged my shoulders in a way calculated to convey that none of her misgivings was of the slightest importance. I wondered how sincere she was, or whether she was just an intelligent woman making use of the people she met. These women from the West had a knack of playing on the imagination of men from the East like myself. We were easily seduced by their smooth white skin, their supple legs, and their long silky hair. She stretched herself lazily as though giving me time to examine her body at leisure. Its beauty showed well in the tight blue jeans and the simple shirt. I busied myself pouring a glass of lemon squash. She pressed the recording button and said: "Could you start by saying a few words about yourself?"

"On condition that you also tell me something about yourself once we are over with the interview. I promise not to tape what you tell me."

Her face was suddenly transformed into a stony mask. She emitted a brief mirthless laugh, and with a quick movement pushed the small recorder nearer to me and said: "Will you please begin."

It was almost one o'clock in the morning when I walked out into the road bordering the Nile. By the time I had walked to Bab El Louk station it took me almost an hour. I found the last train brooding silently near the platform. I chose an empty seat near the window. My heart beat with a strange happiness mingled with anxiety. I felt on the verge of a new and unexpected stage of my life.

When I arrived home I turned the key in the door, closed it behind me without turning on the lights, and went straight to the bedroom. I sensed a movement in the bed and heard Amina say: "Is that you Khalil? I've been home since seven. I was getting rather worried. Where have you been?"

She didn't wait for an answer. I felt she was happy to be back and wanted to talk. "Ah. I'm so exhausted. My friend Zeinab literally ran over me with her problems. How are you Khalil? I really missed you. What time is it? Have you had an enjoyable evening?"

"It's three o'clock in the morning." I hesitated. Should I tell her where I had been? Without looking her in the face I said: "I was at Farouk El Maghrabi's place. After I left I decided to walk to Bab El

Louk station. It's a beautiful night."

"All the way from Boulac El Dakrour!!? Then you must be really tired. Undress and come and lie down. How is Farouk? It's so long since I saw him. How did you manage these past days? I was thinking about you all the time."

"I also missed you Amina. The house seemed so empty without you."

She held me tight and kissed me. I lay motionless in her arms, unresponsive. She asked: "What's the matter?"

"Nothing. Nothing at all. I'm just tired."

"Then you probably don't feel like chatting. Let's go to sleep." She pronounced the last words a little curtly.

I put out the lights, and darkness enveloped us. My body needed rest, but my mind was wide awake.

About a couple of weeks after Amina returned from Minia I entered my office one morning to find an oblong white envelope lying in my tray. I recognized Saïd's handwriting. What could he want? I hadn't seen him for some time, since the day we had that argument over the Larochelle contract. I had refrained from getting in touch with him. I felt that he was trying to use me in the struggle against the agreement, without caring much what might happen to me. I was angry that he had placed me in an awkward position. It looked as if I was scared of standing up for what was right. Nevertheless, I should have taken the first step and got in touch with him. He had always been the one who visited us, sharing our meals, or staying overnight. His domestic situation did not permit him to invite us back. Of course, the thought had never occurred to me, but he might have felt ill at ease after our heated discussion. Despite his practical attitude to life, he was very sensitive and proud. Yes, I should at least have sent him a note to ask why he had suddenly stopped visiting us. I pulled the single sheet out of the envelope and started to read:

My dear friend Khalil
It is some time since we last met. I have been rather busy, but that is not the main reason. After the difference of opinion between us over the new project with Larochelle, I felt you were angry with me, and needed time to think over our relationship. My deep friendship for you has perhaps exaggerated my reaction, and this is the only real excuse I can offer. I passed by your house last Thursday evening, but no one was there. I was in a hurry and had neither pen nor paper on me, so I didn't leave any message. I think it's important for us to meet and talk things

over. I prefer not to visit you in the office. The atmosphere is tense these days, and I don't want to provoke unnecessary rumours. The people in the administration seem to be losing their nerve, in particular the "Horse", who apparently has sworn to punish anyone "conspiring" against the best interests of the company. I suggest we meet in the Glass Coffee House next Sunday, at six in the evening. If this is not convenient send me a note through Mostapha Ramadan, otherwise I will assume you are coming.

My greetings and affection to you and Amina.

Saïd Abou Karam

I put the letter in my pocket, and leant back in my chair, thinking it over. Things in the company were no longer as stable as they had been. The agreement with Larochelle was causing a lot of anxiety among the workers. The trade union committee had distributed a few hundred copies of the report which I had given to Saïd. He had been wise enough to introduce changes to make sure that the chairman would not recognize my text, and had also added a review of some of the workers' opinions. It had been circulated extensively, and helped to mobilize effective opposition to the agreement. I wondered whether Saïd knew that subsequently I had presented an amended report to the chairman in which my original criticisms were substantially toned down . . .

What did it matter? I knew best what was right for me. He was still young, full of enthusiasm, but lacking the experience necessary to navigate in the troubled waters ahead. He didn't realize that the struggle would be long, very long. I was barely twenty-five when I first joined the socialist movement; now I was close on fifty — a quarter of a century. Sometimes it seemed that things were at a standstill, that it was the socialists who needed to have their minds liberated. But what right had I to be critical? I sat with the spectators most of the time. Why did Saïd want to meet me next Sunday? I didn't feel like involving myself in the strife which was building up daily before our eyes.

Ruth had promised to get in touch with me as soon as the tape had been transcribed. A long time had passed since that Thursday night, or at least so it seemed. What day were we? Monday? No, Tuesday. I counted the days on my fingers. Eleven days. That was not so long. After the interview we relaxed on the terrace, with a light meal and a bottle of wine. A soft breeze was blowing across the Nile. Now and again I felt the touch of her fingers when she took my glass, or smelt her faint perfume. She talked most of the time. Her husband had worked in India with the International Bank for Agricultural Credit; and

47

they had lived there for three years soon after marrying. I listened to her voice softened by a hint of melancholy as she flitted from memories of the autumn trees at home, to the Himalayan peaks bathing in the colours of dawn.

I went to meet Saïd in the Glass Coffee House on Sunday. I found him sitting alone, waiting for me. He was smoking a *Narjeela*, his dark face pouring with sweat. He stood up to shake hands with me, then clapped to call a waiter.

"What will you have?"

"Coffee with just a strain of sugar."

I looked at him and asked smilingly, "Since when have you started smoking a *Narjeela*? You look on the verge of suffocating."

"I arrived about an hour and a half ago. So I said to myself why not try something new? But the damn thing has nearly choked me."

His laughter rang out. He pushed the *Narjeela* aside, leant across the table and suddenly became serious.

"Khalil let's get straight to the point. I heard something about you which has made me very sad."

My heart sank; I sat motionless, waiting for him to go on. He looked at me steadily.

"There's a rumour that you have retreated from your original position on the Larochelle contract, and submitted another report in which you make substantial concessions."

Despite all the secrecy the matter had got out. Probably through someone in close contact with the chairman; his secretary had access to the confidential files. The trade union people were everywhere.

"Who told you that?"

"I was the first one to ask questions. I want to know if it's true."

I hesitated for a moment, then decided there was only one possible answer.

"Yes, it's true. But I still want to know how you found out."

He pondered my answer, then said, "I wonder if you'll believe me?"

I looked at him with amazement, "Of course I'll believe you. I don't think you've ever lied to me."

"The 'Horse' told me."

My body went rigid. I took a deep breath.

"The 'Horse'?!"

"Yes."

"But why? He of all people?"

"He wants to kill two birds with one stone. First, he knows we are good friends and would like to see us fall out. Second, he hopes I'll spread the news around and turn everybody against you."

My heart began to jump in irregular beats.

"And are you going to spread it around?"

"Frankly, I haven't yet decided. Honesty impels me to tell people about your position. I know we are heading for a conflict, and everyone's position must be clear, so that we know who will be on our side at the crucial moment. I don't think the chairman trusts you any more. He must have discovered that you gave the trade union committee a copy of your report. He wants to prove that you can't play games with him and get away with it. A kind of warning so that you think things over again. But he also wants to burn your boats with the workers and employees in the company, discredit you in their eyes so that you're left with no alternative but to stand on his side. And like a fool you get caught. I've been thinking of this all the time since he told me, wondering whether I should tell the others, or just pretend not to know. What worries me most is you, the friend in whom I've always had hope. I say to myself it's wrong to put my personal feelings before the interests of the workers. Yet so far I don't know what to do. Maybe because I'm still not sure what would best serve their interests. I have never felt so bad before."

He put a hand to his head as though in pain. "How can I stand up in front of the workers and say: "You know Khalil Mansour Khalil? The man who was a militant for so long? Well, he's decided to band with the filth at the top and sell what is ours to the foreigners. He's abandoned those who sweat to earn a living, abandoned the wives and kids who'll be thrown into the streets if this agreement comes through."

He stopped the headlong rush of words. I felt his fingers tightening around my arm.

"Well, what have you to say?" He shook me violently and repeated "I'm asking you — what have you to say?"

He gazed into my face with fury, released my arm and pushed it aside with a gesture of disgust, "Of course you have nothing to say. Cursed be the day when I met you. At least our enemies we know. But those like you who put on socialist trappings are a hundred times more dangerous."

I felt my heart stuttering to a stop, as though I would die at any moment. I remained motionless. If I could have said something, or cried out an insult, or even wept, I might have been relieved. But what was there to weep about? I was finished. The present, the future, no longer existed. Even the past was dead. Now I was alone. Nobody would want a man who had betrayed his friends. Not even Amina or Saïd. And my old comrades . . . I could see them shrug their shoulders and say: "He chose to play their game. To lick their boots . . . like a fawning puppy." And they would turn to more important things, to the problem of coming elections or the changes in leadership, to decisions about who should be promoted to the Central Committee and who should not. And perhaps to a battle or two if things became hot. Bitterness rose in my throat and flowed into my mouth, as though I was about to vomit.

Saïd suddenly pushed his chair back and stood, staring at me for a long moment in silence, and then walked out without looking back. His tall, lithe body disappeared in the crowd, and I sat on, staring at his empty chair.

Saïd Abou Karam

I was busy registering the production figures for the current month when I heard someone call out my name. I lifted my head and saw Mohamed Aboul Fadl, one of the security guards standing at the other end of the big hall which housed the tabletting section. I beckoned him and returned to what I was doing. Whenever I saw one of their hounds these days a muscle in my neck started twitching. I watched him approach out of the corner of my eye. When he was two or three paces away he said: "Good morning. They want you upstairs.."

"Who?"

"The boss."

"Personally?"

"Yes, personally."

I put down my pen, closed the register and stood up.

"Don't wait for me. First I'll tell the head of the shift where I am going."

A few moments later I walked into the office of the chairman's secretary. She was sitting at her desk biting into a bar of chocolate.

"Go straight in. He's alone," she said.

I stood in front of his desk waiting. He was holding the telephone. listening intently, and taking down notes. Every now and then he said a few words. "We will do exactly as you say, Your Excellency . . . Of course, of course . . . Yes, I understand perfectly . . . No, no we will never permit that . . . You can have complete confidence in us, your honour. We will not fail you . . . we have taken all the necessary precautions, and I personally am following the situation closely."

He replaced the receiver, and stared out of the open window, his fingers tapping slowly on the desk. He sighed and then turned to look at me. The small eyes were bloodshot. People said it was his addiction to hasheesh, or perhaps even opium. He examined me questioningly as though unable to recall why I was there.

"Yes?"

"You sent for me, Sir."

"Ah, exactly, Saïd", emphasizing with heavy sarcasm. "One of these days I will give you this file to read." He held up a thick yellow file and shook it at me. On the cover it said "Strictly Confidential" and "Security Unit" printed in black letters. He let it fall back on the desk and added, "It is your file."

"I already know what's written in it."

"Of course, since it describes in detail what you say to others, and what you do. I have warned you before to stop inciting the workers."

"I have never incited the workers against the company."

"That's a lie."

His hand searched automatically for the packet of cigarettes on the desk, pulled out one, and lit it with a silver plated lighter. He blew out a cloud of smoke in my direction before resuming. "I repeat, what you said just now is nothing but lies, and were it not for the fact that your cousin is an excellent cook, I would have fired you from the company a few months after your appointment. Right from the beginning you have shown yourself to be a person who does not hesitate to bite the hand which feeds him."

I felt the blood rush to my head. He was no more than a common thief. Nothing entered or left through the doors of the company unless he took his toll, and yet he had the effrontery to speak to me like that. Now he was preparing to put the whole company up for auction.

"Nobody feeds me. I work to earn my living. Only dogs are fed by people, and there are dogs at all levels.''

A metallic glint in his eyes, like the edge of a razor, emerged for a split second. I had come to know him well. A shrinking rabbit with those who had influence, a roaring lion with subordinates. But with me he was more careful. He knew I could stop the machines at almost any time.

"Don't be insolent. One of these days you'll find yourself in the streets, if you don't watch out. I've warned you several times, but this will be the last. Don't play around in matters which concern only the higher levels in our company, especially if they are part and parcel of general policy in the country. The era of closed doors and high walls is over, and we need foreign expertise and know-how.''

"What does 'know-how' mean?''

He threw me a rapid glance as though he had sensed the hidden sarcasm in my question.

"It means the technical knowledge and the expertise required to produce a particular commodity.''

"And do we lack the expertise necessary to produce the same drugs we have been producing all along?''

"I suppose you've heard that from Khalil Mansour Khalil? He gave you a copy of his report didn't he? Or am I mistaken on that count too?''

So he did have his ways of finding out what was going on. His stooges in the union for one. It was not easy to get rid of them. They had been elected by a large majority, making good use of their connections to get all sorts of services for individual workers. I drifted back to what he was saying.

"As I said this is my last warning to you Saïd. Be wise; try to understand what's going on around you. You're an intelligent man. Don't throw your chances overboard. I'm willing to help you, once the agreement is signed. We'll send you to France for training. You'll earn money, and gain technical experience. You might even be able to catch yourself one of those pretty French girls. They're crazy over black skins.''

He emitted an obscene laugh, then quickly became serious again, as though he had forgotten himself.

"Think over what I have told you. The trade union committee will only land you in trouble. One day you will remember my words to you and thank me for them. And remember, keep away from Khalil Mansour Khalil. If you associate with him you'll run the risk of marking yourself for life. When you came into the room I was talking to the head of the SSSPS in Helwan. That means matters have entered a critical stage. So keep your wits about you. Ah . . . by the way, before you leave, I have something here which might interest you. Khalil Mansour Khalil withdrew the first report about the Larochelle contract. I've made a photocopy of his new one for you. Here . . . And now go. I can't afford to waste the whole day with you."

I went out with my head in a whirl, came to a halt at the end of the corridor and sat down on the messenger boy's empty chair. After a while I noticed him standing at a distance, eyeing me curiously, so I got up and went on. I descended the stairs holding tightly to the banisters, crossed the courtyard and automatically headed for the tabletting section. On the way, one or two people said something to me, but I paid no attention. When I reached my desk, I pulled out the chair, opened the register and sat staring into space. Time passed. At one moment I put my hand in the pocket of my overall and it struck against a sheaf of papers. I pulled them out. On the first page was a title: "Report on the Joint Production Agreement between the Thebes Pharmaceutical Company and Larochelle Chemicals." My eyes ran over the lines:

On the 30 June 1978 I presented a report concerning the proposed agreement between our company and Larochelle Chemicals in which I attempted to clarify the harmful effects of the above-mentioned proposal on the present and future status of Thebes Pharmaceuticals. However, after more ample study of the project agreement in relation to the situation prevailing in our company, I have come to the conclusion that in my first report I failed to highlight sufficiently the benefits which could accrue from the setting up of a stable partnership with an international concern like Larochelle, known to have at its disposal enormous technical capabilities and financial resources.

In this first report I might also have tended to exaggerate the negative effects of such an agreement on the present activities and future development of our company. For we should not forget that the national drug industry in general, and the "Thebes Pharmaceutical Company" in particular has accumulated sufficient experience to enable it to avoid any mistakes or pitfalls which might arise, at one or other stage, in the implementation of the agreement.

I have had detailed discussions with the chairman, and these have permitted me to arrive at a more objective appraisal of some aspects which received insufficient attention, or were overlooked in the first report.

53

"Overlooked." I had never known Khalil overlook things so easily. Perhaps that was the real problem. His mind was always wide awake. But his heart, where was his heart? With the workers or the brokers? I was not going to let him off so easily. The struggle was going to be hard, but we had to fight . . . fight to protect our daily bread, fight to keep our heads high. We'd had enough of retreating, of being herded like cattle from one pasture to another, sick of the deceit.

The next morning I sent Mostapha Ramadan with a note for Khalil, and told him to leave it on his desk. It seemed wiser to avoid getting in touch with him directly. An atmosphere of impending strife hung over our heads. I also decided not to go to his house. I wanted to meet him on neutral grounds.

I went to meet Khalil with a heavy heart. The sky was like a metal lid, the air was thick. At the coffee house the windows had been left open in an attempt to create a draught. The noise of the street seemed louder than usual. I felt like running to my room, closing the shutters, putting on the fan, and abandoning myself to the calm. I sat at a table near the far end and for the first time ordered a *Narjeela*. The usual clients started drifting in. I knew most of them. For years I had been coming regularly to this coffee house. The radio was emitting hoarse voices . . . a play about queuing in front of co-operative stores and the need to keep strictly in line. A group of middle-aged men, their heads streaked with grey, were watching a game of backgammon. At another table a number of young workers were concentrating on a game of cards. The sound of the discs rattling into the wooden box contrasted with the soft whisper of the cards. I asked for a cup of coffee and let my thoughts wander, puffing at the *Narjeela* from time to time. Sweat poured from my body.

I looked at my watch. It was almost a quarter past six. Night was settling over the city. I glimpsed him stepping into the coffee house and looking slowly around the tables. He seemed thinner than usual, his shoulders drooping, and the street lamps threw a jaundiced light on his face as he moved slowly over the paved floor. The eagerness of the early days had gone. Everything seemed enveloped in a sickly shadow, in noxious fumes. These days no one was immune. I stood up and shook hands with him. He spoke in a low voice. "I'm sorry to be late. A last minute telephone call from a relation I have not seen in years."

"How are you Khalil? You look a bit tired."

54

He shrugged his shoulders indifferently, looked at the *Narjeela* and asked laughingly about it. His gaiety seemed forced, without heart. I felt he was going through a crisis.

When the coffee he had ordered was in front of him, I decided to speak. As we talked I felt that the man sitting opposite me had already submitted. Something kept telling me he had already made his decision, and didn't intend to renounce it. As we argued my anger mounted, and several times I was on the verge of exploding. I felt like standing up and raining blows down on him, but I struggled to maintain my calm.

I spoke to him frankly, hiding nothing, but he kept circling, or refusing to respond. He was like a reptile, crawling under a stone to hide. I reached a point where I was on the verge of suffocating and could stand it no more. I suddenly stood up and walked out, leaving him seated at the table alone.

Once outside it seemed that I could breathe again. The vendors were lighting their gas lamps on carts piled with water melons. A huge man dropped rounded, greenish discs of *Tamia* from his enormous paw into a cauldron of boiling oil. People crowded round the taxi-cabs anxious to get home, and a slight breeze stirred fitfully giving hope that the heavy metal lid of the sky was about to be lifted. A girl stood at the corner of the street smiling up at her friend. I moved my arms and legs, lifted my head, felt the blood coursing through my veins, as though life having fled for a while was now returning. I caught sight of myself in a shop window and smiled, white teeth shining in a dark face.

Part II

Khalil Mansour Khalil

I glanced at my watch and yawned. It was a quarter past eight. The long hours of the day stretched out before me. Were it not for the salary they paid me, and the need for somewhere to go instead of staying at home, I don't know whether I would have come any more. I hated the familiar sight of my desk, the in-tray full of correspondence, and the files piled up in one corner. But how many people really enjoyed their work and found themselves in it? How many people rushed out enthusiastically each morning because they had something interesting before them? Who said work would one day become a need and a source of pleasure? Marx? Was it the dream of an economist, the imagination of an artist, or merely the hallucinations of a madman?

I liked to let my thoughts wander this way. They took me out of the humdrum of everyday life ... Today I felt like a boat adrift, carried away by a slow current. I would let myself float, and watch the river banks go by ... Suddenly the telephone rang. I looked at it in bewilderment as though caught unawares, then put out my hand and picked up the receiver to hear the chairman's voice, husky from too many cigarettes and late nights. What could have brought him to the office so early? There was something he wanted to discuss with me. Only an important matter would bring him here this early. Yet it could easily be some trifle or other. Perhaps the Director of Administration had once more tried to entice one of the female employees to his flat on the Mokattam Hills, and someone had let the cat out of the bag. He revelled in these stories. They were an outlet for the sexual hunger he concealed by posing as the defender of morals and honour when such incidents occurred. If required, he could use them later, to exert pressure on the parties involved. But he was not the only one in the enterprise who played these games, nor was he the worst of them.

I found him firmly ensconced behind his desk; the expression on his face indicated the seriousness of the matter for which he had called me. He was freshly shaven, heavily perfumed and wore a light beige suit, tailored in the latest fashion: narrow lapels and tight-fitting shoulders. We exchanged greetings, and he then handed me a folded sheet of paper. It was a cable indicating that Monsieur Jean Rocard would arrive in Cairo on Friday 22 August, flight number AF 494. The aim of his visit was to resume negotiations between Larochelle and the Thebes Pharmaceutical Company. He would be staying at the *Meridien* and requested that the first meeting be held on the company premises, on Saturday at 09.30 hours.

I lifted my eyes from the cable to find the chairman examining me silently, as though trying to divine the effect of this news on me. He lit a cigarette and said: "Sit down and listen to me carefully. Now we are entering a crucial phase in the negotiations. This Monsieur Pacard . . ."

I interrupted him. "Rocard."

"Pacard or Rocard or shit I don't care which — is bringing a new project agreement." He lapsed into silence for a moment, examining my face again.

"You notice I said a new project agreement. We are supposed to study it and give him a definite answer before he leaves Cairo the following Thursday. They have written me a letter saying it is not possible to delay matters further, and that this is our last chance to conclude an agreement with Larochelle."

I said nothing. It was better to have him finish what he had to say.

"I see you are silent. Is there something I have said that you do not like?"

"Whether I like it or not makes no difference. I'm waiting to hear what exactly is required of me."

"I want you to study the document, and prepare a detailed report, with your conclusions in a separate section."

"Again?"

"Yes again. Let me speak to you frankly." He held out a packet of cigarettes and said: "Cigarette?"

"No, thank you. I stopped smoking about a month ago."

"Why?"

"It's better for my health. Besides, with prices going up I was spending over twenty pounds a month on cigarettes alone."

"Twenty pounds?! My dear man, I spend over seventy pounds on the damn things." He prounounced the figure with a hint of pride. "Anyway, let's go back to what I was saying. I have not lost hope in you yet. You are one of those rare people endowed with exceptional talents. I would even go further and say very honestly that I have so far never worked with anyone who has your ability for studying all the aspects of a problem in detail, and then extracting what is essential, so that what needs to be done becomes clear. I am prepared to swear an oath of divorce, if necessary, in order to convince you that my intentions towards you are nothing but good. I need your help. In return I am prepared to give you the key to opportunities of which you have never even dreamt: material gain — although I wonder if that attracts you — travel abroad, and facilities for scientific research. I don't think I need to tell you what the name Larochelle signifies in the field of chemical and drug research."

"No, you don't."

"In comparison we are nothing but a drop in the ocean." His lips curled in disdain. "Heh . . . so what do you say?"

"What you are asking me to do is part of my job."

He chased away a fly which had settled on his desk with an irritated sweep of the hand.

"Don't put on an act with me. That is not what I mean, and you know it. What I am driving at is quite different. From the moment I hand you a copy of the project, you are to consider yourself one of the people on whom I can depend. This new situation will entail certain responsibilities, and of course lead to benefits. One of the first things expected of you will be an unquestionable loyalty to those in charge of this company — that is to me personally — and an unimpeachable loyalty in protecting any secrets confided in you. Meaning, that from this moment if you say anthing about the proposed agreement with Larochelle to anyone, apart from myself, you will never set foot in the Thebes Pharmaceutical Company again. I hope that is clear."

My mouth went dry. He lifted the telephone receiver without taking his eyes from my face, staring insistently, as if trying to see what lay inside my skull. Now I was at a crossroads, and there was no retreat. I had to choose either to join all the filth beneath which the country was becoming submerged, or to stand by such truth and honesty as remained. But he was trying to corner me, to force me to choose his side. If I said "No" he would consider me an opponent and take whatever measures he felt appropriate. I thought quickly, egged on by the ferrety searching of his eyes. Then I must say "Yes". "Yes" would leave me a choice. But that I would think about later.

I heard him say: "Soheir. Please send us two cups of coffee." He looked at me questioningly: "One of them with only very little sugar?" When I nodded he put the receiver down. I could hear the clock on his desk ticking off the seconds. He was still waiting for my answer; further hesitation would make him suspicious. I took a deep breath and said: "All right I agree to your proposal." He showed big yellow teeth in a smile of satisfaction.

"May I congratulate you. At last you have shown that in addition to your professional competence you also know where your interests lie."

He stared at me as though trying to allay his remaining doubts.

"Don't forget. Not a word about what has passed between us. Monsieur Pacard is arriving at half past nine. I will meet him alone, first, then send for you. He might wish to explain a few things about the contract to you."

There was a knock on the door and the messenger brought in the coffee. The chairman was silent until the man had closed the door behind him.

"Do not forget that in this company the walls have ears and even eyes, some working for us, and some against us. I suppose you know nothing goes on without my finding out about it. Why don't you drink your coffee?"

I lifted my cup and took a sip. My thoughts still whirling round.

"How's Amina?"

This was the first time he had asked about my wife, using her first name to boot. He usually behaved towards me as though I had no existence outside the company. But now we were cronies.

"Thanks be to Allah. She is fine."

"If either of you ever needs anything don't hesitate to tell me."

I nodded, rapidly swallowed a few sips of coffee, and stood up. As I left the room I could feel his stare boring into my back.

I met Monsieur Rocard early on the following Saturday afternoon. He was sitting on the sofa when I entered the chairman's room. He was a tall man and when he stood to shake hands with me his eyes inspected me from a height. They looked with the coldness and distance common in the eyes of men accustomed to command, without the need to concern themselves with the petty details of life. He wore a dark jacket and tight well-fitting grey trousers, pronounced his French with an almost mechanical precision, and was conversant with Arabic, which he spoke with an accent difficult to define. He had spent several years in Algeria when it was still under the French colonial administration, and disliked de Gaulle intensely, whom he said had not realized "that we live in the era of transnational interests, in which narrow nationalist thinking must take a back seat, if the West is to face the menace of Soviet communism."

I sat contemplating him. Everything about his person was neat and polished, from his close cropped hair and manicured nails, to the soft leather bag which he opened with a code lock. When he asked for anything it was with an extreme politeness, as though we were in the court of some French king. But he sprawled on the sofa with his legs stretched out, like a man relaxing comfortably at home. He tried to draw me into a political discussion but I veered away by asking about the price of the chemicals we would be importing from Larochelle. He submitted gracefully, and before I left the room gave me a copy of the project document which he said would answer at least some of my questions. I realized that the chairman must have mentioned to him that I was one of his assistants. His aim was double: to involve me in the game as early as possible, and to show the Frenchman that his assistants were not just nobodies, but men of calibre who could do a good job.

I slipped the project document into an envelope and left the office a little earlier than usual. My mind was in a turmoil. I needed to walk, to exert some physical effort and release the tension that had mounted up throughout the day. As I passed along the corridor I noticed that things were unusually quiet. All the doors were closed, nobody seemed to be moving, and voices were reduced to a distant murmur. At the bottom of the staircase I glimpsed a group of employees in deep conversation, but when they saw me they fell silent and dispersed. In the front compound a black limousine crouched between the buildings waiting for some signal to move, and at the outer entrance the faces of the time clerks and guards looked gloomy.

I walked rapidly along the road. I thought of calling on Amina, but I knew she was busy getting ready for her exhibition; her mind would be elsewhere. I could imagine her eyes wandering into space after the initial comments of interest or surprise.

I took the train from Helwan and instead of getting out at Dar El Salam I decided to go on to Bab El Louk. There was nothing to do at home, I wanted to think things over, to let my legs carry me along while my mind tried to find its way out of the maze in which I found myself.

At eight o'clock in the evening I was still walking aimlessly around. The streets of the city seemed to hunt me down, with the girls in white hats selling paper tissues, police vans weaving a passage through the traffic with their shrieking sirens; sand bags piled up on the pavements, metal helmets, automatic rifles; with promises ringing in my ears, travellers cheques and cold eyes. My feet moved wearily, and my mind was still confused. It was useless to tramp the streets of this monstrous city all night. Better to go home, put on the lamp, pull the document out of its yellow envelope and read it. Once finished with the report he had asked me to write, I could perhaps reach some conclusion.

I don't know how I reached home. My legs seemed to move automatically. The suburb was buried in a deep silence, and the click of the lock when I turned the key sounded so loud that it seemed that I must have awakened the whole neighbourhood. I changed into my slippers, and made a big cup of coffee. I sat down at my desk, took out the project document and started to sip my coffee. Slowly my mind grew clearer and soon I found myself completely absorbed in preparing the report. Several hours passed before I lifted my head at the sound of a car passing in the street. Suddenly I realized that Amina was not yet home. I made an effort to brush away a wave of anxiety. These days she was busy preparing for her exhibition. From the moment she finished her work in the factory it was a continuous race from one place to the other. She seemed to have completely forgotten my existence: I, too, was preoccupied and tended to spend most of my time alone. Sometimes I wondered what Saïd was doing these days. The plant was very quiet now, quieter than usual. The workers must have seen the Frenchman arrive, and the news had probably spread. A delegation from the trade union committee had met the chairman. I heard later that he had promised them that the coming period could be one of prosperity for everyone in the company. He advised the members of the delegation to concentrate on production and to avoid circulating rumours, or raising issues which could lead only to unrest and strife. It was essential, he said, to unmask those who were trying to disturb the peace and stability the company had enjoyed for so long. He wanted them to consider him as an elder brother or father who could be depended upon to look after their interests, and repeated several times that they had absolutely no cause for worry.

I was amazed to hear that they had contented themselves with listening to what he had to say, despite the fact that he did not attempt to hide the existence of a new project agreement. I could not imagine that Saïd was convinced. But why had he kept silent? Perhaps out of fear. This explanation gave me some satisfaction. I was not the only one . . . But Saïd . . . Fear . . . ? of course he knew fear, but he was not one to retreat unless there was no other way. No . . . it was something else. Some design he had in mind . . . some plan.

A few days later I was in the chairman's office discussing routine matters when he suddenly sprang a question on me, as though it had just occurred to him.

"What do you think of the trade union committee?"

I was at a loss what to answer. To give myself time I countered with a question.

"What aspects of the trade union committee are you asking about?"

"How do you think it will react to the agreement with Larochelle?"

Now I understood. He was trying to make use of my experience in areas other than in that of research. Why not? The most rapid way to climb the ladder; but if I went along with him in such matters, where would it end? This was a way of no retreat, a trap with no escape. I had seen how it operated before with others. More than my principles were at stake now. It was my very being. I felt sick. I might have my weak points but *that* . . . I struggled to get a hold on myself.

"To be quite frank, I haven't thought of it. Perhaps instinctively I have tried to avoid even thinking about such matters."

He gave me a quick questioning look.

"Are you quite sure that your instinct has not driven you to do just the opposite? After all you know — one's past . . ."

I shrugged, as though the subject was of little interest to me. A flat denial would only arouse his suspicions.

"Do you think they will submit to the inevitable?"

"But you promised them that all would be well."

He burst into raucous laughter, greatly amused by what I had said.

"We both know very well to what the agreement will lead in fact."

I said nothing. "We both know." Why did I allow myself to be implicated in all this? Why not be content with a modest vantage point, eschew this degraded world where men stabbed each other in the back? Live in my books and research, and watch Amina as she worked? From time to time she would ask me "What about that study you intend to resume. Have you started it yet?" and I would smilingly say: "No, not yet, I'm still waiting for inspiration." Every time I pondered things these days I despised myself.

"I'm still waiting for an answer."

"I don't really know. Of course there is a chance that they might think of doing something. But at the same time you can't completely exclude the possibility of their deciding to remain quiet. It all depends on how they see the situation."

"Stay quiet?! I doubt it. That negro Saïd Abou Karam is behind everything the workers try to do. He's never satisfied unless there is trouble. I often think of firing him, then perhaps we could have some peace."

He gave me another quick glance. He knew quite well Saïd was my friend, and probably hoped I would repeat what I had just heard. It might plant some fear in his heart. Or was it just a feeling that he could trust me? Rather unlikely. He trusted nobody. Suspicion was a prime factor in everything he did. Sometimes this was fortunate. Before embarking on any action he would weigh the risks a thousand times.

"You must have some idea of the situation. You've always been interested in worker's movements haven't you?"

"I was."

"Well, I think you still hanker after the past. There is something stupidly loyal about you. Apart from that I appreciate your talents. That's why I'm trying to attract you to my side. It's a pity to waste yourself on these nobodies."

A strange character. Sometimes he displayed a sense for people perhaps made more sharp by his peregrinations from one area of activity to another, and the fact that he had witnessed the struggles that went on in each of them.

"Heh . . . still taking refuge in silence?! Then I'll continue. Your friends don't know how to judge people, or put them in their proper place. That is why they keep losing the best people they have."

The cunning bastard. He knew how to strike where it hurt. Christ once said: "Verily take the truth from the mouths of children. For they shall inherit the Kingdom of Heaven." He was sometimes like a child. Nothing could restrain him from expressing his thoughts. A mixture of the most profound and the most nonsensical things could flow from his mouth, and he could swing from extreme caution to outright foolhardiness.

I caught him smiling at me sarcastically as though he had read my thoughts.

"I think it's one of your leaders who once said: 'We must learn from our enemies. They're sometimes right in what they say about us.' It was Lenin wasn't it? By the way I read about him in a book by Hassanein Leheita. I tell you that in case you start imagining I'm a Marxist like yourself."

He laughed uproariously, seemingly very pleased with his own humour. He was in high spirits this morning. The new agreement had apparently given a boost to his morale. These days his kind were having the time of their lives.

He broke off and came back at me again. "You haven't really said anything yet."

"I tell you I don't know."

He narrowed his eyes as if weighing what he was going to say carefully.

"Good. If you don't, then I do. I know exactly what they are envisaging."

There was no need for me to encourage him. If he had decided to tell me what he apparently considered an important secret, he would do so of his own accord. I waited.

"They are preparing for a strike."

"A strike!?" I attempted to sound incredulous.

"Yes, a strike. Imagine that. They're nothing but a bunch of half-wits. It is I who will strike, and with an iron fist. I'll break the snake's back before it bites. A strike is not a matter which concerns us alone. It encroaches on national interests and on the rule of law. The state will never allow it — it knows that a strike is like an epidemic which can spread all over the country."

Why was he telling me all this? I could not believe that it was a sign of his confidence in me. I was still on probation. He would test me once, twice, three times, maybe a hundred times. He might continue to test me to the end of my days. I remained guilty until I could prove my innocence, and sometimes guilty even if I did. People like me were governed by the law of suspicion, living beneath the sword of Damocles. No, it certainly was not that he trusted me. He had an aim. To transform me into an unwitting instrument. If he could make me believe that a strike would have very serious consequences for the workers, I might rush off and try to convince them to drop the idea. He hoped I could influence them through Saïd. The man was not as simple as I thought. He had pondered the matter deeply, and come to the conclusion that the most important thing was to avoid any disturbances in the plant before the agreement was signed. He was afraid that Larochelle would back out at any signs of unrest. If my deductions were correct it meant that the only effective course of action was to strike, and that at the earliest possible moment. I felt like an old veteran dozing in his rocking chair who had been awakened by the sound of a bugle.

I leaned back in my chair and closed my eyes. Where did I stand in relation to all this? Why had Saïd not come to see me? Or why had I not gone to see him? In a crisis of this kind did pride have any place? Yes, of course! What was a man without pride?

I pushed my chair back from the desk and walked over to the window. A beautiful autumn night. The stars looked down from a velvety sky and an infinitely soft breeze flowed from the fields. Life could have been so much better. Amina was fortunate. Once absorbed in her painting everything else was of minor importance. What was happiness? An absorption so total that even the sense of time is lost. I had known the feeling in my youth, but older now, I was pulled in different directions; I had lost the still centre, and was caught in powerful currents at a time when my strength had started to wane. If Saïd did not come to me then perhaps I should go to him. I closed the shutters and returned to my desk. As I passed in front of the mirror I smiled at myself. What did the proverb say. "The Piper may be dying but his fingers go on playing." The "Horse" had insight. He had seen through me. The clock in a neighbour's house chimed the twelve strokes of midnight — time to go to bed. I started to collect my papers when suddenly the telephone rang. Who could it be at this time of night? I hesitated for a moment, but then lifted the receiver and said: "Hello."

I heard her say in a rush: "Khalil. Is that you? This is Ruth. I'm sorry to disturb you so late. I tried to get in touch with you all day."

"Don't let that worry you. I'm glad to hear your voice. Very glad."

"I also am happy to have found you. How are you?"

"Not so bad. Where were you all this time?"

"I had to leave at short notice for the States, and I got back only yesterday."

There was a long silence as though each of us was searching for words, then she said: "I have finished transcribing your tape. When can we meet?"

"Any time you wish."

"Tomorrow, in the evening, after seven? Here in my flat."

"That's fine with me."

There was another long moment of hesitation. Then she said: "I'll be waiting for you Khalil. Good night."

The receiver clicked in my ear. I would like to have prolonged our conversation, but her unexpected call had taken me unawares. I felt happy and disturbed. I fumbled with the papers on my desk, and after several attempts managed to get them back into the yellow envelope. Amina was not back, but in any case I did not feel like talking. Tonight I preferred to be alone. I extinguished the lights except for a night lamp near the door. Each heartbeat seemed to say "Ruth" . . . "Ruth" . . . "Ruth" . . .

Saïd Abou Karam

The weeks passed rapidly and autumn came almost before I realized it. I was plunged to my ears in work — the plant during the day, the trade union committee, or the Federation of Chemical Workers at night. Every week I snatched a few hours to walk along the bank of the Nile, or sit in the coffee house chatting with friends or playing backgammon. To us it seemed as though the agreement with Larochelle had died a natural death, and been buried in the files for ever. From time to time an anxiety would awaken within me, for this apparent end to the matter perhaps augured something we did not expect.

I remember that day very well. It was the first Saturday in October. After the weekend holiday there was that hint of laziness in the air before we caught up with the rhythm of the machines again. I was talking to one of the chemical engineers about some difficulties we were having with a new product. We stood in the outer compound under the sun, watching the grey smoke belching from a chimney into the clear sky. I noticed an unusual activity near the entrance and turned round. A black Mercedes crept through the open gates, slowly drove up across the open space and came to a halt at the bottom of the steps to the administration building. Out of it stepped a tall man in a dark suit. His eyes circled round the compound slowly taking in the details; he carried a small leather bag. The chairman came out to meet him, smiling broadly, his hand outstretched. They shook hands vigorously, exchanged a few words and then disappeared inside the building. The car moved silently away like a huge insect. An obscure fear dispelled the feeling of well-being with which I had started the day. I took leave of the young man and returned to the tabletting section to await the news I felt sure was on the way.

Just before the lunch hour one of the female administration employees brought me the first items of news. A representative from Larochelle had arrived and had been closeted with the chairman in his room all morning. As the employees passed through the corridor they threw anxious glances at the red light burning over the door like a warning signal. The secretary was refusing all telephone calls, and all visitors, even those with an appointment. The eyes of the workers remained fixed to what they were doing. Any voice which rose above a whisper immediately drew attention to itself.

But the news soon filtered through. It crept through the door of the chairman's office, along the corridor, down the stairs and spread in all directions to the various sections of the plant. The atmosphere of cautious anticipation gradually changed into something like a slow, long/drawn-out but intense combustion.

During the first few days a lot of contradictory things went around, but before the week was over the real facts became known. The French concern had withdrawn the original patents agreement and replaced it with a new merger project in which 49% of the total invested capital would be contributed by the Larochelle group.

The outward calm in the plant shattered. Workers kept coming to my desk to ask me questions, or to discuss what we should do, and the telephone rang all day. An interminable discussion broke out again. In the room where the trade union committee met we sat amidst clouds of smoke, arguing hour after hour. In the new situation the workers would bear the brunt of whatever changes were made. Gradually other details leaked out. The foreign investors were in a hurry. It was necessary to speed things up. And so it had been decided that instead of wasting time with the patent agreement Larochelle should opt for a direct merger. A representative had been sent with the new proposal. He had taken the night plane from Paris and next morning was driven from the Meridien Hotel, along the Nile to the premises of our company in Helwan.

My heart was heavy with the threat this man posed. My thoughts were like a hornet's nest aroused by an intruder, but gradually they became calmer. I don't know why I remembered Khalil at that particular moment. Perhaps because since we became friends I had got into the habit of seeking his advice when some problem arose.

Why not get in touch with him again? I quickly brushed the idea aside, but it kept coming back to me. After the position he had taken how could I ask for his advice? At last I decided to consult some of my comrades in the committee. The atmosphere of crisis was building up and we had to move fast. But this time it was necessary to ensure there was no leak.

When I broached the subject to my comrades there was a tense silence followed by an outburst of disapproving voices. After a time the storm calmed down, and we began to discuss the matter more quietly. At last they agreed that together with Mostapha Ramadan, I could visit Khalil and ask him what he thought of the new project, in the hope that he might be able to give us some advice. We badly needed a copy of the new project document to study in preparation for our campaign, and perhaps he could get us one. But most important of all, and this had provoked the most resistance, we agreed to ask for his views about the strike unanimously decided upon by our committee, although the exact date had so far been left open.

I telephoned Khalil several times before I found him at home. His tone was very reserved, and were it not for the effort I had made to convince my comrades I might have dropped the idea. But after my obstinate insistence how could I tell them that I had changed my mind, simply because he had not shown much enthusiasm on the phone. We went to his house in the evening about eight o'clock.

It was plunged in darkness and for a moment I thought no one was at home. I rang the bell and he opened the door. He looked worn, and had gone grey at the temples. He asked us to sit down, and brought us minted tea which we drank in silence. I tried to dispel the frigid atmosphere, asked him about his news, what he was doing, what books he had read recently. Then I asked him about Amina, and when she expected to give birth to their child. He answered in monosyllables, and all my attempts to draw him into a conversation failed. Even when I started to remark on the political situation, he sat there gloomily, paying almost no attention to what I was saying. Mostapha Ramadan kept shifting his feet, and throwing glances at me which gradually became more insistent, as though he was trying to convey to me that it was better for us to leave. But I ignored his signals. This meeting was related to the strike, and that was no small matter. Besides it hurt me to see Khalil in this state, and I felt it necessary to make a last effort to keep our relations going.

I decided to take the bull by the horns and go straight to the subject.

"Khalil I assume you have heard of the recent developments in our company?"

"What recent development?"

"The new project with Larochelle."

"Of course. Is there anybody in the company who has not heard about it?"

"And what do you think?"

He hesitated for a long moment. He knew me well enough to know that I was not asking questions just out of curiosity.

"It's a change which needs to be studied."

"And has the Director of the Research Department not yet studied it?"

"As you know, I am no longer consulted on such matters."

"Then you have not even read the project document?"

"Why do you ask?"

He had not denied reading it. Perhaps he was leaving the door slightly open. It was best to put matters bluntly to him. Surely what he had inside him was not completely dead.

"Khalil, you know this new proposal will be a catastrophe for the majority of those employed by the company. At higher levels they are not thinking of anything except the profits the minority will be pocketing if Thebes becomes a foreign investment subsidiary. Our fate will be different. Those who are kept on may get higher wages but these will soon be swallowed up by rising prices. Many of us will be thrown on to the streets. The new production methods and processes they intend to introduce will lead to the dismissal of many workers. Even in the administration the new systems will create a labour surplus."

"That's progress."

"No, it's not, at least not for the workers."

"What is it that you want of me exactly?"

"Tell me first. Have you read the project document, and if you haven't can you get us a copy of it?"

He looked me straight in the eye. He would not lie to me, that I knew. But his voice was barely audible as though he was abandoning himself to the inevitable.

"Yes I have read it" he said, "However I am wondering what it is that you are envisaging, and whether you have carefully weighed the consequences of anything you might do."

"What we intend to do, that we will discuss with you in a moment. But let me ask you first. Are you prepared to make a study of the project document for us?"

He took a deep breath. I could see that the struggle inside him was hard, perhaps the hardest ever. I had the sense of a candle, burning weakly but still alive, a flickering flame somewhere deep down inside. There was a great weariness in his face. The silence seemed endless and all-enveloping. Time stood still, and all movement died on the way.

"The chairman instructed me to make a study of the new project and I have already completed it."

My heart beat with joy. I stretched out my hand to him, but he ignored my gesture and left it foolishly suspended in the air. I felt angry and humiliated. Why was he treating me like that?

"You just want to use me again. As usual, you don't care a damn about what happens to me. I am to pay the price, to be sacrificed in the interests of capital, but also on the altar of socialism and worker's rights. You want to take, but never stop to ask yourselves a very important question, 'What do we give in return?' "

"What can we give if we don't have anything?"

"You can be awfully trite sometimes. So you don't have anything to give? What about friendship, solidarity, understanding, protection for those who run the risk of helping? Small human things. But no . . . You're too busy with the big problems."

"We barely have the time to take our breath. It's one problem after another."

"If you have no time to breathe, how can you have time to think?"

I was beginning to feel furious. What impudence he had, standing on a pedestal and making speeches, lecturing us to show how bloody wise he was. But when we needed him, he put his tail between his legs and ran off. I sat staring at him, waiting for the wave of hatred rising within me to subside. I had not come to pick a fight.

"We came to ask for your help."

"I know. But before that you did not think of coming."

"I'm sorry. I thought it was better that way."

"No. You wanted to teach me a lesson. But that's something I never did with you."

"Let's settle these matters between ourselves later."

"I've told you what I think, and for me the matter is settled. If I agree to co-operate with you again are your people capable of keeping the secret?"

"Of course."

"Like last time?"

For a moment I didn't know what to say. I muttered quietly, "No, not like last time. We have learnt our lesson."

"Then you can count on me."

I put my arm around his shoulders and hugged him. This time he responded. I caught him wiping his eyes quickly with his hand, then he smiled and said: "When the piper dies his fingers go on playing."

We laughed. I felt very happy. All was well now. My friend was with us again. I was moved to see the smile on his face and, overcome by my feelings, I said nothing for a while. Then remembering, I looked at my watch.

"We have stayed too long. Our comrades are waiting for us in the coffee house, and by now they must be very restless. Let's go Mostapha."

We stood up. Khalil remained seated and with a calm smile said: "And the strike?"

We looked at him in amazement.

"Do you see how well you keep your secrets? They know you are preparing to strike. The chairman said to me, 'We'll teach them a lesson they'll never forget. As for you Mister Khalil, let me give you some good advice. If I ever so much as hear that the contents of your memorandum have been made known to them, you will never put your foot in this company again'."

We dropped back heavily on our seats at the same moment, as though our legs had given way under us. We said nothing for some time. Then I asked in a voice which sounded as though it was not mine, "And now what do we do?!"

He began to comb his hair with his fingers in a gesture characteristic of him when he was thinking deeply.

"You must hurry with the preparation for a strike before they have time to do anything."

"That means you approve of the strike?"

"Do you have any other alternative? If the agreement comes into operation, about two hundred workers will lose their jobs, that is about twenty percent of the labour force. The others who remain will have their salaries raised. That way they hope to split your ranks, and convince the majority that the signature of the agreement with Larochelle is in their interest. Each individual worker or employee will be hoping that he is among those who are staying on. It is therefore vital that you go ahead with the strike. Try to enlist the support of the Federation of Chemical Workers."

My thoughts strayed. I could imagine what we were in for in the coming days. The small muscle in my neck was twitching again, and

74

something like an icy current seemed to go through me. I sighed and stood up.

"We really have to go now."

I stretched out my arm. Our eyes met as we shook hands in silence.

Amina Tewfik

It was almost seven in the evening when I turned my key in the front door. During the train journey from Minia to Cairo, for reasons I could not explain to myself, I suddenly became a prey to all sorts of dark forebodings. Perhaps it was the depressing story I had lived through during the previous two days, the long hours spent listening to insults, to words which were meant to hurt, to violent arguments. It was as though each of them was digging up all the painful memories and unpleasant incidents in their life, in a wilful attempt to destroy anything that might have remained between them. He maintained that she was keen on continuing with her job because she was having a love affair with one of her colleagues. She begged him to use his reason, to ignore the rumours being spread by an employee whose advances she had repelled. How could they possibly feed a family of four on his earnings, with prices jumping higher every week? I saw the fear and the pain in the children's eyes each time the word divorce lashed out in the tiny flat, or whenever it seemed they would come to blows.

I looked out of the window at the dark brown earth ploughed by tractors. The sun setting behind a row of palm trees, spilling its crimson and ochre colours into the waters of the stream, and the fine arterial canals branching out from it, bringing life blood to the green fields. Black-eyed buffaloes brooded at a crossing, watching the train. A dark peasant woman walked along the road, her robe flapping, her tall body upright, and at her side shuffled a shrivelled old man — beauty and misery side by side, everywhere.

Throughout the journey back from Minia I kept thinking of Khalil. The house was silent when I arrived. I went to the bedroom thinking he might be resting, but he was not there. I undressed in the bathroom feeling the cold freshness of the tiles under my bare feet. I filled the bath with hot water and gently slid into it. I could see the tips of my breasts and my rounded belly emerging at the surface, and feel my body throbbing, the muscles tense, the blood coursing through my veins. I let myself sink in the pleasurable caress of warm water. This short separation had reawakened my desire.

I put on a nightdress of fine cotton and stretched my tired limbs on the bed. I must have fallen into a deep sleep for I awoke to the sound of his key turning in the lock. He came straight to our room and put on the lights. I was happy to see him and said: "I missed you these past few days. When I got back and did not find you I felt depressed." I watched him undress, glimpsed the movement of the muscles under his brown skin, felt the desire mount up within me again, powerfully. He lay down by my side almost touching me, but I felt that his thoughts were elsewhere, as though he had just passed through an experience which had struck a deep chord within him. Where had he been this night? Another woman? I moved slightly away from him. I had pride, and I hated dealings which were underhanded. I expected him to respect my feelings just as I had always respected his. I could get on quite well without him.

I turned over on the other side. I was very upset and it took me some time to fall asleep. Meanwhile he lay there without moving, as though trying not to draw attention to himself.

When I woke up in the morning he had already left the bed. I found him in the bathroom standing in front of the mirror and shaving with the same concentration he put into everything. Whenever I watched him do anything I couldn't help smiling. Even if it was the simplest thing he would lean over it with an earnest look on his face, pucker his brow and lick his lips from time to time, like a child.

I put my hand on his shoulder and said: "Good morning Khalil. I'm so happy to be back." I had forgotten my ill-feeling of the previous night. I never like to burden myself with worries, or mope over the past, and I welcome each new day with open arms.

We sat at the small table in the kitchen drinking tea. He kept glancing at my belly. I was now in my seventh month, a strange yet familiar being was moving inside me. It kept kicking gently as though demanding attention or trying itself out. Sometimes it remained quiet for days and nights and I would begin to worry. Why had all signs of life subsided? Perhaps it was suffocating inside. I would be seized with terror, with a desire to tear my body apart and look inside. I did my daily work but my mind was elsewhere, occupied by this amorphous,

76

throbbing part of my life. I wanted it to be a boy, not because boys were better than girls, but because if I lost Khalil he could make up for my loss. It was like an intuition that came to me from time to time. I would call him Esam. I had carried him in my body, and in two months time I would give birth to him from between my thighs. I could see the questioning look in Khalil's eyes. I loved him when he tried to understand what only a woman can fully realize.

Nobody was closer to him than I was and I cannot dispel the feeling that the evening when I travelled to Minia was crucial. For although no life is made of a single instant, and no one is made or destroyed in one night, yet surely there are moments when more is done or undone than at any other time. Perhaps working with colours, and shadows and lines had made my imagination too fertile. Yet for every man and woman there is a time when the struggle within them reaches a crisis. Then there is a need for someone by your side. Maybe that night he felt I was abandoning him when he needed me most, that I was too busy with my paint and brushes and designs, too busy forging a path for myself.

When the telephone rang in our house that night it was as though fate had already decided. How could I consider myself even partly responsible? He would have gone to meet this woman whether I was there or not. And yet he was lonely ... and loneliness can be dangerous.

Inside, the questions go on. Why did I leave him at that precise moment? Was it an accident? Why did I agree to go to Minia that night? Was it in sympathy for Zeinab? Partly. Yet the real reason probably lay elsewhere. I was tired of hearing about the problems in his company, tired of his moods, his friends, of the anxiety which haunted us day and night. True, we had much in common; even his political interests were not alien to me. But I was an artist, engrossed in putting down on canvas what I discover with my body and my mind. Sometimes I asked myself what use these daily battles were? What he had gained from the years of sacrifice, from abandoning the career for which he had worked so hard? Yet there were moments when I felt he had been through an important experience of which I knew nothing. I had begun to feel the strain of all this uncertainty. So I decided to escape for a while, to get into a train and abandon myself to the rhythmic thud of the wheels, and the restful green of the fields for a few hours, to breathe in the acrid smell of cotton twigs smouldering in an oven fire. I wanted to leave behind the wearisome details of everyday

77

life, the expression on Khalil's face, harassed by his memories, unable to decide whether he preferred the pleasures of peace, or the thrill of joining the struggle. I was thinking of myself, not of him, so I went to Minia that night. It was my right. But the question remains. Did I have to leave him just at the moment when I knew he needed me?

When I recall what happened after I returned, I realize that my departure was not the result of a decision taken on the spur of the moment, but of a consistent pattern. My resentment against him had continued to build up. Yet I did not know of his relationship with the American woman. I felt he was hiding something. So I decided to turn my back on him, to occupy myself with what interested me in life. I left him to his affairs as though they were no concern of mine, and plunged myself into the preparations for my exhibition. When I learnt that a representative from Larochelle had come out to discuss a new project, and that Khalil had written a memorandum about it, I neither showed interest in these developments, nor asked him any questions; and he said nothing. Even when I heard the word "strike" during a discussion with a group of workers in the house one night, I did not try to understand what was being said. I wonder how I managed to do that, but at the time I had taken a firm decision not to occupy myself with such matters. As far as I was concerned they were of little importance. I was an artist, and it was essential to avoid anything that could interfere with my work. These daily activities were a waste of time. Since I resented the way Khalil was behaving with me, I began to resent everything he did. For I had not yet learned that whether we like it or not politics cut deep into our personal life. Instead of following my feelings, I calculated the losses and gains, and made a choice. But the most careful calculation can lead one wide of the mark. Very often it's more important to follow the dictates of one's heart. I had forgotten for a while that love is rare, and an effort must be made to keep it alive.

So the days went by without my knowing how things were developing. I left the house very early in the morning, and was rarely home before midnight. I arranged with the Town Council of Helwan to hold my exhibition in an annex to the Institute of Fine Arts. When I visited the place I found it in a terrible state. Hundreds of old files and papers were strewn all over the floor, old broken-down furniture displayed dirty stuffing, rusty wire, splinters, and torn covers. Greasy finger marks, ink splashes, names scrawled in coloured pencil, or scratched with sharp instruments covered the walls, and scattered piles of cement, gypsum, and chalk mixed with cockroach and rat droppings covered the floor. It was impossible to hold my exhibition there.

I spent another two weeks running from one official to the other, trying to find a new location. Each one referred me to the next, until I ended up in the office of the chief Councillor — a fat man wearing a waistcoat. Over his fleshy lips hung a big hennaed moustache. His eyes examined my breasts with a dull glint, and then travelled down my body. He told me that I would have to come back on Thursday evening, since it would be difficult for him to find time to examine the matter except when the routine work of the week was over. When I walked out of his office I had already decided not to return, for I knew that a second visit would expose me to much more than a distant scrutiny of my body.

Khalil and I were in the habit of going to work together, but during this period he began to wake up late, as though he had developed a dislike for the job he was doing. As a result we met very rarely. But he continued to take interest in my exhibition. Whenever we met he asked me how it was faring, and offered to help. Sometimes he went with me to meet the officials concerned. But time was flying and I had still not found what I wanted. He suggested that I accept the annex to the Institute of Fine Arts and do whatever was necessary to clear it up and have the walls painted and the floor varnished. We could discuss the matter with the Director of the Institute; he was ready to accompany me on a visit to him, since they had been students together at the same school in Tantah.

The man received us warmly. He was very enthusiastic about the idea of the exhibition, expressed his readiness to help, and promised to suggest to the students' union that a small group of volunteers be gathered to make whatever changes were needed.

When I visited it about ten days later I almost cried out in wonder. The change surpassed my wildest dreams. Everything had been cleaned. The walls were white as milk, the floor shone like a mirror, and shaded lamps were placed in all the places I had indicated. I almost wept with happiness, and returned home on wings. Khalil was there; for the first time in weeks I took him into my arms. He had grown very thin, as though burning with a hidden fever. He inquired about the hall, and when I told him his face lit up. He suggested that we visited the Institute, to thank the Director and the students.

The next day we met the Director and spent some time chatting with him, then went to the room where the students' union secretariat was lodged. We had tea with those boys and girls who had formed the group of volunteers, in the midst of laughter and happy voices. Khalil was in the best of moods, asking them questions about their studies, and other things. His face was so changed he looked almost like one of them. He told them stories about his youth and childhood, and the gathering ended with everyone telling the latest jokes. The boys and girls seemed to have developed a liking for him very quickly. Few were the occasions on which I had seen him so happy, and we left the Institute in the best of spirits.

On the way back he took my hands and said: "I love you Amina. You are a wonderful person and I hope this exhibition will mark a new stage in your life. Whatever may happen never doubt yourself. You will go a long way." I came to a sudden stop, put my arm around him, and kissed him. I remember that embrace on the road. It had something special about it, something beautiful and pure as though we were both children again. Our hands remained clasped for a long moment and we came to ourselves only at the sound of a train rushing over the crossing.

Every hour brought me closer to the moment for which I had waited so long. I slept only a few hours each night, and woke long before dawn. I lingered in bed listening to his regular breathing. Sometimes I felt him shiver in his sleep, and moved closer to him, as though my body could chase away the images he was seeing. Before the darkness of night lifted, the voice of the muezzin's call to prayer would drift across to where I lay. I did not see his lashes lift, or glimpse the naked white of his eyes, or the jet black of his pupils, yet I knew his eyes had opened, that he was remembering, that his mind had travelled far off. Once more his naked feet moved over the ground slowly, his legs sagged under a load of weariness, sweat poured out of his body on to the sand. His skin was covered with a white layer like a ghost, and over his head the stars shivered. He strained his ears to hear the sweet sadness of the voice carried by the wind, the song of a soul in exile, searching for comfort in the heavens, in an almighty powerful Allah, reaching out to the sun that will rise, to those who were left behind, to a woman or a child. I could see him walking with slow steps between the sleeping tents surrounded by barbed wire, at peace with himself, with the effort made, with the sweat on his brow, and the white loaves browning in the oven.

The call to prayer dies away, and the universe around us is silent, enveloped in the eerie shadows of the early dawn. I turn on my side, nestle up against his slender back, seek for the feeling of closeness we seem to have lost. I watch the light of day filter through the shutters, get out of bed, prepare the tea, put a fine loaf to heat on a slow fire, boil the milk, and place the sugar basin and cups on the table.

After a while he pokes his tousled head through the door and I hear him say, "Good morning". From that moment onwards I forget everything, even his presence, and live for my paintings hanging on the walls, on the flame which burns inside me, and the cup of morning tea which scalds my lips. I rush out of the house into the street, glimpse my neighbour leaning on the window sill with her breasts bulging out of her flimsy nightdress. My feet carry me like wings along the pavement, up the steps to the station, and my head is a space peopled with coloured shapes and wooden frames.

Khalil and Saïd, with the help of a few workers, distributed posters and cards for the exhibition to the industrial establishments in our district and to the offices of the Town Council. We went around the houses, schools and shops in Dar El Salam; I put up a few posters in Helwan Station, and Saïd took care of the district of Basateen.

Suddenly the opening day was upon us; we threw the Institute gates wide open. During the first half hour nobody came. My heart slowly sank. But after a little while the first visitor arrived. He put a hesitant foot on the threshold of the entrance, and suddenly found himself surrounded by a circle of youths, as though they were trying to prevent him from escaping. I saw the poor man wipe the sweat from his bald head with a big handkerchief, and surrender himself to the escorting group. He quickly disappeared inside, but his arrival was like the drop that heralded a rainstorm. People started to gather in large numbers in front of the entrance and walk in. Some visitors came in family groups. I stood half dazed near the entrance to the hall. What had brought all these people? The majority probably did not know what a painting meant, and the rest might have heard some chance remarks. I could not assimilate what was happening, and was overcome by emotion. I realized of course that Saïd and his comrades had played an important role in attracting so many people. I suddenly felt a terrible exhaustion; I had strained every fibre of my being throughout the weeks, and now there was no strength left inside me. I was like a doll whose stuffing was coming loose, leaving a useless flapping body. I sat down in the hall, barely moving my eyes to follow the people, as they came and went. Some of them just passed by looking at the paintings curiously.

A few stopped in front of them or came closer, or moved to an angle and examined some perspective anew. I saw a man with grey hair approach. He had young eyes full of vitality in a face that was old. I heard him say, "Congratulations, that painting of the hunter is beautiful. I can see him straining every ounce of strength in his body. Nothing will stop him from attaining his goal. Congratulations."

I felt the tears drop from my eyes, wiped them quickly in embarrassment, and smiled. He looked at me sternly and pressed my shoulder with his fingers. The next moment he was gone, and I sat there looking at the empty space he had left behind. From this hour onwards I would never be the same. There was no going back now. Why had these people come in such numbers? Partly out of curiosity. But mainly because I had said to them "You are my people and not stupid or ignorant. Come, you might be able to see something in my paintings. For it is through you I learnt that truth should be expressed with simplicity."

I felt Khalil's hand on my head. No other hand had ever touched me like that. It was capable of raising or calming a storm within me. Its fingertips moved along the lines of myself, and reached recesses which none had reached before. They brought to life things which had died, and others not yet born. I looked around at him and smiled. He said: "Congratulations. Today seems to me like a dream. It's been a wonderful day and now it's over. The night is waiting for you, waiting for its star to come out. The fishermen are laying their nets under the moon, and somewhere near the Nile is a table prepared specially for you. Come, Amina, you are our star tonight."

He put his hand on my arm guiding me quickly through the compliments and goodbyes, the exclamations of wonder, the shining faces of the boys and girls, the snatches of conversation, the laughter and the smiles, the sound of heels on the tiles, the purring cars and their blinding headlights. My head was turning. He led me gently into the night. At last we were alone and everything was quiet.

When I woke up in the morning he had already left the house. It was a Friday, and I wondered why he had left so early. He had said nothing last night. I felt depressed. I was looking forward to spending the day with him, to relaxing from the strain of past weeks and enjoying a few hours of laziness. We could have had our tea in bed, and talked about the exhibition and perhaps . . . But he had decided to go out this day in particular. I got out of bed slowly, but my head kept going round, and I moved my body with difficulty. I went out into the hall. On the table was a note folded under the monthly *Colour*. I opened it and scanned the lines of neat, regular, handwriting.

Amina,
Awfully sorry. I was obliged to go out. Saïd phoned up at seven in connection with the strike. I would have liked to spend the day with you, but hope to finish as early as possible and come back. If I find a telephone within easy reach, I'll get in touch with you. It looks as though it will be warm and pleasant today, so if you feel like going out, don't wait for me since I do not know when the meeting will be over.

Kisses.
Khalil

P.S. I boiled the milk and put it in the refrigerator.

My heart skipped a few beats. During the last few weeks I had heard the word strike repeated several times without much effect on me, perhaps because I had been so absorbed in other things. But now it had a different sound. Why was happiness always so shortlived? I should try to live as long as possible in what happened yesterday, turning it over slowly in my mind.

It was better to stay home and think of what had happened during the past weeks. I decided to wait for Khalil. I went to the kitchen and made a glass of tea, then took it back to the bedroom. The newspaper headlines never seemed to change: "A dwelling for every citizen within three years." I pushed the paper aside and stretched myself out on the bed. My belly rose and fell with a regular movement. I caressed it, feeling a solid body move under the gentle pressure of my hand. He was swimming in my fluid. I smiled at the vision of a small face, and tiny fingers curling over the edge of his gown. Whom would he resemble, me, or his father? It would be good if he took the best from both of us. I heard the telephone ring in the hall and heaved myself up as quickly as I could. Khalil's voice came to me as though from a distance. I was unable to hear what he was saying and asked him to repeat it. The second time I caught the words more distinctly.

"Amina, I was told a few minutes ago that the workers in the company are going on strike tomorrow at twelve noon. I'm going to have lunch with Saïd and then come home, probably not later than four o'clock. Don't mention what I have told you to anyone. The strike must remain a secret until the Trade Union Committee announces it. Can you hear me?"

"Yes, I heard everything you said."

I went back to bed. My belly rose and fell, with the same regular movement, but the image of the small face had disappeared from my eyes. "A strike?!" I had never seen a strike before. It was a word that awakened a deep anxiety in me. Images flitted through my mind. Angry crowds . . . Policemen in black. Shields and truncheons and bullets and armoured cars patrolling up and down. They kept talking of calm and stability day and night. Whose stability were they talking about? Our stability, or theirs? The stability of those at the bottom or the stability of those on top?

Khalil Mansour Khalil

We had met only once before, but already we were like intimate friends. She seemed to meet me unreservedly, and made me feel that to her I was more important than anyone else. It was something I had not experienced before.

"What's wrong? There's a change in you this time. You look worried, preoccupied."

I smiled. "It must be your prolonged absence."

She laughed. "I must look out for myself. You people in the East have a knack of saying things beautifully."

"Why not? It makes life more colourful."

"Not always. Sometimes it's a mere formality, a way of evading action, or of hiding the truth which is what you are doing now."

She was looking me straight in the eyes. I didn't answer. It was not yet as easy as that for me.

"I see you have sealed your lips very effectively. I want you to speak, but I don't intend wheedling it out of you. Your expression usually tells me what I want to know. But tell me, what would you like to drink tonight? Whisky, or fresh lemon squash?"

"Your face expresses the innocence of a child but I'm discovering very quickly that it could be misleading. Are you not at times a hard person to deal with?"

"There's no contradiction between the two. Don't you think one should be able to be both? It depends with whom one is dealing?"

"And with me?"

She got up without answering. I heard liquid being poured into a glass followed by a splash of ice. She returned and placed two glasses on the table, then tucking her bare feet under her curled up in the opposite corner of the sofa as though putting distance between us.

"My question still stands."

She turned to me with an earnest look puckering her brow in deep thought.

"With you I don't know, or to be more precise I haven't yet decided."

"And why have you not decided?"

"Because I don't know you."

"That's not so difficult."

"It is. You belong to a different world from mine. We walk through life with a naked self, but you carry yourselves inside."

"I don't agree with you. Our cunning is naive. It reflects the simplicity of our life. Perhaps that's why it's difficult for you to understand us. But your world is a complex one, so you have to be cunning in an intelligent way. The stakes where you are concerned are usually much greater."

All expression faded from her face and her eyes became blank, unseeing, like those of a statue.

"Are you angry with me?"

She shrugged her shoulders, as though the thought of anger had never even occurred to her. I realized that she had been hurt by what I said, but refused to show it.

"If you are angry I apologize. I would like to be able to say to you what passes through my mind."

She gave me a quick look of reproach.

"Don't apologize, for that is exactly how I also feel. Sometimes in a new friendship there is some misunderstanding at the beginning. Each one is feeling his way to the other."

"And sometimes my fingers are clumsy."

"On the contrary, your fingers are very sensitive."

"You are responsible for what is happening. I can think of two reasons for saying so. The first one is this." I waved my empty glass.

"And the second?"

"The second is the more important. You oblige me to be myself."

"And that is better of course."

"With you, I don't know. Or to be more precise I haven't decided yet."

She laughed merrily.

"*Basrra*, as you say in Egypt. Let me fill up your glass. I want to know what you're hiding. It seems that I'm going to find out things really worth knowing."

"You could be disappointed."

I held my glass away from her.

"No, I don't think so. Give me your glass, and don't be afraid. Tonight I am happy, very happy, and happiness overcomes all wickedness."

She stretched out an arm and switched off the ceiling light. I saw her breast lift under the robe, and the shadow of her armpit exposed.

"Would you like something to eat?"

"No thank you. Tonight I want to float. To live on wine and the transparency of our souls."

"You can help yourself to as much transparency as you like. I personally need food to satisfy my hunger."

She disappeared into the interior of the flat. I looked round the room. The wide windows were open. I could see the night sky, the stars, the silhouettes of the buildings on the other side of the Nile. I had better be at work early in the morning, keep a clear mind and not drink too much. I was tempted to stay where I was and let things go their own way. But no, when she came back I would ask about the interview and then leave.

She returned with a tray of food and two glasses of whisky. I exclaimed, "What beautiful colours. Red tomatoes, black caviare, white cheese, and green lettuce."

"You'll eat with me won't you?"

"No, really, I must go. I'll just finish my drink and leave." She said nothing so I added. "I would like to stay and share your meal, but . . ."

"But what?"

"It's better if I leave now. Before I forget, what about the interview?"

She bent down and pulled out a neat plastic file from under the table and handed it to me saying: "Please check it carefully and note down any remarks you may have, so that we can go over them next time we meet."

"Fine . . . Thank you for the enjoyable moments I have spent with you."

"I am really grateful for your help, and for everything. We will meet again soon I hope."

I stood up. At the door she leant forwards 'and kissed me on the cheek quickly. I felt her lips touch my face for an instant, and her soft hair on my ear.

"Please phone me any day after six."

I floated down the successive flights of stairs to find the porter, ghost-like in his white gallabeya, leaning against a pillar. He gave me a quick, hard look which landed like a pebble in a placid lagoon, raising widening ripples of anxiety. A taxi was standing outside as though waiting for me. It took me home racing through almost deserted streets. I opened the front door. The night light shed its shadows over the silent hall. I collected the papers from my desk, put them into my briefcase, and went into the kitchen. The breakfast table was already laid for the morning. Amina was as dependable as ever, not like me. Her roots were deep in the ground, like the giant mulberry tree in front of our house. I used to stretch out under it in summer and let myself be lulled to sleep. I longed to take refuge in Amina, but I hated this feeling. A long time had passed since I walked out of the prison gates, but I had still not settled down. The word "failure" echoed in my mind. Yet there were millions of people who lived their lives and went their ways without worrying over ideas like mine. Why not settle down and forget the past?

There must be some way out of this unending conflict of the mind. Amina always faced me with the facts, laid bare the contradictions in my life; perhaps that was why I kept running away from her. But Ruth was different. She exercised an attraction I found difficult to resist. Was it just the fascination of the unknown, of visiting another world where everything is there for the asking? If only things were simpler, more straightforward. A shiver went through me as though some danger was lurking nearby. The voice of caution whispered inside me. I smothered it and returned to a vision of her slender body in my arms.

I woke in the morning to Amina's face leaning over me. "Good morning. Aren't you going to work today?" I looked at my watch and leapt out of bed.

At the breakfast table we were silent. Recently we had continued to drift apart. I was busy with my company, and preoccupied with the situation which was getting more strained every day; and she was preoccupied with preparations for her exhibition. But she continued to ensure that our daily life went on without disruption. Now it had narrowed itself down to the routine things; the intellectual and emotional exchange to which we had been accustomed had disappeared. I watched her belly grow, and yet could not bring myself to ask her even the normal questions about how she felt. Deep within me was this feeling of guilt, and the longer I refrained from communicating with her, the more difficult it became, as though together we were constructing an insurmountable barrier.

I stood up, rested my hand on her shoulder and bent to kiss her head. She remained seated at the table staring in front of her without moving. I gently pulled her up from the chair and buried my face in her neck. She patted me on the back as she would a child. I felt she was struggling to overcome the distance that separated us. She smiled, and patted my back again. I felt a slight movement in her belly. She abandoned herself inertly to my embrace. I wondered whether the barrier between us could ever be broken down.

"How are the preparations for the exhibition going?"

Her face brightened up a little as she answered. "The canvasses are all ready. But I have a problem."

"What's that?"

"The only hall I have been able to find is in a deplorable state. It's been used as a dumping ground and has not been cleaned or painted in years."

"Where is it?"

"In the Institute of Fine Arts."

I lapsed into silence, thinking over what she had said. Suddenly I remembered. "The Institute of Fine Arts? But I know the Director very well. We were at school together. Sometimes he used to spend a few days with me on the farm. What do you say to our paying him a visit together?"

"Yes, that might help. When can we go?"

"Tomorrow."

The following day, when I walked through the door of the Director's office, he clasped my hand for a long time. We sat down, drank coffee, talking of our school days. When Amina explained her problem he suggested that the necessary work could be done with the help of the students' union. When they had finished, Amina visited the hall. She came back almost leaping over the ground with joy despite her pregnancy. I took her in my arms, and held her in a long embrace. For the first time in months we felt close. For the rest of the day we kept hopping from place to place doing things in the house, singing at the top of our voices, laughing and chattering until it was time to go to bed.

Came the opening day. I knew her heart was filled with anxiety. At first I thought the right thing was for me to be by her side, to share her happiness if the exhibition succeeded, and to console her if it did not. But after much thought I decided to keep away. This was her exhibition, her day. She had to reap the results of her work — good or bad — alone.

I did not return home after the day's work, but instead agreed with Saïd to arrange a little celebration for Amina, and asked him to reserve a table at the Nile Shore Casino. He welcomed the idea enthusiastically: "Sometimes I feel I haven't seen the Nile in years. I walk along the banks without even noticing it's there."

I sat in a small coffee house in the depths of a narrow lane on the outskirts of Helwan. A number of labourers were sitting on wooden benches and rickety straw chairs. They looked like construction workers from Upper Egypt. At one of the side tables, separated from the others, I noticed a compact group of men. From their stocky, powerful bodies, bushy whiskers, and the white turbans wound around their heads, I could see they were labour contractors. They were pushing big wads of greasy money into the inner pockets of their gallabeyas, or pulling them out, or thumbing through them. One of them was noting down something in a black notebook, while the others argued. I contemplated what was going on for some time, but suddenly wondered why I was sitting here while Amina stood in the exhibition hall confronting what was perhaps the test of her life? Why was I not at her side? As usual I was running away. But from what? From failure? From success? Probably both. If it was a failure I preferred not to face it. And if it was a success it would only remind me that so far I had gone nowhere. I was ashamed of myself. That was what I was evading by not going there. How had I allowed myself to fall into this snare?

I put a few coins on the table and stood up. I saw faces turn towards me, and eyes examine me curiously for a moment before turning back to the accounts. I walked down the lane rapidly making my way through groups of children playing noisily, swarms of flies, and pools of smelly water. I emerged into more open space and started running down a road, jumping over pavements, rubbish, and piles of stones. My body felt light, and my lungs breathed the air in and out, as I threaded my way through the throngs of pedestrians on the road. They turned to look at this grey-haired man in a well-cut coat, running like someone pursued by a police patrol. I ran unmindful of the curious stares, and suspicious looks, for Amina was there, standing alone. I glimpsed the coloured lights on the outer wall, the posters, and the crowd of people at the door. I crossed a courtyard, climbed a few steps, and went through one door, then the next into the hall. The walls were a dazzling white under the lights, and I came to a sudden halt. My eyes travelled over the paintings in wonder as though I was penetrating for the first time into her world. It was a world of colour and beauty, an impressive embodiment of her effort to remould reality into an image of her own. As I turned round I saw her sitting on a chair near one of the pillars, quietly contemplating the visitors as they walked along, or stood opposite one of the paintings on the wall. There she was a woman alone, her fingers restless with creativity, a new life in her womb.

I put my hands on the remembered warmth of her shoulders, their familiar contours; many times I had lifted her long hair from them, caressed their naked beauty, rested my head in their hollows. She looked up at me with shining eyes. I said: "Let us go. We must celebrate your success. A new star is born tonight."

We threaded our way through the crowds, the chatter, the laughter, the sound of cars, of children running around, and walked out into the night, into a world which was ours. I took her into my arms and kissed her mouth. The earth under our feet seemed to drop away and we floated high up.

Near the river we sat at a table, she, Saïd and I. We ate slowly, talked, and laughed as we had never laughed before. And all the time a thought revolved in my mind: "Drink Khalil, drink. Dispel the shadow that follows you. Drown the voice that says inside, 'Maybe this is the last cup of wine'."

I slept in her arms that night with peace in my heart. I was a body without memory or pain, swimming in a strange happiness at the edge of the world. I dreamt of my mother who died the day I was born. I saw her laughing eyes and heard her call. My head nestled in the hollow of her shoulder. I could see her breast, naked and full. In my nose was the smell of her body like earth moistened by dew, like flowers and trees washed by the rain, like fresh linen and soap, sweat and endurance.

In the morning I opened my eyes, gradually climbing the steps to consciousness. Behind the closed door was a faint ringing. I swung out of bed, dug my feet into the slippers quickly, and tiptoed into the hall. When I lifted the receiver Saïd's voice came to me slightly hoarse: "Good morning. Sorry to disturb you so early, but I want to see you as soon as possible. It's urgent."

"Where are you now?"

"In the Glass Coffee House. Some committee members are here."

"What are you doing?"

"Discussing the date of the strike."

I said nothing for a long moment. I heard him exclaim a little anxiously: "Hey, Khalil, what do you say?"

"I'll be with you in an hour's time."

"We'll be waiting."

I replaced the receiver and looked at my watch. It was seven o'clock. I sat down to collect my thoughts. Reality had caught up with me again. I shuffled over to the bathroom. After a shave and a cold shower to brace me up, I dressed quickly, while Amina slept peacefully on. I felt a strong urge to kiss her as though I was leaving on a long journey to a distant place. I was filled with a deep foreboding of dangers ahead. But it was better not to disturb her. She needed sleep and I could leave her a note telling her where I was.

I went to the kitchen and put the milk to boil, made myself a cup of strong coffee, swallowed it quickly, and left the house. A soft morning breeze was blowing across the fields, and the sun rose quickly into a clear blue sky. What was it that I feared? Things would be all right. I recalled the exhibition and our celebration. What more did I want? Somehow I was never satisfied, never able to savour what life had to offer. My mind kept leaping forward into the future before I had time to enjoy the present.

It was exactly eight o'clock as I slipped through the door of the coffee house. Inside I found Saïd, Mostapha Ramadan, and two other committee members: Hassan Eid, and Ali El Sharkawi. When I asked about the remaining members they said that those present had been mandated to take a decision. If all the committee members were seen together they might draw unnecessary attention to themselves. It was important that the security people got no inkling of what was going on.

I sat there listening. They were envisaging a strike as soon as possible, before the agreement was signed. Since all the necessary preparations had been made Saïd suggested it began the following day. Everything had also been done to ensure the full support of the Federation of Chemical Workers. It was clear that the outcome of their action would have wide repercussions on investment policies and therefore on the future of the workers. He was against any postponement which could only result in a loss of momentum and give more time for the undermining activities of the company stooges and security agents to have their effect.

The discussion was heated, but I preferred not to intervene, since I was not a committee member and they probably tolerated my presence simply because I was Saïd's friend. He was their leader and they trusted his judgement. But every now and then I caught a questioning look in the eyes of onė or other of his three companions which seemed to say: "This man is not one of us. He belongs to another class, to the higher levels of authority in the company. What has brought him here? What is his interest in all this?" A moment later it would be gone. I realized that if they had doubts about me, it was only natural. Nevertheless I felt a growing irritation. I was reminded of the past when I had comrades among the workers who considered me mainly as a source of financial support for the movement, or as someone who was not completely dependable. I was often furious with them. By joining the party and participating in the struggle I had made much greater sacrifices than they had. Was it not Marx who had said that the workers have nothing to lose but their chains? However, as time went by I became more realistic, and tried to understand the reasons for these feelings. They were afraid that people from other classes would try to have the upper hand over them. Sometimes I wondered where people like me could finally settle. Under capitalism they were oppressed, and with the socialists things were often pretty rough. In some ways they were in the same boat as women. As I listened to them talking it seemed to me that the distance separating us was growing. I felt like a spectator watching from the shore while the others sailed off to some unknown adventure. No one had asked me what I thought. So far my presence seemed to have passed unnoticed. Why had they asked me to come then? Even Saïd Abou Karam seemed oblivious to my presence. Maybe he was not to blame. From the moment they felt that the strike was imminent, signs of hesitation began. Phrases like: "Choosing the right moment", "Avoiding risks" or the "need for caution" were being repeated more and more. They well knew what they would have to face, and perhaps their caution was an attempt to foresee the answers to all the questions going through their minds, to make sure everything had been weighed carefully.

I sat there watching little bits of the future being born, as it travelled along the deep lines of the faces with the sweat of emotion, took shape between the hands roughened by work, developed in their minds as they made an effort to understand where they were going. My ears caught the words shooting back and forth between them like the shuttle of a handloom weaving textures of thought. I could see reflection being transformed into a mobilizing force, organizing hundreds and thousands in factories and offices. I could sense the collective will being born, ready to march forward, to retreat, to advance once more with enduring force. I watched ideas struggling, clashing, wrestling with each other and then meeting in calm waters. And little by little I felt caught up in the process. My constant, nagging doubts were forgotten, my personal pains dissolved. Once again I lived exhilarating moments. I heard Saïd's voice announcing something I had been waiting for: "Comrade Khalil. We have not heard your opinion yet."

I saw their eyes turn towards me. "I am not a member of the committee, and I have no right to vote."

His hand made a gesture of contained anger. "I don't think I need to answer that remark. This is hardly the moment to settle private accounts, or are you just trying to evade my question?"

"Neither one nor the other."

"Then go ahead."

"I think we should strike as early as possible, before it's too late."

There was a long silence. Everyone seemed preoccupied. I wondered what could be passing through their minds. Perhaps they would never experience anything quite the same again. My glance strayed to the window. A small boy stood near the end of the lane, urinating. I turned to catch the expression on Saïd's face. I had never seen it so totally rigid. Not the smallest twitch of a muscle.

In the morning I went to my office as usual. I closed the door and tried to concentrate on some files, but I kept reading the same lines over and over again. At times I seemed to hear voices shouting in the distance. I stood up, walked to the door, and strained my ears. The telephone rang suddenly and I jumped. The director of administration wanted to know what I thought about one of the female employees in my department. Was she efficient? Polite? Dependable? I hated the man. His smooth, always closely-shaven face, his urbane manners, and his meticulous way of dressing. He had worked for a long time with the intelligence services and been transferred to the company as a part of more general changes in the institutions of the country. Every time there was a new step in the policies agreed upon with the Americans, and a shift in the internal situation, changes of personnel were made in the key sectors. The man had found himself transferred overnight from his spacious office overlooking the presidential palace to a small room in the company, where the only view he could brood upon from his window was of an inner courtyard where rows of barrels of chemicals were stored.

I asked him to send me a note, and replaced the receiver. My room was in the west wing of the administration building, at the far end of the corridor, next to the library. It was a quiet corner into which the noises of the plant made little intrusion. Usually all I could hear was a distant buzzing, with an occasional light vibration. I opened the door and walked out of my room and became immediately aware of an uncanny silence, as though everything had suddenly stopped. I forgot what had brought me into the corridor, and stood straining my ears, trying to catch some sound. I went to a window overlooking the inner compound. The courtyard was deserted except for three guards who had left their shacks, and were now gathered together, gazing at the plant buildings, as though they had seen something unusual. The messenger boy's chair had disappeared. I walked towards the library, passing in front of the big hall reserved for the typing pool. There were none of the usual sounds from the room. I knocked and opened the door. The room was empty. My eyes moved over the room registering a cup of coffee, its contents untouched, a handbag on a small table, an open box of carbon paper, a lighted cigarette on an ashtray, a waste-paper basket fallen over and spilling its contents. I closed the door and continued on my way to the library. Here again there was no one, just piles of books on the green baize table, a necktie hung over a chair with one end dangling on the floor. The atmosphere was strange — objects and tasks people had suddenly abandoned. I realized the strike had begun. I returned to my room and sat in an armchair, listening to the sound of my own breathing. Then the telephone rang. I lifted the receiver, and the voice of the chairman came over the line sounding unusually quiet, like someone preparing himself for the worst. He said:

"Mr Khalil, please come to my office immediately."

He was seated on the divan, smoking. His face was pale, and the lighted tip of the cigarette glowed all the time. He waved me to a chair and looked me in the face for a long moment before saying: "Of course you must know Khalil that the workers went on strike at exactly a quarter to twelve."

"On strike!"

"Yes, on strike."

I don't know why at that particular moment I remembered Ruth. I felt that her spirit had departed suddenly leaving an empty shell. Death seemed to float in the air. My fingers clasped one another nervously, as though hanging on to something invisible. My palms went cold.

"Did you hear what I said?"

"Yes I heard."

"Then why don't you say something?"

His tone seemed to rise of its own accord as though he was seeking an outlet to his tension.

"What do you expect me to say?"

He looked puzzled. What did he think I could do? Come to his rescue? Give him advice? I was glad to see him in this predicament. Let him reap the consequences of what he had sown, he and all those of his kind who had made friends with our enemies, cringed and crawled at their feet, obliged us to swallow our humiliation each day as we watched television and read the headlines.

"I intend to contact the Minister of National Security."

"Immediately?"

"What do you expect me to do? I can't shoulder the responsibility for what might happen." He stared gloomily into space for a while. "They're going to spoil our reputation with the foreign investors. They'll begin to say to themselves, 'Where is the peace and stability so much vaunted in Egypt?' And Larochelle . . ." He broke off to light another cigarette, and launched one of his questioning looks at me. "I have no alternative."

"Why not go to them and have a discussion?"

"I!? Go to them!? Are you crazy? They'll think I'm scared of them. No . . . impossible. If they want to discuss matters they can come to see me, I mean, their delegates."

They were all alike. The arrogance which grows with ignorance. To meet their delegates was a way of emphasizing the unity of the workers. But in a general meeting it was sometimes possible to manoeuvre more effectively. Perhaps he preferred to play a waiting game, to depend on his stooges. I felt a wave of disgust. Why the hell should I be giving him advice? I was really stooping to impermissible levels.

I came back to him staring at me with a curious look, as though he wanted to approach me, but was scared at the same time, a desire to be friendly with a hint of dislike. "I want you to go and review the situation in the plant and give me your assessment."

Now what exactly was he aiming at? He had a knack of puzzling me sometimes. Maybe I was imagining a depth of intention in this man which did not exist. Probably all he wanted was some kind of an idea of the general atmosphere among the strikers. I knew he had been taken by surprise when the strike broke out. He was not expecting it so soon. He lifted the receiver and dialled a number.

"Hello, is that the SSSPS. Give me Lieutenant-Colonel Adel Mashhoor. I am Abdel Aziz El Kabani Chairman of the Thebes Pharmaceutical Company." He looked at me and said: "You go now, and come back after you've been round the plant."

Maybe he thought I would tell them about the telephone call he was making. He probably still had my relationship with Saïd in mind. I descended the stairs slowly, crossed the courtyard, and slipped into one of the buildings to begin my tour.

I found the men and women workers sitting on the floor, chatting quietly. Now and again I heard a laugh quickly stifled, as though its owner had felt it was not yet time to laugh. At some points in the various sections young workers were on guard. All the lights were out and the machines silent. I realized they had disconnected the electricity, but some light filtered through the windows. The whisper of voices, the white uniforms, the silent shapes of the machines appeared strangely impressive, even awesome, like a silent strength. People flitted by like ghosts, and the atmosphere was charged with the tension of unknown possibilities. Groups of three of four workers were gathered near the red fire extinguishers that hung on the walls; the administration staff were mingling with the others, their jackets contrasting with the white coats of the workers.

Towards the end of my tour I noticed women workers spreading newspapers on the floor and arranging packets and cartons of food on them. Then everybody gathered around and they started eating. The guards remained in their place until the others had finished, then squatted down to eat.

96

I looked for Saïd everywhere but did not find him; I wondered what he was doing. They must have formed some kind of strike committee, and he was probably busy in one of its meetings. The quiet and order which reigned everywhere indicated that they were well organized. I refrained from asking where he was, or from giving any outward sign which would betray how I felt about the strike. But I did spend some time talking to a few of the workers, women as well as men. They seemed to have no hard feelings, as though once the fight had begun they preferred to keep their energy for other more important things. I could see they were well-informed about the issues at stake.

By the time I got back to the chairman's room, it was almost time to leave work. He was seated behind his desk, but no longer alone. Apart from the director of administration, and the head of the security unit (a bald man with bulging eyes, and a prayer button on his forehead) there was a third man. From his dark glasses and his choice of words, I gathered that he was an officer. The chairman introduced me saying: "Lieutenant-Colonel Adel Mashhoor." "Mr Khalil Mansour Khalil." I sat down, and at his request described what I had seen, sensing the eyes of the officer fixed on my face from behind his dark glasses. When I had finished he said abruptly: "If we hit at the head, everything will return to normal." Then turning to me he queried. "Is that not so Mr Khalil?"

Why had he addressed himself to me in particular? It could be fortuitous; I was perhaps over-sensitive. However it was unlikely that he did not know who I was. "I'm afraid I did not get your meaning exactly."

"If we get rid of the leadership, the head, the body will lose its capacity to act."

I said nothing. I noticed the chairman was standing near the window and making signs at me. I went over to him and he pointed outside. My heart contracted. At a short distance was line upon line of helmeted policemen, carrying rubber truncheons and shields. They looked like an army of yellow ants which had invaded the roads and fields, and almost covered the ground around the walls of the plant. Two big dark blue vans stood at some distance, their long steel aerials jutting from the roof; and behind the rows of police squads a grey armoured car with what looked like a squat machine gun protruding from the front.

At half-past three I slipped out of a side door guarded by a man wearing civilian clothes. The black butt of a revolver poked out beneath his coat. I ran quickly down the road impelled by an inner anxiety. During the past two weeks Amina had begun to look very tired. The summer had been very hot, and what with the exhibition and her advanced pregnancy she was exhausted.

When I got home I found her lying on the bed on her back. She was moaning in a low voice. I asked her what was wrong and she explained that severe pains were shooting round from her back to the lower part of the abdomen. Her face was pale, and her brow was beaded with sweat. She kept arching her back and letting it drop flat on the bed when the pain subsided. I said that they were probably labour pains. She nodded quietly in assent, then suddenly shrieked. I said I would get a taxi to take her to the hospital, rushed out of the house and started running towards the station. I found a taxi pulled up near the kerb. The driver was listening to the radio with a dull sleepy look on his face, and did not hear me the first time. I jumped in and gave the address to the driver. Amina had put on a loose gallabeya and prepared a small bag with the baby's clothes and a few other things. We got into the taxi, and drove quickly to Agouza hospital, and at two o'clock on the morning of 25 September 1979 my son, Esam, was born.

I sent a registered letter to the chairman informing him that my wife had given birth to our first child, and that owing to some minor complication she would be in hospital for a week. I asked him to accord me leave during this period. But Amina had to spend two weeks in hospital because of a high fever a few days after Esam's birth. I did not have sufficient confidence in the hospital services to leave her alone, and there was no one from her family or mine to take care of her. Perhaps, deep down, I welcomed this chance to be away from the company during the strike.

I spent most of the time by her side. When she went to sleep I would walk out on to the balcony to smoke a cigarette, and think of different things. Sometimes I remembered that far away in Helwan squads of police were camped around the plant, while I sat here staring into the dark. I read the newspapers carefully and listened to the radio, hoping that something would filter through about the strike, but in vain. The event seemed to have been intentionally surrounded by a wall of silence. I tried to phone the administrative offices, but there was no answer to my repeated calls. I sent a second registered letter asking for an additional ten days leave. On my return I would settle the matter without difficulty, and in any case, no one knew how long it would take, until the situation in the company returned to normal.

Now and again I would experience a wave of anxiety over the fate of Saïd and the others, and wonder how things would end for us all. One day I woke up early with the firm intention of going to the company to find out what had happened, but as I was getting ready to leave I noticed that Amina's temperature had shot up again, despite the antibiotics. She began to shiver and I was so scared that I almost collapsed myself. I watched her face getting more and more drawn, clasped her thin fingers in my hand. She was the closest and dearest person I had ever known. Throughout the time we spent in the hospital I hardly noticed Esam nor did I realize that I had a son until the moment when I stepped over the threshold into our house, and we opened the windows. I saw Amina lay him down on the sofa, and at that very moment he turned his head round, and looked up at me. I moved up close. His wide open eyes were the same as Amina's. They stared at me with a questioning look. But the fingers, curled tightly around the edge of his blanket, were the exact miniatures of my own.

Three days went by. On the fourth, around eleven o'clock in the morning, the front door bell rang just as I was preparing to put him in his cot. I laid him down and opened the door. The postman was standing outside carrying the usual bundle of letters. He smiled and said: "Good morning. A registered letter for you, sir."

I signed the delivery slip and closed the door. I shivered. I knew the feeling well, could trace it back to moments when I was tracked down, or cornered, to the cold light of dawn and the grey van waiting outside the door. I pulled a single sheet of paper out of the envelope and rapidly scanned the typewritten lines.

Mr Khalil Mansour Khalil
Director of Research.

Greetings:
We wish to inform you that in view of your absence from the company for a period of fifteen consecutive days without prior permission, the Board of Directors has endorsed a decision to end your services with the Thebes Pharmaceutical Company as from the 11 October 1979.

We would be obliged if on receipt of this letter you immediately contact the concerned officials in the Administrative Department in order to complete the required formalities.

Please accept our respectful regards.
Mokhtar Hussein
Director of Administration
Issued 12 October, 1979
No 1712/12/10/79

Part III

Saïd Abou Karam

It was half past eight on that Friday evening when I left the coffee house. At least we had reached a decision. Tomorrow the strike would begin at 11.45 hours exactly. I walked slowly along the pavement observing the crowds of people in the street. Nothing seemed to have changed. A small boy sat on the ground, his head bent over a tin filled with cigarette ends. He lifted his head when he heard my footsteps and I glimpsed a fleeting panic in his eyes. Under glaring white lights the shop windows displayed coloured summer shirts and gallabeyas. The butcher stood in his shop wearing a white apron as he cut into a hunk of dark red meat hanging from a hook. A small group of customers followed the movements of his hands with anxiety whenever he added pieces of fat or gristle or bone to the balance. My senses seemed to have become sharpened a hundred fold to what was going on around me. I perceived with exceptional clarity, floated with the evening breeze, in a kind of transparency.

I hastened my steps. It was important that I call in at the Federation to make sure that everything we had agreed had been done. Nothing should be left to chance. Every step had been carefully calculated, yet so many things remained unknown. Who knew what could happen with human beings when they started to revolt — human masses on the move? The unpredictable, that was what made me so nervous. I walked along the street but my mind was elsewhere, busy going over all the details again. Throughout the past weeks I had lived a divided life — a divided mind, a divided self. Part of me had become a thinking machine, its little cogs and wheels turning unceasingly, drawing up the plans for the coming battle in black ink on white paper, weighing each factor however minute, calculating everything with a newly acquired, almost uncanny precision. The other part still lived in the eyes of people, in the evening breeze as it blew softly around my face and into my lungs, in the laughing voices wafted to my ears as I walked with long strides over the pavement, in the creamy foam topping the glasses of iced sugar cane juice and tamarind, in everything which reminded me of the life that flowed strongly through the streets of the city and the veins of my body.

I climbed the stairs of the old building in the dim light of a single dusty and fly-blown lamp, slipped quietly in front of a man fast asleep with his head resting on the reception table, and walked into a room at the back of the offices. Inside were two people: a girl in blue dungarees sitting on a beach chair, and the president of the federation, a shrivelled old man hemmed in behind an ancient desk. His hair was grey, and his small eyes looked out from between a mesh of wrinkles spun with the infinite patience of time. When he spoke there was a note of worry in his voice.

"Welcome Saïd. Where have you been? Let me introduce you to my daughter Aleya", waving to the girl sitting on the chair. "This is Saïd Abou Karam, Chairman of the trade union committee in the Thebes Pharmaceutical Company."

I sat down on a cane chair in the corner before answering. "I was in a meeting."

The president said nothing for a moment, as though giving me time to take my breath then asked: "And what have you decided?"

"We have agreed to go on strike starting tomorrow at a quarter to twelve exactly."

The sound of breathing in the room was suspended. For a moment there was complete silence, then I heard something like a deep sigh. The old man's face turned to carven wood. The time had come. The first battle, like a clenched fist raised in defiance. He looked out of the window at the dreary back lanes, and dark shadows of the ramshackle houses leaning against each other for support.

"We have printed a declaration expressing the solidarity of the federation with your struggle. Tomorrow it will be distributed to all the factories from Alexandria to Aswan immediately you inform us that your action has begun."

"Is that all?"

"In addition, if any violence is used against the workers, or any attempt made to forcibly expel them from the plant, a one day strike of all workers in the chemical industries will be launched in support of your struggle. We have included this as a warning in the declaration." He pointed to a brown paper parcel placed on top of the cupboard. "There are two hundred copies which I have kept for you here for distribution in your plant." He stood up. "And don't forget. Be on your guard against sabotage. Strengthen the fire squads and protection groups around the machines and in the storage places. Do you want anything else?"

"No."

"Then good luck till we meet again. And Allah be with you, comrade."

He held my hand firmly between his strong fingers for a long moment before letting go. The girl stood by his side, looking at me with wide open eyes. I noticed how beautiful they were, with long black lashes surrounding the milky whites. She said: "I am the Trade Union production secretary in the Abou Zabal Chemical Factory. Be sure of one thing. You will not be alone in this struggle."

"I am grateful to both of you. Allah willing we shall meet after the strike is over."

I descended the narrow spiral staircase. I knew its steps one by one, and could run down with closed eyes avoiding the smooth slippery steps, the broken ones and those which were about to crumble. I emerged into the lane, breathing in the cool air. I felt lonely. On a night like this how could I possibly fall asleep? I needed someone with whom to talk until morning. I wondered what Khalil was doing. I could always drop in and spend the night with him and Amina. I knew they would welcome me as they had always done, but I hesitated. Our relations were no longer the same. There was a small wound on the surface and it would take some time to heal. All I could do was to return to my room in Basateen, to the bare white walls, the wooden bench, and the iron bed. There was no reason to grumble. Things were not so bad. Each life had its path. It was a choice that one made. I lifted my head. The North star shone brightly in the darkening night. I must sleep for at least one or two hours. I wondered whether somebody had remembered the arrangements for catering during the strike.

In the morning I sat at my desk, noting down the production of the previous day. The atmosphere was one of quiet expectancy. Nothing showed on the surface, except for a fleeting anxiety which I sometimes caught in the eyes of a worker as he passed by, or a questioning look thrown in my direction by a group of young workers concerting in a corner. Or perhaps I was only imagining things. I looked at my watch more often than usual, and caught my leg shaking with an involuntary movement which I stopped at once. Every now and then I went to the toilets, and as time passed I found it more and more difficult to keep still. But I suppressed my urge to move around. It had been agreed that I should stick to my desk, in case anybody should want me at a moment's notice. The hands of my watch advanced with a maddening slowness, like flies in a bowl of molasses. Each hour seemed to be divided into a thousand minutes. The delegate of the tabletting section in the strike committee kept throwing rapid glances out of the window, and the fingers of the female workers fluttered like restless butterflies around their machines. My mind jumped from one thing to the other, flashes from the past mingled with the present in a chaos of images which led nowhere. I saw myself as a child running barefoot on the shores of the Nile. My feet were black but the soles underneath glimmered palely. The ripe dates in my lap were crimson. I sank my white teeth into their flesh. In the evening I sat on the ground close to my mother. She fed me with pieces of cheese and bread. Her coloured bracelets tinkled with a comforting sound in the silence of the wide open space. Suddenly I felt someone lean over me. Mostapha Ramadan's voice came to my ear like a distant whisper "I have made the necessary arrangements for catering." My mind returned to the images rushing through my head. The face of the president of the federation with its web of lines. When he migrated from his village to the industrial town of Mehallah the workers used to sleep eight in a room. He had to lie stretched out on his back without turning over. The working day was divided into two shifts of twelve hours. Eight workers would come back from the day shift to sleep, and the eight who had slept in the room during the day would go out. On their way to work they would drop in to the local bar for a bowl of *bouza* to give them energy, and again on their way back. He spent part of his life cleaning sewage pipes, plunging in the icy black water, his naked body rigid with cold. His skin became covered in dark scabs, and no matter how much he washed the smell clung to him, and whenever he came near people, after a little while they would start to move away. He learnt how to read and write when his daughter Aleya went to school, sitting with her in the evenings while she read from her books and prepared her lessons. What would happen if they brought in the riot squads and went for the workers? It could become a real massacre. I had seen it happen before. If the strike was a success they would raise me to the heavens, but if it failed . . . God only knows. It could become hard. I could imagine their eyes evading me as I passed by, their voices falling silent every time I walked through their lines. That's if I'm not fired. At moments like this I say to myself, "Thanks be to Allah". Neither wife, nor child. Their hungry eyes would be enough to break a man's spine.

Seventeen minutes to twelve. I heard the hum of voices, and saw the arm of our section delegate rise into the air. Suddenly the machines slowed and then stopped. There was an awesome silence, something like the end of time, then words, a few spoken through trembling lips. The delegate stood up on a chair, and lifted a red and white striped handkerchief over his head. Slowly they gathered around him, the

106

shuffling of feet subsided, and once more there was silence. I heard him say. "Brothers and sisters. From this moment onwards we are on strike. All information and directives are to come to you through me. Do not listen to anyone else. Protect your machines, and arrest anyone who so much as touches them, or tries to cause any form of chaos or disturbance in our ranks. Avoid conflicts, and do everything in a quiet and orderly way. We have arranged for light meals and tea, until we can see more clearly how the situation will develop. We have constituted small fire and machine protection squads. If they ask for any assistance do not fail to extend it immediately. Apart from this, any other directives must come from me. If anything should happen my replacement is comrade Awad El Meligi."

I looked around the hall slowly. Everything was quiet, in perfect order. I could almost hear my heart beating. The tension that had been bottled up in me subsided. The battle had started, and there was no room for further doubt or hesitation. We had stepped over the threshold into a new stage, into the future. I returned to my desk, opened a book and started to read.

An hour later Mostapha Ramadan came quickly up to my desk. He was almost panting, his face pale. I could see he was making a great effort to maintain an outward calm. He said in a low voice: "Come, let's go up to the roof. We'll have to use the stairs since the electricity's off." He took hold of my arm and we walked towards the main entrance to the section, up three flights of stairs, and emerged suddenly into the bright sunlight. For a moment I was blinded and shaded my eyes with one hand, until they got used to the light. After a while I began to see what was around us. The green fields surrounding the plant looked as though they had retreated into the background. In their place was row upon row of policemen in khaki uniforms, with helmets and visors pulled over their heads, and short grey truncheons in their hands. They constituted a compact inner mass. An outer circle was composed of two or three lines carrying automatic rifles with stumpy bayonets attached, their steel flashing occasionally in the strong sunlight. At the rear were a couple of armoured cars with a short cannon muzzle jutting out at the front and a couple of radio vans, their fine antennae rising like needles into the air. Automatic rifles, cannons, and radio!! What was this? A mere demonstration of force, or preparation for a real massacre? No one could tell at this stage. They would hide their plans until the very last moment.

We went down again to the tabletting section. The delegate walked over to me and said: "Mr Khalil was touring the section a few moments ago." What had brought him here at this time? In any case even if I had been at my desk, we would have been unable to speak to one another. We had to appear to be in separate camps. It was time for me to go round the other sections of the plant. I did not expect any problems yet. Our main enemy was time, for with time fatigue and doubt could creep into body and mind. We had made preparations for everything, for food and drink and rest, and even for entertainment. The siege could be long. On the other hand they might think of evicting us from the plant with tear gas. What then? If the sit-down strike developed into a pitched battle things could get out of control. Everything should be done to prevent such an eventuality, and to avoid any form of provocation. The federation should intervene at the right moment. It could save the situation. We could not face the violence of the state alone. That was something we had all agreed upon. But what I feared most was that the federation would hesitate at the last moment. For quite a number of years now it had fallen under the influence of government circles, and most of its leadership had won the elections as a result of direct interference from the authorities. However, during the last months resentment had been rising everywhere. Prices were jumping crazily and pay rises were negligible. The government maintained order simply by clamping down on any form of democratic rights.

I lifted my eyes from the book. Some faces smiled at me in confidence and expressed calm; others looked anxious. I could feel a strong undercurrent of tension in the way their eyes were shining, in the movement of a hand, in a sudden high pitched tone of voice, or the drawn features of one of the workers emerging under the dim light of a window. Some of the women seemed to be less nervous than the men, perhaps because their husbands had a job, or because they had never lived through a strike before and seen how matters could deteriorate in a moment.

I stood up and walked towards the room we had chosen for the meetings of the strike committee. There I found Hassan Eid and Ali El Sharkawi waiting. After a little while the others joined us. We knew that two of the company stooges were members of the committee, and had decided that certain questions should be discussed only in their absence. So we limited ourselves to a discussion of the arrangements for catering and entertainment and for protection against fire or sabotage.

I returned to my post in the tabletting section, and sat down with the others in a big circle on the floor. I asked each one to tell us something about himself or herself. It was a way to occupy their minds, to evoke their interest in one another and bring them closer. For who could tell. Many of them might have spent years working in the same place without really getting to know one another. Little by little we found ourselves plunged into this rather novel experience, and the time flew by, so that no one noticed the appearance of one of the security unit men at the entrance to the hall. He approached our circle slowly, and stood at a short distance following what was going on. Something made me turn my head at that moment. I saw him standing there, wearing tight blue jeans and a striped shirt. When he realized that I had seen him, he came closer and said in a loud voice: "The boss wants you in his office Saïd."

I ignored him and continued to listen to what one of the girls was saying. He hesitated for a moment, then repeated what he had said the first time, but in a lower voice. I turned towards him and said: "Firstly, you are supposed to say 'Good afternoon' to the people sitting here. Secondly, you should excuse yourself for interrupting them. Thirdly, when you address me please do it in an appropriate way. That's if you want me to go with you to meet the boss."

I saw him look at me with fury, so I left him to swallow his anger and said to the girl "Please go on with what you were saying Nagwa."

I saw the expression on their faces as they looked at me. A hint of satisfaction mingled with tranquillity. No doubt that the situation was in hand if I could permit myself to speak to the security people like that.

He cleared his throat and said: "Peace be with you. Can I interrupt for a second?"

The girl stopped short in her account. I looked at him and returned his greeting. "Allah's peace be with you, and his mercy and blessings. Please sit down."

"No, thank you, Mr Saïd. The boss wants you in his office."

I stood up and made a sign to the delegate of the strike committee. I took him aside and whispered in his ear: "Ahmed. If I do not come back in a couple of hours at most, send this note to Mostapha Ramadan with one of the workers whom you trust. Under no circumstances should you leave your post here."

He gave me a rapid, slightly anxious glance and said: "I'll do as you say."

I gestured to the security man. We crossed the hall, slipped out through the entrance down a short flight of steps to the deserted, silent courtyard. The reddish disc of the sun had dropped to a level just slightly above the wall. At each corner of the big building stood a small group of three guards. One stood upright on duty, while the other two rested on the ground. We passed through a back entrance into the administration building, climbed the stairs and walked along the corridor to the chairman's office. I saw a man standing at the door, but he continued to stare vacantly in front of him, as though he had not noticed us approaching. His hair was long, and he wore dark velvet trousers. "New generation secret police" I thought. I knocked at the door and walked in without waiting for an answer. Inside was a small group of people deeply engrossed in a conversation. They fell silent the moment I walked in, as though they had not had the time to switch over to something else. The chairman was sitting on the couch, and next to him was a person wearing tight blue trousers and a brightly coloured shirt. He was clean shaven and looked tall. He wore dark glasses which accentuated the coldness of his features. Something told me that he was the SSSPS man probably responsible for the industrial district of Helwan. They sat facing another man whose small body was sunk deeply in a huge armchair. His head was completely bald, except for a few black hairs around the ears. His face attracted attention by its extreme pallor almost suggesting severe illness or extreme pain. His mouth was coarse, and over the top lip was a fine moustache, like a line of mascara. He was wearing a thin, dark brown summer suit. At a respectful distance from the others was the director of administration perched on the edge of his chair and carefully dressed as usual.

Their eyes examined me openly, circled around me, slowly absorbing the details as though I was an animal they had never seen before. I stood in the middle of the room waiting until someone spoke. At last the chairman broke the silence.

"Saïd, this is Mr Lotfi El Sabe, deputy minister for National Security," nodding towards the man with the pale face sitting in the armchair, and "Lieutenant-Colonel Adel Mashhoor, director of the SSSPS branch in Helwan," looking at the man next to him on the sofa. "Perhaps you already know him?"

"I have not yet had the honour."

There was another long silence as though they had not expected my answer. The chairman gave an irritated frown in my direction and then resumed.

"This is Saïd Abou Karam, head of the Trade Union Committee in our company." He stopped for a moment before continuing "We want to discuss the strike with you Saïd."

I waited for him to go on. Nobody had asked me to sit down, but there was no use getting worked up about that; that's how they were. It was better to concentrate on essentials. Perhaps to remain standing was better. That way I was looking down on them.

"The deputy minister for National Security has come in person to investigate the matter, and listen to the viewpoint of the workers. To start with he would like to know why you have had recourse to a strike without passing through the usual preliminary stage of discussions and negotiations with the authorities in the company?"

Apparently they had agreed that the chairman should direct the discussion as he saw fit, since only he knew me personally.

"In so far as the company is concerned you know that we discussed the matter with you several times during the past year. In addition we sent you three memoranda concerning the project agreement with Larochelle. I met you once here in the office on my own. And on each occasion you assured us that everything would be all right, and that no harm would befall the workers. Yet all of us know that as a result of the agreement at least two hundred workers will lose their jobs."

"But you never said you would strike."

I looked at him with some amazement. This man sometimes surprised me with his stupidity, or was he just trying to look as though he couldn't understand?

"What you really mean is that we took you unawares by starting it earlier than you expected?"

His eyes swung from side to side as though he was cornered. Apparently he had not informed the government authorities that a strike could break out. Now the beans had been spilt, and I had spilt them. He had tried to show that he was in complete control of the situation, and that everything was going smoothly. He knew quite well that we had been thinking of a strike for some time, but wanted to take both sides unawares. To conclude the agreement with Larochelle and oblige the workers to accept it as an accomplished fact, and to force the French concern into a situation where it would have to throw its weight against the workers since it had become a major owner in the plant. Thus he hoped to bolster his position. With the multinational in the game the highest authorities were sure to intervene. But now the tables had been turned. The agreement was not yet signed and there was a strike which could dissuade the new partners from coming in, or at least make them postpone a final decision.

My eyes settled for a moment on the man in the armchair. His pallor seemed accentuated by something which my instinct told me must be an inner hatred. I felt like running out into the open air. On the table I noticed a jug of fresh lemon juice. I poured out a glass for myself and drank it slowly. I saw their faces turned towards me in surprise. The director of administration looked at me as though he might faint at any moment. The officer wearing dark glasses shifted his feet, leant slightly towards me and addressed me for the first time. "Saïd, I assume you have studied the situation in all its aspects?"

I waited for him to go on but he remained silent so I said: "Of course."

"And know that there are several possible outcomes to this strike?" He stopped again as though reflecting on what to say next. "The first is that it should succeed and end in the workers obtaining their demands. The second is a compromise solution in which both sides make concessions which will be defined through negotiation. The third is that the government authorities should intervene with all the means at their disposal to break the strike, means which I am sure you would not make the mistake of minimizing, especially as they can have a direct bearing on the future of the workers, and of their leaders in particular."

I could see that dealing with this man would not be easy. He expressed himself unhurriedly, with cold lucidity. "Do you agree that what I have just said is true?"

"Yes."

"Nevertheless, I would like to add just one idea for your consideration, which I think is also perfectly true."

Once again he stopped. This time I had the impression that he was testing me to see what kind of a person I was, whether I was prone to be hasty or to get the jitters easily.

"This idea leads me to believe that in fact there is only one possible outcome to your strike."

I refrained from commenting. He stared at me for a moment from behind the dark glasses, and gave an imperceptible smile before asking: "Don't you want to know what it is?"

"Yes I do."

"The third possibility. To my mind the third outcome is inevitable."

112

"And why the third only?"

"Because your strike has implications not only for the future of Thebes Pharmaceuticals alone, but for the whole policy of the government. That is why I would have preferred not to have it sprung on me like this without prior warning, as though I had no inkling of what is going on in the industrial district for which I am considered responsible by those in charge of national security. In short, I would have hoped to be informed right from the beginning; right from the moment when it was still a project floating in the air, or in someone's imagination."

He was aiming a few of his barbs in another direction for the moment. But I knew very well that the workers would remain the principal target, and that he was not going to allow himself to be led astray by secondary considerations. Maybe later, when the main battle was over, he would settle his accounts with the chairman. He looked at me again from behind the dark glasses.

"That is why you will be facing things that you have never thought of even in your wildest dreams. Saïd, you are one of the few who know full well that any policy is based on a limited number of premises, and that if one of these premises is undermined the whole policy will collapse. No workers before have ever dared to strike as a way of combatting the government's investment policies. If we allow you to do that, the result is obvious. That is why to my mind your strike can have one, and only one outcome. To be crushed, completely, at once, without hesitation, and with all the means at our disposal."

The word "crush" resounded in the room like a whiplash. I still stood upright listening silently to what this man was saying. He had not told me yet what he wanted of me. If I was patient I was sure to find out.

"Therefore, if you are really thinking of the interests of your fellow workers, their families, and their children, of the trade union leadership in the company and of yourself in particular, then you will go back to them and say. 'We must end this strike.' Think of everything that can happen Saïd. Do not continue blindfold along the path you have chosen. The blood of innocent victims will keep you awake at night."

All around me was a circle of faces, with black, staring eyes and pale sneering features. I rested my hand on the back of an empty chair to hold myself up. My knees were giving way under me and I longed to sit down. I tensed my muscles, fighting the exhaustion which was

113

overcoming me. We had fought step by step to convince the workers of the need to strike, discussed it almost with each individual worker, in the courtyards, on the road, in the homes, coffee houses and places where they ate. How could I climb the stairs, my head high, my body upright, and go back to those who had sent me, crawling in the mud like a worm? How could I try to convince them that now they should do exactly the opposite of what I had fought for step by step? And why should I? Right from the start we knew the difficulties of the struggle we had decided upon. Nothing had changed, except perhaps that this man sitting in front of me had expressed all the possible consequences we faced in a way that made them brutally clear. Through the window I could see the riot squads standing in rows, the automatic rifles and snub-nosed machine guns, imagine the whine of bullets, the cries of the workers, and their blood flowing over the ground. These same images had passed through my mind before, but this time they were a hundred times more vivid. I made an effort to pull myself together. If I envisaged defeat right from the beginning everything would be lost. It was imperative to remain in control of myself, to be calm, to remain the fighter who had taken a decision after calculating all the risks and was prepared to go through with it right to the end. If I could have borne the consequences alone would things have been easier?

"It's no use wasting your time trying to convince me to call off the strike. We weighed the risks very carefully before taking a decision. We are against violence and bloodshed. We want to work and live in peace. We are using legitimate forms of struggle in the face of the means of oppression, torture and death which you have imported into the country. We believe in upholding our democratic rights."

The white face buried in the depth of the armchair seemed to grow even whiter. I had never seen so much hatred concentrated in one man's eyes, and in the distortion of his features. He pronounced his words quietly, but in the silence they fell like the strokes of a hammer. "Then you refuse to co-operate with us to avoid a conflict in which the workers will be the first to pay the price?"

"If co-operation means surrender then we prefer to pay the price. It is better for a man to be whipped and fight back, than to crawl on his stomach and ask for mercy from the enemy."

I heard the sound of something metallic fall to the ground. I looked around quickly. The paper cutter had fallen out of the fingers of the officer in dark glasses on to the ground. The small muscle in my neck twitched rapidly. He bent down, picked it up and held it by the handle, pointing it in my direction. I glimpsed the metallic blade flashing in the sun. He got up slowly, walked out of the room and returned a few moments later with an officer in uniform, and made a gesture in my direction without saying anything. I saw the steel bracelets shine for a moment in the light, and smiled, the officer in uniform said: "Put out your hands."

I felt the thin edge of the bracelets bite into one wrist, then the other, giving out two simultaneous clicks. I found myself being led out of the room, down the stairs to the entrance of the building. In front of it stood a van with a closed box and iron grills on the small windows. So they were starting with me. I wondered whether they would take us one after the other, or all together. Perhaps they would wait to see the effect of my arrest. The van drove out of the gates followed by disguised looks of sympathy from the guards; but no one waved to me or said anything. The rows of riot squads looked like heavy yellow clouds closing down on the plant from all directions. Our vehicle sped down the road. I glimpsed the black ribbon of the road rolling out behind us, and trees shrunken and dried from the factory smoke and fumes. Everything green in our country was being destroyed. After some time the van came to a sudden halt. One of my guards jumped out and beckoned me to follow him. The white building of the police station sprawled in the sunlight. Near the entrance four sentinels were taking refuge from the heat in their small wooden shacks, and three lorry loads of riot police waited at a distance ready to depart. Near the station was a small eating place with tables and chairs half visible inside. Behind the glass windows were big bowls of tamia, fried egg-plant, and boiled eggs. I felt my stomach contract with hunger. The red disc of the sun hung close to the horizon. We pushed a way for ourselves through the throngs of people at the door. No one looked round at us. The sight of a man in handcuffs was familiar. I stood in front of the officer on duty. He was busy talking to one of his colleagues. After a while he wrote a few words in the register on his desk, and resumed his conversation. They took me down a flight of stairs into the depths of the building. I found myself facing a dark green door with a small round opening in its upper part. Keys screeched in the lock, and a moment later it closed behind me. I heard the bolt crash into its socket, and the lock turn rustily, leaving me in a complete silence. A pale yellowish light struggled with the dark somewhere near the ceiling. I looked around at the dirty smudged walls, the pail of water, the rubber receptacle which served as a toilet and from which

115

emanated a penetrating odour which mingled with the smell of humid rot in the air. I felt my stomach turn, took off my shoes and sat on the frayed mat which covered one corner of the floor.

The hours crept past. They had taken my watch, together with my keys and pocket book. I could not even observe the alternation of night and day since my cell had no window, and was lit all the time by the yellow lamp high up on the ceiling. Rotten air penetrated into it from a small hole way up at the top. I spent most of the time lying on my back on the mat, in a state much closer to semi-consciousness than to sleep. Frightening images kept flitting through my mind until the moment when suddenly my ears were almost pierced by the screech of the lock, and the rusty noise of the bolt being shot back into its socket. I came to gradually, and found myself staring at a pair of huge boots occupying the open space between my eyelids. I sat up and heard the man say: "Get up and follow me."

I put on my socks and shoes, and pushed my shirt into the top of my trousers, then splashed my face with some of the water from the pail. A stubble of beard had grown around my face, and it itched every time I touched it with my fingers. I followed the guard out of the room and climbed the stairs with the feeling of rising out of a deep cave into daylight. I stood in front of the same officer who had received me when I arrived. He was talking to a dark man dressed in a gallabeya and wearing a fine, white shawl around his head. He left me standing until he had finished with the man, pulled out a letter from a torn dirty file and said: "Take the things you left in deposit. The SSSPS has sent us instructions to release you."

I walked out of the police station. Near the entrance I recognized the grey hair and lined face of the president of the federation. He came quickly towards me and hugged me to his chest saying, "God bless you Saïd. I'm glad they've set you free." He examined me closely. "You've lost a lot of weight. What happened?"

"May God bless you too. To start with let me ask you . . . What day are we?"

He looked at me with surprise.

"Friday the 2nd of October."

"They took away my watch and put me in an underground cell without windows. There was a weak electric bulb burning day and night, so that after the first day it became impossible for me to know how long I had been kept in it."

"What about food. You've really lost a lot of weight you know."

116

"Three small loaves of dry bread and a pail of water."

"But we were sending you food enough for three regular meals a day."

"Nothing reached me."

He spat on the floor and said: "Sons of a bitch."

I asked him anxiously: "But what about the strike?"

He smiled happily, his small eyes almost disappearing in the web of his wrinkles.

"A victory, comrade. A real victory. Larochelle cabled your chairman to tell him that they had decided to withdraw the project agreement, but . . ."

"But what?"

"Four of you have been fired from the company. You, Mostapha Ramadan, Ali El Sharkawi, and Hassan Eid."

I took a deep breath, slowed down my pace, and tightened my hold on his arm. "So despite everything they found out what we were trying to conceal."

"Yes."

"We shouldn't let it go at that. This time we must understand how it happened. Somehow the police manage every time to strike in the right place."

"Almost every time. Let's forget about that now. This is not the moment to remember the police."

"I know. The strike has attained its objectives and that's the most important thing. But tell me first, where are we going? I must eat else I will die of hunger. A whole week on bread and water!!"

"Let's go home. Aleya has prepared a special meal to celebrate the success of the strike, and your release from jail."

"With pleasure. Seven days and nights all alone is no joke. I have as great a need to talk, as I have to eat. Let's walk faster. Those hunger pangs are really playing havoc with me inside."

"Oh . . . by the way, I forget to tell you something about Khalil Mansour Khalil. They say he ran away from the plant during the strike. He was absent since the 25 September and has not come back."

"That's strange!!"

We crossed over the wide street and started to walk in the shade of the trees on the opposite pavement. What on earth made him disappear like that? He could only draw attention to himself. Just one week and yet so many things had happened. And here I was again without a job. What did the future have in store for me this time?

Khalil Mansour Khalil

I wandered through the streets of the city lost in the crowds. Coloured advertisements besieged me on every side, offering their services with a clamour of lights. A man emerged out of a dark lane suddenly and whispered to me in English: "Change dollars Mister." In my right trouser pocket I carried the letter of dismissal and in my left three pounds.

A week had gone by after the letter arrived during which I remained completely at a loss. At last I decided to go to the company. I walked down the road which I knew so well, as though I had just returned from another world. The sky was clear, and in the fields buffaloes slowly chewed the green maize stalks. There was no sign of the armies which had surrounded the plant. But there were numerous police cars continually driving up and down, and at strategic points were car loads of riot police, and wireless patrols. When I passed through the small gate a security agent in plain clothes asked to see my identity, and then accompanied me to the entrance of the administration building. As I crossed the outer compound with him I noticed a number of men wearing civilian clothes standing at the doors leading to the various production sections. I mounted the stairs to the chairman's office on the first floor, and entered his secretary's room; she was staring vacantly in front of her. I said: "Good morning. I see everything has gone back to normal."

She looked around as though afraid that someone might be hiding nearby. "The strike is over, thanks be to Allah."

"Over?! But how?"

She refrained from answering for a long moment, looking cautiously around. I almost laughed at the sight of her face, her rounded eyes and mouth, her button nose, like a panic-stricken doll, but I quickly suppressed the desire.

"Larochelle withdrew its proposal."

I stared at her unable to believe my ears. So the problem had been solved as simply as that. It seemed so comic. Suddenly I was overcome by an uncontrollable fit of laughter. I fought hard, and managed to cut it short helped by the sheer fright looking out of her eyes. "I want to meet the boss."

She started to look for something on her desk, and without raising her eyes to my face said: "The boss told me not to let anybody into his office. You can go to Mr Mokhtar. As a matter of fact he is waiting for you."

I walked away without asking any questions (in any case what difference did it make whom I met) and continued down the corridor to the office of the administrative director. I walked in without greeting him, and sat down. One of the employees was submitting some letter to him. The discussion kept going round in circles. He was so meticulous about everything, as meticulous as he was about his neck-tie, his cufflinks, and the way he had of parting his black hair. The perfection of a man who did his work with seriousness and honesty! But I knew that behind the careful instructions and unerring formalities, he hid what he really was.

I waited patiently. I knew he was keeping me waiting on purpose. Since he had been appointed in the company I had always kept my distance. He was the type of person I disliked intensely. He had been brought up in the fold of institutions that considered the private life of individuals as part of the domain which was rightfully theirs to pry into. When he was transferred it was natural, therefore, that he should have been appointed director for administration in the company. Administration, in the view of those who were in authority, was the art of transforming people into instruments for furthering the interests of an individual or a group. He and I were therefore like oil and water. We could not mix.

The employee standing in front of me had ostensibly finished the various matters he had come for, but continued to wait expectantly as though uncertain what to do. A moment later without turning around he started to withdraw with short backward steps, stopping every now and then with the mixture of hesitation, controlled expectancy, and humility one finds in people who have spent their whole life being ordered about. Should he leave the room or remain a little longer? The man sitting behind the desk had not made any movement or gesture which could give him a clue. He was therefore in a quandary. He might make the mistake of withdrawing, whereas the director wanted him to stay. On the other hand he might stay at a time when he was expected to withdraw. Besides, apart from these considerations, was it not true that proximity to one's superiors was a source of great bounty, and just as important as being in close communication with Almighty God.

The director of administration put out his hand to pick up the telephone. I realized that unless I acted quickly he would continue to ignore my presence. I pulled out the letter from my pocket, walked over to his desk, and almost thrust it under his nose. He said: "What is this?"

Picking it up with the tips of his fingers, as though he was afraid it might carry some infection, he started to read through it slowly, and once finished, pushed it aside, with the gesture of someone who considers the matter settled.

"I think the matter is very clear. What do you want of me?"

"No, it's not clear at all. I will not discuss the essence of the problem with you. I know full well that it is not your area of competence, and that in fact there is nothing you can do about it. You are just executing orders. But I consider that the measures taken against me are, from the purely formal point of view, illegal and contrary to the regulations."

"How?"

"I sent a registered letter to the company asking for leave of absence, then a second letter requesting an extension for reasons related to my wife's condition."

"Quite true."

"Why then was a decision taken to dismiss me from my job?"

I saw him smile. His lips parted slightly as though he was making sure that his smile remained within certain well-defined limits.

"The chairman did not agree to the leave you asked for in view of the unusual circumstances prevalent in the company at the time. It is the duty of employees at the higher levels of authority not to absent themselves in an emergency."

There was a long silence. So they had planned it to make sure that the legal aspect was covered. It was perfectly correct that in the labour regulations the timing of leave in enterprises was a matter left to the discretion of the chairman of the board. My intuition had not been far off the mark.

"But before a letter of dismissal aren't I supposed to receive a preliminary warning?"

He smiled again, a broad smile this time. He was manifestly pleased with the situation. I could imagine him rereading my letter of dismissal several times and then signing it with a flourish.

"That is exactly what we did. We sent you a warning by registered letter after you had been absent for eight days."

"But I was not in my home at the time!"

"That is no business of ours. Do you expect us to follow your movements and track you down?"

"Nevertheless do you not feel that the procedure followed with me was highly unusual, and is never used even with employees at the

120

lowest level of the hierarchy. There must be other reasons for the way in which this matter was dealt with."

"That is something you would know better than I. But I did hear that the chairman himself no longer wants you in our company. It has been rumoured that you had relations with the strike committee, and that you divulged certain company secrets to its members."

He gestured with his hand, and asked: "Would you like a cup of coffee?"

I said: "Thank you" and got up. I took the letter that was lying on the desk in front of him and walked out, and went up the stairs to the second floor. When I entered my secretary's room she was taken aback, and looked greatly embarrassed. I asked for some papers I had to sign to complete the formalities related to my dismissal, and for the keys of my desk, and went to my room. I emptied my drawers of all the papers and files, and asked her to keep them for my successor. She looked at me in silence and nodded her head sadly. I put my books and a few tapes of music into a bag and then shook hands with her. She started to cry. I felt a wave of irritation. What was there to cry about? I had no links with this place. At least that's how I felt now. Perhaps the rapid sequence of events since the strike had not given me the time to become really aware of what was happening. It was as though my emotions were paralysed.

I patted her shoulder and said: "Don't cry. I do not regret leaving my job. I gave all I could to it while I was here but received nothing in return. The only thing that I'll miss are some of the people I'm leaving behind, like you, and others. Saïd Abou Karam in particular."

"Saïd!"

"Yes. You seem surprised."

"No. I'm not surprised. Haven't you heard what happened?"

"I heard that the strike is over, and that Larochelle has withdrawn its proposals."

"That's only part of the developments. After the strike ended a decision was taken to dismiss a number of people."

"Apart from myself?"

"Yes, apart from you, sir. Four others: Saïd Abou Karam, Mostapha Ramadan, Ali El Sharkawi and Hassan Eid."

If they had been able to identify the strike leaders, they must also know the details of my involvement, and that I had given the committee a copy of my report. That explained everything. My God! What wonderful protection they gave to those that helped them! What a capacity for hiding secrets! Once again I had made a mistake, trusted people who were unworthy of trust. The strike had succeeded for a variety of reasons, partly related to the timing but partly mere chance. Yes, the authorities had succeeded in doing what the security officer had said. The head had been cut off from the body. It would grow again. Perhaps soon — or it could take years. I too was fated to start again. What had I gained from all this? What had I gained from all the battles I fought?

I had no place in my own land. Everything I touched ended in failure. Saïd and the others would not walk the streets alone. Parents, relations, friends would gather around with the solidarity born of poverty, the daily struggle for existence, shared experiences in factories and the city back streets. Whatever relations I had would not last very long, now that my past had caught up with me again. A visit or two at the beginning, then nothing. I had lived all this before. In front of my eyes danced the prison walls. The family that had disappeared as soon as I stepped through the wooden portico. The friends who had forgotten; and Tahani. Once the sentence was passed, it was as though she had been spirited away to another world. I lived in a house surrounded by wide open spaces, by the whisper of plants and trees. It wasn't luxurious, but perhaps people envied me for its quiet and simple beauty, the white walls, the flowers on the roof, the studio. But it was isolated from other homes, stood out alone. My roots were not deep in the earth, and around me there was no warmth, nothing bound me to a community. I had chosen to walk through life alone, but perhaps it was my fault? Yet I had linked my life to a common struggle, realized it had no meaning without others, only to discover that politics had not saved my soul.

Black smoke rose from the chimneys into a pale sky. Leaves shrivelled on the hot surface of the ground. A black crow perched on the telephone wires seemed to watch me. I arrived home. Amina was feeding Esam, his eyes watched her with an anxious confidence. They were one body, and I stood, a stranger, watching the silent harmony of their union from which I was excluded. I was circling at the margin of my life, away from the essence of things, removed from their substance. Even in this intimate relation between the mother and the child I was only a witness. She took off his clothes, sponged the little body with toilet water, wrapped him up in a clean towel and laid him on the bed. I approached. He gasped for a moment then burst into a shrieking wail. I ran to the kitchen as though seeking refuge.

After making sure that he was asleep she came to the kitchen. She looked worn after the period of childbirth and illness. I caressed her head, touched her face with my fingers. In her eyes, grown wider, I saw the courage with which she struggled to keep things going; and I felt guilty. She smiled at me. We ate the meal she had prepared the previous night. I forced myself to eat so as not to disappoint her. She asked me what I had done that morning. I told her, leaving out the details which could hurt. Usually I told her everything, but these days I had started to be careful, feeling that the problems she was facing were enough without my adding to them.

We went to bed early. Esam was a quiet baby and slept throughout the night. To me he seemed no more than a small creature of flesh. I tried to discover some relation between him and me but failed. Sometimes when I observed him I was overcome by a feeling of wonder. This small creature who was still unable to formulate his thoughts, or pronounce words, was my son. Written on the birth certificate was his name: Esam Khalil Mansour Khalil. But it was Amina who had carried him in her belly, given him protection, given him life. Sometimes when I watched him, or lifted him in my arms, or changed his napkin I felt I was intruding upon a private relationship, a stranger to my child.

That night I felt tired, empty, crushed. There was nothing I could be sure was mine. Nothing I could say was the product of my work. I was not even sure of Amina's love. My mind churned like an empty mill-stone. Half-formed images, splintered memories, chaotic thoughts crowded in on one another. Nothing in it came to completion. It was rebelling against me, abandoning my body, racing ahead like a wild horse. I kept trying to catch up with this mind out of control. My fevered imagination tortured me throughout the night, until with the light of dawn filtering through the shutters, I suddenly fell into a deep sleep.

The following day Amina decided to go out early with Esam. She suggested that I accompany her, but I told her that I intended to start on the second part of my study, and preferred to stay at home. She encouraged me with zeal, and told me it was the best way to occupy myself, and to forget what had happened the past few weeks. The only way to maintain one's stability was to be productive. It restored the feeling of one's own worth and usefulness. I walked part of the way with her and returned, went into the kitchen, washed the plates and cups, put the food she had prepared on the stove, and then swept and cleaned the house. I made a cup of strong coffee, put it on the desk, extracted a sheaf of white paper from the drawer, and arranged my books and documents. I took a few sips of coffee, and opened one of the books, but I had barely read a few lines when the telephone rang. This time I recognized her voice immediately.

"Why did you not get in touch with me? I was worried and angry that you left me without any news." .

My heart beat impetuously. This beautiful creature who seemed to have everything was worried because I hadn't phoned her!

"I'm sorry. Please accept my apologies. Unexpected circumstances made it very difficult to contact you."

"Circumstances? What circumstances? Is something wrong? Your voice sounds different, as though you're worried."

It did not seem that my voice could have betrayed me so easily, and yet somehow the change in me had not escaped her.

"It's nothing really. A very small matter. I will tell you about it when we meet."

"Then we're going to meet?!"

"But of course. Surely you didn't have doubts about that?"

"When you didn't call me, I thought that maybe you didn't want us to meet again."

"On the contrary. I would like to see you, always. I'm not saying it just to please you. It's really true."

"This time I don't believe you. If you had remembered me you would have simply lifted the telephone and asked about me. But you didn't. I am the one who got in touch with you."

I felt happy but also ashamed of myself. What with the strike, and the birth of Esam followed by Amina's illness I had forgotten her. And on top of all that I had been fired. It had been difficult. But now that I had heard her voice, I was seized by an overpowering desire to see her again.

"It's true. I must admit that I forgot. But when you hear the whole story I'm sure you'll forgive me."

She said nothing. I was afraid I might have hurt her feelings. I was getting ready to clarify the matter when I heard her say: "If my intuition is not leading me astray, there are things which make it difficult for our friendship to continue. Why not stick to the truth and say so? I like to be clear about things. You are a man with responsibilities. You live in Egypt, and I am an American woman. I may be here today, and gone tomorrow. It's no use exposing yourself to all sorts of questions for the sake of this new-born relationship. Is that not what you're thinking?"

"My answer is no. I admit that such thoughts did pass through my mind after our last meeting, and in particular when I noticed the way the porter of your building looked at me when I left. But I decided that to see you was more important than anything else."

She laughed. "The porter! And what does the porter have to do with all this?"

"You do not understand. Most porters here work as spies for the security section."

There was an abrupt silence. I said: "Hello. Do you hear me?"

"Yes. I heard you." Her voice was subdued.

"What's wrong? Did I say something I shouldn't have said?"

"No. It isn't that. It's just that things like that have a way of dampening one's happiness."

"I'm sorry. You told me I should not hide anything from you. But let's leave all this aside. I want to see you Ruth. Is that possible?"

She said nothing as though thinking my question over, or perhaps punishing me with moments of silent uncertainty.

"Of course it's possible. If it were not, I would have refrained from getting in touch with you."

"When?"

"Today if you like. I'll be at home after seven in the evening."

"Can't we meet somewhere else?"

"Why?"

"Just for a change."

"Where do you suggest?"

"At the Guezira Casino."

"How do we get there?"

"I have no car. Can we meet there?"

"No. I prefer to meet here in my flat, then we can go together. I do not like appointments in public places. Either of us might be late, and then the other has to wait."

"Then I'll drop in on you around half past seven."

"I'll be waiting."

I heard a quiet buzz followed by two clicks, then the receiver was silent. I frowned for a moment. That noise. I put back the receiver slowly. Moments from the past seemed to repeat themselves, and made me relive them just as they had happened before. I shrugged. What more could happen than had already happened before? I went back to the book but my thoughts kept straying.

That evening there was a fine crescent moon. As we emerged from the building the porter rushed up smiling. No doubt she tipped him handsomely. Her fingers guided me with their touch on my arm. Sitting by her side as the car purred into life, enveloped by her closeness, her barely perceptible scent, I knew I was running away, downing my arms, enjoying the feeling of surrender.

The coloured lights quivered in the waters of the Nile. My hand reached for hers as I looked into her face, drinking in the shadowy beauty of its lines, and listened to her voice.

"You haven't told me yet what kept you away all this time."

I hesitated. How could I break the spell of this night with the story of all that had happened during the past weeks? There were so many things I would find it difficult to talk to her about. How could I tell her that I had been fired and was now a man without a job. I felt embarrassed.

"Do you insist on bringing us back to the distasteful realities of life?"

"Why do you describe reality as distasteful? To be quite frank I want to find out what you seem so keen on hiding about yourself."

I laughed. "I'm not hiding anything from you. We have met only twice before, and yet we have already spoken of many things people usually avoid talking about, at least at the beginning. Look, how the moon is hanging between the trees on an invisible thread."

"You are an unusual person. You must have a strong leaning for art. Have you never expressed yourself in writing, or painting?"

"When I was a boy I wanted to learn the violin. My father refused. He wanted me to take over managing the land and herds he owned. But I hated looking after land, and doing accounts with the tenants; instead I loved to stretch out under a tree, watch the fields, the water rushing out of the gates into a stream, flowing along the canals, irrigating the wide expanses in sunlit sheets. I felt that being a landowner poisoned my relationships with the peasants, made them curry favour with me, play cunning tricks, lie and cheat. I knew in their hearts they hated me, despite their words of praise when speaking of me. For was I not the son of the landowner who possessed hectares of land and property, and who ordered them about because they depended on him for their daily bread?"

She seemed to withdraw and I felt that an invisible wall had suddenly risen between us.

"I find it difficult to understand you. Sometimes you don't see things as they really are, then you collide with realities and the shock makes you suffer. Life is a struggle and only the powerful survive. I was not born rich. If I was not a strong woman, I would still be living in misery, swallowing my bitterness as a sales girl, or as a female factory hand. In fact I did spend part of my life that way. Now I try to forget those days." She said nothing for a moment, then resumed. "Why don't we go back to what we were saying about why you avoided meeting me?"

She pressed my hand and smiled. I felt in the palm for her warmth which seemed to escape me now.

"If you insist then you will have only yourself to blame."

There was a long silence. I hesitated like a poor swimmer getting ready to throw himself into deep waters. "To cut a long story short I was dismissed from my job about a month ago."

Her face registered surprise. She gave me a questioning look. "You're joking, of course?"

"Joking?! I'm not fond of bad jokes."

"I'm sorry. I was not prepared for this." She fell into a long silence, staring at me as though trying to guess what I might be thinking, or searching for the right things to say.

"But how did it happen?"

Should I tell her? Why not? Nobody else had taken so much interest in what happened to me. I was like a sick man looking for somebody to care for him. I remembered Amina. She had turned her back on me recently. Perhaps it was the baby; before that it had been the exhibition. But why was I leaving her alone while I sat by the Nile holding hands with a woman whom I barely knew, telling her about the most crucial things in my life? Amina had tried to encourage me in her own characteristic way. "Don't worry yourself over what has happened. I still have a job, and I'm sure you'll find work very soon. Try to be occupied with something. It's the only way to rid yourself of depressing thoughts. That study . . ."

I tried to find excuses for her. She was so busy. But what I needed now was not advice. Whenever she talked about the study it emphasized the feeling of failure I carried around. And when she spoke of her work it reminded me that she had a job, but I had nothing. Perhaps I was wrong after all, without her job things could have been much more serious. Besides, were we not supposed to support one another? Nevertheless, I felt she had hurt my pride. I was overcome by a greater sadness than I had ever experienced before. The day when I

127

walked out of the prison gates and found nobody waiting for me I felt sad, but not like this. For then I could still live in the future, make plans, imagine all the things I would do. But now all my hopes were destroyed. What I needed most was not to be told what to do with my life, but friendship and love that was simply given.

I heard her say: "You seem to have wandered far away."

I had almost forgotten her, yet she had accepted that. She gave me a sense of freedom, allowed my mind to travel. Her eyes expressed many things, but when I looked into them there was no pity. And so I was glad. I wanted love, not pity. I wondered if this woman was really prepared to give, or was taking what mattered to her? But what could she get from me? She still faced me with the same questioning look.

"Yes, my mind did wander far away. I was thinking of many things — that my life had made a complete circle only to return to the beginning, thinking of love and friendship, of Amina and my feelings towards her, of what loyalty means. And I was thinking of you Ruth."

She smiled at this. "But you have not told me yet what made them dismiss you. Or do you prefer to close the subject?"

"No, since I have spoken to you about it, there is no need for me to conceal anything. Our company had started to negotiate a partnership deal with a French concern called Larochelle. One condition was the modernization of production processes which entailed the dismissal of a substantial proportion of the workers. The result was a strike."

"But I don't see why this should have affected you."

She was staring at me intently.

"The chairman accused me of co-operating with the trade union committee and providing them with a copy of a memorandum I had written concerning the deal."

"And was that true?"

I felt the kind of reserve which instinctively seized hold of me whenever I was being questioned. But I had nothing to say that was not already well known. "Yes, quite true."

There was a silence.

"But I thought you had severed relations with the left, and now limited your activity to research writings."

Why was she so interested in this affair? She was an American and these days there were so many men and women like her. They had invaded almost every field of activity, formed an efficient network. Was she one of them? How could one tell? It was almost impossible to find out. Doubts like this could spoil even the most genuine friendship. I glimpsed the crescent suspended in the night like a scythe ready to descend on our heads, and her face opposite me was a statue carved in white marble.

"What do you mean by 'left'? Are all those who go on strike, or protest, or oppose the policies imposed by arbitrary laws, or by forms of terror which use a technology imported from your country to be considered part of the left?"

She detected the angry tone and retreated, but her eyes still looked at me calmly.

Neither of us moved or spoke. I picked up the glass of beer in front of me, swallowed its contents with a gulp.

I stretched my legs over the soft grass underfoot, and watched a wide-bottomed sailing boat as it crossed the river, bearing a group of tourists. Their voices echoed loudly over the quiet waters. My heart was torn between the melody of a native ballad and the mad rhythm of disco music. The evening breeze carried the voice of a woman singing in English. "Your embrace was so warm last night, my darling."

I leaned towards her and said: "Maybe we can leave now, if you don't mind."

She shook her head as though it made no difference to her whether we stayed or left. I paid the waiter and we moved away. I heard her murmur: "Would you like to drive?"

At every moment she seemed to know what I needed most; or perhaps she wasn't in the mood for driving. The tips of her fingers were cold as they handed me the key. The engine purred gently, and the silver shadow cut through the night with a growing speed. Her arm touched me now and again, as the car swerved round a corner, or avoided some sudden obstacle. I glimpsed her profile, the tilted nose, full lips and the curve of her neck. I fought against a wave of desire that mounted irresistibly and fixed my attention of the black ribbon of the road. When we reached her building I stopped the engine and prepared to get out when she said softly, "Come up with me Khalil."

Amina, the child, and so many other things were waiting for me — better to leave her, and take the last train home to the little house standing near the fields. I sat immobile in my seat.

"Please . . . we must not part like this."

She took the key from me. "Wait for me. I'll put the car away."

In the lift she stood close, and looked straight into my eyes. When we stepped out I went quickly through the long corridor like a thief eager for the treasure awaiting him.

"Rest here for a while; take off your shoes. Fatigue is always greatest in the head, heart, back and feet."

I took off my shoes as though throwing off my remaining reservations. Tension slipped away and I felt wonderfully relaxed. She looked at me teasingly and asked: "What will you have? Whisky or fresh lemon juice?"

She threw her head back and laughed delightedly. She unclasped her hair, tossed it back over her shoulders and moved towards me. I caressed her hair with tender fingers. There was shadow in her eyes, the shadow of a woman hurt before, a look of tentative, fearful hope. Her fingers moved over my eyelids, my lips, my hair. I unfastened her robe, trembling with the wonder of coming moments, with the beauty that was hers. And suddenly she was naked. I followed her beautiful lines with my fingertips, traced her curves with the eagerness of the blind, felt my heart swell, looked into her eyes and read a question: what will you do with me my friend? I searched for her lips with mine, felt her responding and resisting at the same time. My fingers travelled more boldly, over her firm breasts, the curve of her belly, the shadow of her thighs. Now her mouth searched eagerly for mine, led me away feverishly, prepared our encounter. Together we tasted the wistful springs of tenderness, our bodies fused together, drowning our aloneness, seeking the hidden veins of love with the powerful drill of desire, deeper and deeper, higher and higher on a rising wave of pleasure, then down from the peak, over an avalanche, dying, slowly returning to life, to the muffled beats of my heart, and her bare foot close to mine.

She looked at me with shining eyes, kissed me again and said: "Thank you."

I awoke in the morning to the sun streaming through the open window, and turned my head to where she slept, the shadow of her armpit was mysteriously provoking. I looked around the spacious room, with a strange feeling as though I had returned to where I belonged after a lifetime of wandering. Yesterday seemed very distant, its faces shrouded, obscurely fearful . . . I looked at the woman sleeping by my side and laid my hand on her shoulder. She stirred, and for a moment stared at me, unseeing, through a layer of glass, or stone. Then suddenly she smiled. She put her arm around me, nestled close and I felt the touch of her body, seeking mine.

"Good morning. How happy I am to waken and find you by my

side. You look so healthy and brown in the sunlight — not like my insipid white skin."

I laughed happily. "I find you more beautiful."

"Perhaps others see what we really look like." She broke off to hug me, then added: "What are we going to do this morning?"

I pondered. "I really don't know."

She spoke quickly, as though trying to prevent me from pursuing my thoughts: "Then stay with me. Relax, while I make breakfast. Gaafar is on holiday."

"Gaafar?! Ah . . . the servant."

"He's not exactly a servant. He's educated, can type in Arabic, cooks, cleans and drives the car."

"Rather unusual, to find a man with all those talents. You must find him very useful."

She looked at me steadily for a moment, then said: "What do you want for breakfast?"

"Do you insist on having breakfast now?"

"No, I can wait. We can sit on the terrace, or would you prefer to swim?"

I looked at her for a long moment then asked abruptly, "Do you know what I would like?"

She smiled at me with a slightly quizzical expression as though trying to guess.

"I would like us to become one again, as we were last night."

She whispered softly, "So would I. Wait a moment, I'll be back."

When she returned she slipped into my arms with a movement I hardly felt, and in one brief moment she threw off all barriers and carried me off with a passionate strength.

We lay on the bed, stretching our bodies with fatigue. She whispered, "I love you. I have never known such pleasure. Never known a man so tender. I will never harm you, never."

"I love you too . . . But why talk of not harming me? Did you at some time intend to?"

Momentarily she looked sad, withdrawn, then she was transparent, herself again. "No, of course not. I have silly ideas sometimes, irrational things. Perhaps one is always afraid of happiness . . . that something will destroy it."

"Do you feel insecure at this moment?"

"No, with you I feel secure. In your arms I feel that the world can be a safe place."

131

"I trust you too, yet there are moments when I am afraid."

"Afraid? Why?"

"When I feel that suddenly you are no longer with me, that you have gone where I cannot reach you — as if you are no longer the same woman, but someone else. Then I ask myself are you the woman I know, touch, love and with whom I share thoughts and feelings, or this other woman whom I don't know? Which is the real Ruth Harrison?"

She put her hand on my arm and said: "Khalil, please. Sometimes you see more than you should. In everyone there is a dark corner. Love does not mean that you can invade a person, take everything over. I need to feel you trust me, and believe I will never do anything to harm you. You are very dear to me, I never thought that I could become so close to anyone."

I touched her nipple lightly and watched it shrink, and then swell like a rose. She murmured, "Stop that, or we'll make love all day."

"Why not?"

She laughed. Then turned serious. "Yes, why not? But I have things to do. What about you?"

I felt my heart contract, "No . . . I have nothing in particular to do."

"I have a suggestion; we'll have breakfast, then go for a swim."

"Yes, let's have breakfast. But after that I will leave. Tell me, are you married?"

"Yes."

"And your husband?"

"In the States."

"But you have no children?"

"How did you know?"

"From your nipples."

"You seem to know about women."

"On the contrary, my relations with them have been limited."

She leant over me, and rested her lips on mine for a long moment then moved away.

She returned a few moments later dripping with water, and kissed me again lightly.

I took a cold shower and dressed. We ate breakfast at a small round table on the terrace. The sun rose above the buildings in a blue sky. The Nile flashed with a million ripples flowing with the deep calm and certainty carried down from ancient times.

I said: "Now I must go."

132

"I've found an excuse to delay you. I want to ask something . . ." She broke off. I waited for her to continue.

"I don't want to interfere, but suppose I can help you find work, have you any objection?"

I was taken aback and a little displeased by her question. I preferred to keep our relations on a different plane. Yet with the intimacy now between us how could she not be affected by what happened to me? I wanted to feel that we stood on an equal footing, and if she helped me to find work I would be indebted to her. And yet why not?I needed someone who could help. But I disliked this feeling of need.

She kept silent. I watched the waters of the Nile as they flowed by. The struggle had been going on year after year without respite, and yet people like myself were still being hunted down.

"On principle I have no objection. How can a jobless pauper like myself refuse a helping hand?"

"If you ask me to forget what I said I will never mention it again. You know what is best. But I don't like to see you unhappy, and just sit here looking on helplessly. You have good reason to be bitter about many things, but bitterness will not solve anything. Sometimes you imagine things."

"Imagine? What we are living through these days is not a figment of imagination, but hard reality. You people are playing an essential role in creating this reality."

"We?"

"Yes, you, the Americans."

She seemed to be fighting hard to keep calm.

"Let's be clear that I don't want to be drawn into a political discussion because I'm sure we'll disagree. But first, each country's government and people are responsible for what happens in it. So don't look for excuses, for something on which to hang your own failures. Secondly, the American government is composed of human beings, and human beings sometimes do things well, sometimes they make mistakes. We are trying to help you, but maybe the problem lies in the methods we use."

My anger mounted . . . was she pretending? How could someone with her qualifications, doing research into the problems of the Third World, talk such nonsense?

"I'm not trying to hang our faults on anyone. Recently we have lost our independence, and fallen into the grasp of the neo-colonialist powers. Today America is behind most of the policies followed by our

133

government. This talk of good intentions and mistakes are arguments not even used by the ruling circles in the States. They talk quite openly of the need to defend their interests in the Middle East and the Gulf, and the need to support Israel."

The atmosphere was very tense. There was a look in her eyes I had not seen before, as though a woman capable of killing confronted me. I heard her say pleadingly, "Khalil. Let's forget this useless argument. It's only spoiling things between us. I'm thinking about what is more important, I don't want us to quarrel."

I took refuge in a stony silence.

"Khalil, what do you say?"

I loved the way she pronounced my name — the genuine tenderness in its intonation. How long was I going to fight on all fronts at the same time?

"I'm ready to listen to any suggestions you may have."

"First you must tell me whether you prefer to work with the public sector, the private sector, or an American company."

I decided to ignore the words "American company". Could she really help me to find work in whatever sector I chose? An idea flashed through my mind. Why not suggest it to her? It would help to reveal the scope of her connections.

"I think the best thing for me would be my original post in Thebes Pharmaceuticals."

Her face registered disbelief, and irritation. "But why?"

"It suits me for a variety of reasons. The company is close to my house, and I am familiar with the work. Perhaps too I want to hit back at those who treated me so unfairly, to be reinstated in my rightful place, even against their wishes."

"But perhaps this won't be easy."

"From what you said I got the impression that you have influence, and can find me a job almost anywhere."

Once more her look was one of displeasure. Perhaps she felt that some of the things she had said had been indiscreet. A number of questions had started to revolve in my mind, which when we were close I tended to forget.

"I don't have so much influence. I'm only trying to think of a solution which would please you. But that doesn't mean I can find exactly what you want. My research has helped me make friends, and establish relationships with certain institutions."

"And what price do I have to pay?"

This time she was angry. "I need nothing and ask nothing in return when I help a friend. If you're going to hate me because I'm trying to help you, if you cannot deal with life simply but insist on poisoning the relationship between us then let's drop the whole thing. How can you take advantage of my feelings in order to hurt me?"

I was overcome by a wave of regret. Why was I behaving like this? I was behaving despicably towards Amina, and now this scene with Ruth. What was wrong with me? If I didn't stop it where would it end? Only a month since I was fired and already I was losing control.

I sank into a long gloomy silence then at last I raised my eyes to her face. She was sitting opposite me without moving, her shoulders drooping.

"Ruth. Let's discuss this another time. I'm not in my normal state at the moment, and I don't want to hurt your feelings any more than I have already done. I'm sorry. Please forgive me. I think it's best if I go now. I'll get in touch with you very soon."

She accompanied me to the door. I held out my hand and felt her fingers clasp mine for a moment with a cold reserve. The door closed behind me with a thud.

When I returned home, the house was empty. I felt a pang of anxiety. Where could Amina and the baby have gone? Perhaps tired of waiting she had taken him for a walk, or was looking for me. My feeling of guilt grew. Maybe she had decided to leave me? I was seized by a wave of panic. Surely not, especially in the present situation? After all, I had slept out for only one night. But I had never done it before, and always phoned if I was likely to be late. And yet was it so serious? My sense of guilt made me see one night away as a crime. Could she have found out where I had been? I shivered at the thought. No. That was impossible. My imagination was running away with me! I would soon be having hallucinations! She would be back with Esam, then I would discover she had simply gone for a walk. But what was I going to say to her? Previously it had been much easier for me to invent some tale. My relations with Ruth had not gone as far as they had now. True, I had an uneasy conscience right from the start. Yet from the moment her voice echoed in my ears that night, I felt the die had been cast.

I moved aimlessly around the house. The emptiness filled me with a deep depression. She might return at any moment. What would I say to her? I could not lie. She had always been loyal and straightforward. How could I lie to her? And yet where would I find the courage to tell

135

her the truth, to sit on this chair and calmly say: "You know, I slept in another woman's arms yesterday, and my feelings for her are real?"

Amina Tewfik

We returned home about two weeks after Esam was born. When we got out of the taxi Khalil unlocked the door and I stepped over the threshold with a feeling of relief to be home again. I had escaped without damage. My belly was as flat and firm as ever and my legs strode over the ground with my usual steady gait. I was filled with a deep happiness and I put Esam on the bed, climbed the stairs to my studio and wandered around in it touching the colours, the brushes, and the canvases stretched tightly over their frames, as though I was discovering the most precious things I had ever seen. This was my world; the studio, the house, Khalil and now our child, Esam. I spoke his name softly to myself and smiled.

But two or three days after we had returned I was in my studio when the front door bell rang. I heard Khalil speaking to someone, then silence. When I came down Khalil was sitting in an armchair motionless. I could see that he had just received bad news, but he didn't seem to notice me, so I asked, "Who rang the bell?"

He stretched out his hand with an envelope. I opened it, and read rapidly through the typewritten lines. At first I didn't understand their meaning, as though my mind was blocking out something I didn't want to accept. I read them again, more slowly. It was a letter from the company notifying him that he had been dismissed because he had been absent for more than fifteen days without permission. I felt a wave of anger rise within me, and it took me a few minutes before I was able to say anything.

"They are low people without principles. Don't worry Khalil. Right is on your side; you are sure to get your job back in spite of them. And even if you don't go to the company it makes no difference. We'll manage until you find another job."

I got up and squeezed myself next to him in the armchair resting my head against his shoulder, hugging him close as though trying to infuse some of my confidence in him. He said nothing for a while and when he spoke his voice was so calm that it sounded almost lifeless.

"It is not so simple Amina. They must have heard of my role in the strike, and are taking advantage of my prolonged absence to fire me."

"But you sent two registered letters asking officially for leave?!"

"Yes, that's true. But the chairman has the right to give, or to refuse leave, according to his assessment of the situation, and the needs of the company. This permits him in fact to withhold leave for whatever reason he may think. And if he has done that in my case it will mean that I have been absent for more than fifteen days without the company's permission."

I stared at him. Was it possible that people's rights could be thrown to the winds as simply as that? Surely he was exaggerating? His past experiences had made him too suspicious. And yet he could be right. His life had taught him that the struggle was merciless, that the law could be used to deprive people of their rights. I looked at him out of the corner of my eye. I had seen him a victim to internal conflict before. But this time there was something different. His body seemed to have shrunk, and his face expressed utter despair. It was as if he had lost the will to fight back.

I tried to lift him out of this mood, asked him to come with me to the studio, and help put things in order. He did what I told him, but without enthusiasm — like an automaton. I tried to keep up a conversation but he would answer with a word or two and nothing more. My heart was heavy, and I began to be really afraid. I had seen him at difficult times but never like this. I thought perhaps he was ill. His trembling fingers, his pallor and his restless eyes. An image kept intruding itself on my mind, an experience from the distant past. Alexandria in October was almost empty after the holidays. I sat on the beach in the early morning, lifted my face to the breeze, and gazed at the infinite expanses of blue sea stretching to the horizon. Suddenly I saw a man drowning opposite me, without emitting the slightest sound. His body would rise to the surface and then plunge deep down. He neither moved his arms nor cried out, but seemed to be letting himself drown, unable to fight back from sheer exhaustion, or seeking to die. I stared at him, and at one moment he looked at me with open eyes, full of a despair so total that it no longer asked for help, surrendering silently to the fate he had chosen. It was as though he was saying. "Don't interfere. Just let me go." I felt paralysed where I sat, invaded by the

137

indifference which looked out at me, joined to him by some spell, by an oath. My whole life seemed to be concentrated in this one moment. I watched his body float gently with the current and then sink. I realized he was dead; the spell was broken, our tacit agreement had lasted only as long as he was alive. I rushed screaming along the beach until someone heard me.

This man at my side whom I loved was letting himself slip into a dark abyss, cutting all his links with our life. At one moment I thought he might commit suicide. But when, after a while, I returned to my normal state of mind I realized he was not the kind to end his life of his own free will. I felt myself come closer to him again, and with closeness my fantasies disappeared. He was facing a crisis and my role was to help him and to do all that was possible to ensure that life ran its normal course.

Three or four days after receiving the letter he went to the company. When he returned he said his deductions were correct. They had dismissed him because of his role in the strike preparations, though, of course, this was not the official reason. All the necessary formalities to ensure the legalisation of the decision had been completed, including a letter instructing him to return to work immediately. I tried to encourage him, to convince him that he would soon find another and better job, and that meantime my salary was enough. I suggested he should take advantage of his free time to resume his study of the trade union movement in Egypt. I took Esam out of his cot, so that he could play with him, and talked of the days I had spent as a boarder in the Helwan High School for girls. But all my efforts seemed in vain. It seemed that he wanted only to withdraw to some corner where he would be left alone. After lunch I went to the bedroom to rest. After a while I heard a distant sound and realized he had switched on the washing machine. When I woke up I found that he had hung the clothes to dry and left the house.

After a few days I realized it would be better if I returned to work. The long hours we spent at home with little to do were leading to friction between us, and things were getting worse. I was increasingly exasperated by the sight of him sitting for hours sometimes reading, but mostly staring into space, or watching television. But going to work meant that someone would have to look after Esam. It seemed natural that he should do that while I was away. But when I told him of my decision, he became angry, and asked why I should relinquish the remaining period of maternity leave which was my right? To avoid hurting his feelings I didn't tell him the real reason for my decision, and explained that it was perhaps better for me not to be absent from my work for too long. I don't know whether this was a good excuse to give him. I was only trying to do the best under difficult circumstances, accentuated by his extreme sensitivity. Perhaps sometimes I was unable to do the right things, or say what I should.

Despite all this I tried to bear everything with fortitude. I kept telling myself it was not his fault, and that my problems were nothing compared with his. He was without work, and work for a man is like fresh air. My days were full, with my job, my painting, and the child who filled me with a happiness I had never known. When I looked into his eyes and saw him smile, life seemed to shine with hope. And when he sucked at my nipple with his two hands resting on my breast, I experienced a deep tranquillity, as though all was right with the world. The most important thing in life seemed the flow of warm milk I was giving to this creature. I felt I was supported by many things and that I should stand by Khalil until this crisis was over. I was certain that he would come through all the wiser, that our problems would soon be solved and we would resume the normal flow of our relations.

And yet, looking back, I did have a vague feeling that some danger surrounded our marriage, but I chased it away. I fought hard to believe in the love which kept us together and in its capacity for survival. But as time went by it seemed to be slipping away, evaporating while I watched helplessly, until that night when Khalil slept out for the first time in our married life.

All that day I had been in a strange mood, feeling that something ominous was hiding around the corner. I noticed Khalil preparing to go out, and after he left, my anxiety mounted for no reason at all. I didn't feel like doing anything so when Esam had been fed and put to bed, I asked Mahassin to come over. She's good company and never short of a story, especially about men, whom she imitates with great talent. When I'm with her I never stop laughing. She makes me feel that life is simple, and that there is no need to worry, or to take oneself seriously and miss what pleasures can be had.

After she left, I waited up hoping he would come back, and went to bed only when the cock crowed in the neighbour's backyard. He had never spent the whole night out, and if he was going to be late phoned to tell me. I wondered what could have happened. He was not normal these days. I kept imagining all sorts of accidents. Maybe he'd been run over by a car, or had suddenly felt ill and collapsed. Last week he had complained of a pain in the chest. And so the hours went by.

I decided to take Esam out until it was lunch time. When I returned, the rooms were still empty, but I saw his jacket on the bed, and a moment later I heard the splash of the bathroom tap. The bathroom door remained closed for some time before he came out. At last he appeared in the kitchen door freshly shaved, and wearing a clean shirt. He said: "Good afternoon Amina. How are you?"

"Not so bad. And you?"

He went up to the stove and took the cover off one of the pots on the fire.

"What are we going to eat today?"

I looked him steadily in the eyes and said: "Before asking what there is to eat, don't you think you should tell me where you were last night?"

"At a friend's house."

"Who?"

"You don't know him. His name is Moustapha El Kashab."

"Why didn't you tell me about spending the night out?"

"I didn't intend to stay so late. When I decided to leave he suggested I stay the night. He has no phone at home, I went to look for one but all the shops were closed by then."

"So you found all means of communication with me cut!"

The note of sarcasm made him look at me sharply. For a moment it seemed as though he would answer back. Apparently he thought better of it, and satisfied himself with a scornful shrug of the shoulders. But I had no intention of letting him get away with it as easily as that. I had spent a terrible night. What on earth could have happened to make him so insensitive?

"Did it not occur to you that I might be worried at your absence!?"

He looked embarrassed. "But what could I do?"

"Take a taxi. Besides, what kept you out until almost lunch time?"

"You want me to pay a pound and a half for a taxi at a time like this when I'm without a job."

"Of course, my tranquillity is not worth that much. How much is it worth then, fifty, or only twenty-five piastres?"

"Oh. Why are you speaking to me like that? I don't want to go on with this discussion. I've had enough."

I hesitated. What use was all this? Clearly he had prepared his story beforehand, and obviously he was lying. But where had he spent the night? There was only one thing he would think of hiding from me. Another woman. A woman! And under these circumstances? Men were really strange beings. Perhaps he was trying to forget. I smiled inwardly. Quite interesting. I had read such things in novels, but this was the first time I had experienced them. Yet, somehow, I couldn't imagine him stooping to that. What kind of a woman would she be? What sort of relations could they have? If it was a woman I would leave him immediately. But how could I abandon him when he was down? If I stayed with him it would only be out of pity, and pity was useless. I still loved him . . . Who could this woman be? What did she look like? Why did he not tell me the truth? Yet if he told me the truth, if it became a fact with which I was expected to live, could we continue to live together? Could I awake in the morning to find him by my side, let him touch me, and kiss me, look into his eyes and talk across the breakfast table? Perhaps things are easier to accept if they remain mere conjectures. But why should I accept such a humiliating situation, and for whom? For a man like him? He was not worth any more sacrifices. And in any case our love was now fated to die.

We ate in silence. I left him to himself, asked no more questions, sought no further explanations. But from that moment I knew that the distance growing between us was now unbridgeable. It was no longer an illusion, or temporary circumstance that could be overcome. Perhaps if we had both made a real effort at that moment it might even then have been possible to rebuild a bridge between us, but he didn't try, and I was too hurt. I decided his life was no longer any concern of mine.

I made up my mind to go back to work immediately, and made arrangements to leave Esam with Mahassin during my absence.

On my way home I collected Esam, and usually when I got home Khalil was there. He had started writing again. And at night he would sit reading. Sometimes we watched television. Now and again he went out in the evening to return usually after midnight. He was very quiet, and we had no problems. On the surface it seemed that our life had resumed its natural course. And yet we knew we had drifted very far apart. We had no conflicts, and he always helped whether I asked for it or not, but the warmth and spirit which had characterized our relations were gone. At rare moments they were like dying cinders in a strong wind, and the love between us would flicker into life. We were like two blind people reaching out for each other. But one night I felt his fingers searching for me as though this time they knew their way, awakening the throbbing nodes of pleasure, chasing away the sadness and the pain. I took him to me with a desperate, violent tenderness, for I knew that the embers of our love were flaring for the last time.

The night went by and we lay on the bed bathed in a shadowy morning light. He smiled sadly at me. I knew we were saying goodbye. From then onwards life flowed by as though we were driven by a will that was neither his nor mine. We made the daily gestures, spoke the daily words, ate the daily bread, breathed the daily air, went out and came back, waiting for something to happen, yet not knowing when, or where or how.

On that day, the hands of the clock in the station were pointing to four in the afternoon when I got down from the train. One of the girls in the designing section had quarrelled with a colleague so I stayed on to try and settle things between them. Everyone's nerves were on edge with the increasing problems of daily life. I passed by Mahassin as usual and picked up Esam, carrying him with difficulty. I was tired and he had grown heavier. Once home I could leave him to Khalil and take a hot bath. I held Esam on my shoulder with one arm and opened the door. All the windows in the house seemed to have been closed and there was no movement. I put on the light. On the table in the hall I saw a note. I put Esam down and read it.

Amina
I left the house at a quarter to three. I have an appointment to discuss matters concerning my work. I don't think it will take long and I'll come home immediately it is over. There's a letter from Zeinab for you which I put near your bed. My warm regards to "Mister Esam"!!
Kisses, Khalil

I read the note through a second time. Something seemed to tell me that these simple lines carried more between them than they seemed to say, and that the uncertain period we were living through together had ended. If Saïd was here I could have talked things over with him, but he had never called to see us since the strike. I wondered what could have happened to him after he was dismissed. Why had he stopped coming to see us? I felt lonely. Khalil and I lived in the same house and despite appearances, at heart we had become strangers, each one of us living in a world of his own.

I put Esam in his cot. I could leave him for hours and he would not complain. When he woke up from sleep, he would stare at the ceiling and exercise his little arms and legs with a rhythmic movement. If I leaned over him he smiled, then put his thumb in his mouth and looked at me shyly. He never cried unless he had wet himself or was hungry.

I left him dozing off to sleep and went to the kitchen. I ate quickly, washed the plates and sat down wondering whether I should have my bath immediately or a little later. I must have fallen asleep, since when I opened my eyes it was already dark outside. I went to the bedroom and put on the light. Esam was lying in his cot with his eyes wide open. He started to move his arms and legs vigorously as though showing me what he could do. I picked him up, changed his clothes and fed him. Then I put him down on the bed, and stretched myself out beside him; I must have fallen asleep again. When I woke the sun had risen, Esam had awakened and was lifting his foot in the sun, and examining it with admiration. I realized Khalil had not come home and felt sad and lonely. But a little while later I forgot myself in the preparations for a new day.

When I woke that morning and found myself alone I couldn't shake off the depression which took hold of me. I left work earlier than usual that day and decided to go for a walk. The winter was rapidly approaching, the air was cool, and Helwan still retained some of its beauty, especially near the Nile.

I slipped out of the gate. In the distance I could see the Thebes Pharmaceutical Company. I remembered how we used to walk down together, the flowers on the window sill of a house, the wondering expression in his eyes. I thrust these memories aside. I felt like doing something, getting to work on a canvas. It was a long time since I'd held a brush. Maybe that was one of the reasons why I felt so unhappy, unable to forget. Once absorbed in something I would cease to worry so much about myself. My problems with Khalil were becoming too important. I must not let myself be dragged from the path I had chosen. Men came and went. What remained would be the things I did with my life. A painting. Yes, that was what I needed. To begin on a painting, then I would become myself.

I hastened along the pavement. My body needed movement, needed wings. My belly was now straight as a drum, and the pulse in my legs was steady and deep. A car stopped at the kerb some distance away and a couple got out. Lovers enjoying the pure air and the sunshine. The moment she sat on the low wall at the edge of the river her hair floated in the air like a flame. A foreigner. I glimpsed a slender figure in a blouse and blue jeans. He stood on the pavement with his back to the road, his eyes fixed on her face. I saw his shoulders slightly bent, the head with a bald patch surrounded by thick greying hair. Khalil! Impossible! What was he doing here with this woman? I couldn't be mistaken — it was him. I came to a standstill for an instant, as though my legs refused to continue. She looked at me over his head. My mind rushed here and there aimlessly. What should I do? Face him with what he was doing in front of this woman? Rain blows on them and scream? Create such a scandal that neither of them would ever forget it? A wave of fury mounted within me. He was like all men, capable of the lowest things. I saw her gazing at me with the same steady look over his head. Suddenly I was seized with panic. Why prolong these ugly moments? It was better to hurry away before he turned and saw me. Everything was clear now. Everything between us was over. Life was like that. I couldn't be expected to win all the time. I was not really the one who was defeated. It was Khalil. The militant had thrown his principles overboard. I had never felt so hurt, never felt so furious. I would ask him to leave our house immediately. I should have faced him on the spot, instead of waiting. But what use was that? Nothing would have changed. I could not make the clock go back. Why appear as though I was fighting with that woman over my man? If I had walked up to them it would have looked like that. They could go to hell, both of them.

I walked with a rapid pace until they were out of sight. I looked for a bench to sit on, but there was not one to be found. Everything could be had, but always at a price. The strongest currency these days was the dollar. Even love could be bought for dollars. She had a big car which helped her to pick up men. I remembered the look on his face as he looked at her spellbound. How could he be so stupid, so easy to be had?

I looked at my watch. It was half past three. I suddenly remembered Esam. It was time to be back, and I still had to take the train from Helwan. I took a side street to avoid the place where I'd seen them. My heart felt sick. What was life worth without a hope of dreaming, when rot found its way to the most precious emotions.

I held Esam to my shoulder with one arm and turned the key. The door swung open. From now on we would be alone, he and I. The rooms were empty and the house plunged in a deep silence. He lay on his back and stared at me with a questioning look. His body was small and his mind still felt its way to the things around him. I had planted my power inside him and it would grow. His eyes seemed to say: "Don't be sad. You won't feel alone with me by your side, and at night in bed I'll keep you warm." I put the spoon in his mouth, looked into his black eyes and felt better.

144

Khalil Mansour Khalil

Everything around me seemed to float in a haze, an invisible cloud, to move slowly, at a distance. I lived on the outer reaches, isolated, watching with a strange detachment. Even those closest to me, Amina and Esam, seemed to belong to another world. I lived on a solitary planet watching the other stars rotate. Breathing, drinking and eating, dressing, awakening in the morning, and going to sleep at night as though I was alone in a universe of my own.

One morning I was in the house alone. Amina had gone to work and Esam was with Mahassin. The window was open, the sky was covered in heavy cloud, and the bare, twisted branch of a tree reached up. I was seized by a feeling that I was shrinking, disintegrating, advancing steadily towards an abyss into which I would soon fall. I shivered with fear, got up and started moving from one room to the other. I climbed the stairs and went into the studio. My eyes circled round picking out a canvas which attracted my attention here and there. I noticed a painting stretched on an easel in the corner. I stood there for a long time, then left the studio, rushed down the stairs and went to Mahassin's house. Something was clutching at my throat, I was overcome by a feeling of suffocation. I put Esam in his pram and ran out into the road. I could see his black eyes, like his mother's, looking at me questioningly. He ventured a tentative smile which hovered on his lips for a moment, then disappeared to be replaced by an expression of reproach, as though he knew I was still unable to come close. I walked on and on oblivious to time, and to the distance I must have covered. I felt a soothing exhaustion. My mind seemed to have freed itself from the weight of my body, and I moved along airy and light.

I came back and handed Esam over to Mahassin. She glanced at me curiously, but said nothing. I went home, sat at my desk, pulled out some papers and started to write furiously. And from then onwards, day after day, I gradually resumed my old habit of writing. But when I read the pages and pages covered with my regular, almost square letters I realized that I had lost the capacity to express myself. This writing was only an escape. For the image of Ruth was constantly before me. She sat opposite me and talked, or suddenly slipped into my arms. I longed for the vitality of her voice, the honey-coloured flame in her eyes.

I still refrained from getting in touch with her. I feared the strong attraction she had for me. I refused to accept my need for her. It emphasized my own weakness, and hurt my pride. But I continued to dream of the moment when she would be close to me again.

It was not easy for me to face up to my situation. Being without work increasingly eroded my morale. I watched Amina walk down the garden path to the street to work every morning, then roamed restlessly around the empty rooms until I made up my mind to go to the kitchen and wash the dishes, then clean the house and make the beds before sitting at my desk. On most days I would fail to jot down more than a few disjointed lines, and this would aggravate my persistent despair. But little by little I began to adapt myself. And perhaps if she had not got in touch with me again, I might have been able to surmount the crisis. I had begun to write more and more each day, and after some time went on without interruption until the sun set. I was completely free, and now that I could concentrate, began to forge rapidly ahead. I refrained from getting in touch with any of my friends and nobody called. The only exception was Saïd. One morning I heard someone at the door; I thought it was Amina, but instead Saïd was standing hesitantly in the doorway. When he saw me a smile lit up his face. I was happy to see him. He seemed to have become even slimmer since we last met. Yet he was as handsome as ever with his finely chiselled ebony features. We embraced, and suddenly the tears started from my eyes.

We sat on the sofa and talked. I told him what had happened since we last met, but of course mentioned nothing about Ruth. He told me some things I did not know. After the strike he discovered that the SSSPS people had been watching him very closely. They had used cars, motorcycles, bicycles and occasionally followed him on foot. Sometimes they stopped for a while in case he had noticed, and instead tracked him by radio. That was how they found out who was on the committee that met in the coffee house, and realized it was the main decision-making body for the strike. But they were unable to find out the timing of the strike, or record the discussions. They had deduced that I had given Saïd a copy of the memorandum, but had no real evidence.

When Amina came home she was very happy to see Saïd, and quickly relinquished Esam to me, so that she could give him her attention. We had lunch together and then sat reminiscing. Saïd was delighted with Esam and carried him around, or played with him until Amina decided to put him to sleep.

He told us that he had been obliged to spend some time in Aswan because the little money he had after his dismissal was soon spent. At first he'd stayed with the President of the Federation of Chemical Workers. He hadn't managed to find a job. "They put me on a blacklist because of my colour and my activities," he said laughingly. None of the enterprises in the region would accept him, but he wanted to stay on rather than lose the relationships he had built up over the years. At one point he hesitated for a moment, and with a hint of shyness explained that a close relationship had grown up between him and the old man's daughter. They were thinking of marrying when he had found a job.

He stayed overnight and left early next morning intending to go back to Aswan the same evening. Something told me we wouldn't meet again for a long time. We shook hands warmly, and I watched him walk down the street with his smooth, supple gait, ". . . like a black leopard" I said to myself. At the corner he turned and waved to me.

From that moment I was like a little boat without moorings. And yet also I was strangely exhilarated. At last I was free of all obligations — light as a feather. Saïd, the symbol of what I had been, the conscience that hunted me out and plunged me back into the struggle was no longer there to see. First Amina and now Saïd. I was being abandoned step by step, left to my crumbling defences, prepared for her voice to beckon me to her side, to the path which awakened my desire for the easy way.

So when the telephone rang that evening the scene was all set. The receiver made a slight hissing sound at first, then came her vibrant voice warm as sunlight.

"Khalil, it's me Ruth. I'm calling from Paris."

"Paris!"

"Yes. I've been here a couple of days. I'll be back tomorrow. Will you do something for me?"

"What?"

"Please wait for me at the airport. Can you do that?"

"Of course. But why?"

"Because I will be so happy to find you there. Isn't that reason enough?"

"Oh yes. I will be happy to see you too. When will you arrive?"

"Gaafar will wait for you with the car at Dar El Salam station tomorrow afternoon at one o'clock. My plane arrives at quarter to two. The flight is Air France 492."

"I will be there."

"Khalil."

"Yes."

"I am looking forward to seeing you very much. I shall think about you on the way back."

I put the receiver down. Luckily Amina was at Mahassin's house. I rested my head on the back of the armchair. It was typical of her to call me from Paris just to tell me that she would be happy if I waited for her at the airport. Why was she so keen to keep up our relationship? With her I felt once more that I was not an ordinary person, not a nobody. I could see her in her seat on the airplane sitting cross-legged, drinking coffee and reading. Her hair shining on the headrest. The man sitting by her tries to strike up a conversation . . . I felt a pang of jealousy. My heart beat as though I was already on my way to meet her. I began pacing up and down. Perhaps at the last moment she would decide to stay a little longer in Paris. She could do anything, but I still lived within the confines of a narrow world, in a suburb where people went to bed at nine o'clock. I lived in three rooms, yet my city stretched out like a giant on the banks of the Nile. Its lights as abundant as the stars, and its bridges alive with cars racing through the night. And here I was, living in the memories of past glories, carried away sometimes by a line in a book, an idea that flashed across my mind, but most of the time chained to a fate others had designed. It was no use trying to read or write. Her face tantalized my imagination. I tiptoed to where Esam lay in his cot. The peace and innocence of a sleeping child! If one could sometimes go back to those days when the world was trees and blue skies, riding a bicycle, my Arabic teacher with his bushy eyebrows, and splashing in a tub of hot water before being dried. I undressed and lay on the bed, staring at the ceiling.

I don't know how I managed to hide the turmoil inside me. The hours followed one another with maddening sloth, and I felt Amina's eyes examining me as we sat at breakfast. I made a tremendous effort to look calm, sat at my desk, started to read some documents and take notes, but my mind was absent. I made endless cups of tea and coffee, drinking a few sips and leaving the rest. When it was almost one o'clock I slipped out of the house, and walked slowly towards the station. The car was waiting, Gaafar sat behind the wheel listening to the news. He wore a smart blue coat and cap.

When he saw me he turned off the radio, slipped out and opened the door. He lifted his hand to his cap in a quick salute, but his features remained as expressionless as usual. I looked out of the window at the high buildings rising up in the middle of green fields. On the other side of the Nile were the three pyramids enveloped in a yellowish haze. The car climbed smoothly up the overhead bridge on its way to Salah Salem highway. From above I looked down on low hills, walls of stone, expanses of sand, tumbledown houses, and narrow streets teeming with people. In my nostrils was the familiar, putrid smell of leather tanneries concentrated in this old part of the city. I sat in the chauffeur-driven silver car and contemplated the gap which now separated me from the life of people below. Once, relations with them had been close. I would walk through the narrow lanes, sleep in shadowy rooms, breathe the humid air heavy with the smell of garlic and sweat. But little by little I had forgotten the people I was supposed to be defending. Sometimes I would see a sick child lying in the shade of a tree, or an old woman bending under a heavy weight. Then suddenly old memories returned to fill me with yearning.

Upon the rocks of sand and limestone rose The Citadel, symbol of tyranny hidden in beauty, its delicate minarets rising like sinful rapiers, its domes flashing in the sun, pregnant with secrets, its walls concealing the honeycomb of prison cells. The road twisted and turned like a black snake stretching through the sand hills. On my right, at the top of a rocky cliff, new buildings, and further on, the city of the dead occupied by the living. A giant city. I had watched it grow, crushing men and women and children under its churning wheels and rising stone. I was filled with a hopeless fear, exhausted; what can a single human being do in the face of all this? Oppression can only be defeated by the efforts of millions. But when would they rebel? And if they rebelled when would they organize? Every day brought new defeats, made the enemy stronger. For how long? The car raced along the road in front of the Industrial Exhibition. Flags flying in the wind. The star of Israel in our skies, and yet Sinai was still occupied, and we had not yet seen the birth of an Arab Palestine. And you Khalil, sit here, your body yielding to the soft seat. The net is strong and well-knit. It surrounds the fish on every side and gathers them in. Faster and faster. The broad streets of Heliopolis. On either side palaces, or luxurious blocks of flats. I had forgotten what it's like to be rich. Perhaps by recent standards I had really never known what it is. These palaces! By comparison my father was small fry. For some time I'd been functioning with one or two digits, with three rooms, like the porters' quarters I glimpsed with the corner of my eye. The road to the airport was wider than all the city's highways. A double lane divided by a garden. I'm tired of fighting losing battles. We live in the era of freedom, witness the posters on either side. Freedom to travel, tour the world, buy things, be happy, emigrate to distant lands. All you need is a cheque book and a bank account, preferably in foreign currency. The era of privation is over, prosperity has come — exactly what the President said on his birthday broadcast. Were it not for the law on Social Peace people would have gone down to the streets and cheered. On either side a long line of yellow lamps, a wide open space and lines of waiting cars. A barrier where we stopped.

The airport. Ruth had perhaps already landed. My heart gave a thump, and all I had thought on the way mattered no longer. Gaafar opened the door and I got out, threaded my way through the people at the entrance, into the waiting room and gazed at the panel. Opposite flight AF 492 was the sign "Landed, 13.45".

I waited at the end of the narrow passage hemmed in by iron barriers. Passengers trickled out, then became more frequent, probably from other planes. They pushed baggage trolleys piled high with cartons, boxes containing recorders, television sets, electric ovens and mixers. The petro-dollar consumer craze which emigrant workers imported with them whenever they came on leave. An endless stream of tourists and returning workers injecting our veins with their values. I had become part of this complicated game. My eyes ran anxiously along the line skipping the men and most of the women, occasionally arrested by a face that had something different in its features. I spotted her at a distance walking with her usual rapid pace, and yet somehow looking as though she had plenty of time. She wore a simple dress and pushed her wine-coloured leather bag effortlessly. A taxi driver walked up and said a few words but she continued to walk along without heeding. I glimpsed the intent anticipation on her face as though important things awaited her. I moved close up to her side and said: "Can you please tell me Ruth where you are going?"

She lifted her hand from the trolley and turned towards me.

"Khalil! Then you did come. I'm so happy. What's wrong? Why are you standing so far away? Aren't you going to kiss me?"

I kissed her on both cheeks. She was close to me for a moment, then moved away and looked at me, her honey-coloured eyes brimming with laughter.

"My! What an official kiss! It seems I'll have to wait until we get home."

I grinned sheepishly. Not only had she asked me to come and meet her, but now wanted me to kiss her at the exit to the airport, where somebody who knew us could easily be standing close by. The fact that we could be seen embracing one another like this didn't seem to worry her in the least. I said: "You know a lot of patience is needed with people like me. Don't you care if somebody sees us?"

"Why should I bother about people. I'm free to behave as I feel."

I took over the trolley from her. I glimpsed the car coming up gently to where we were standing. Gaafar jumped out and said: "Thanks to Allah for your safe return Mistress Ruth!"

She answered with her American lilt.

"Allah keep you safe, Gaafar. How are things?"

"Everything is fine Mistress Ruth. Have you got any other bags?"

"No."

I got in beside her and let her take my hand without responding. She looked me in the face and smiled. I could feel Gaafar glancing at us from time to time in the mirror. She rested her palm on the back of my hand, and asked in a subdued voice: "Why are you so quiet. You don't seem happy to see me", moving her hand away, with a slight hint of temper.

"No. It's not true. Since you spoke to me from Paris I have been thinking of nothing else but this moment. My problem is that I am not used to showing my feelings before others. Please don't be angry."

She came closer to me.

"Throughout the past weeks you've been constantly in my mind. I kept wondering how you were."

"I'm fine. I've started the second part of my study."

"And is that enough to occupy your time, and make you happy?"

"Maybe not enough, but that's all I can hope for at the moment."

"You can hope for much more even now."

"Such as?"

She pressed my arm with her fingers and said: "We'll talk of it later, at home."

"Aren't you tired?"

"No, on the contrary. The trip was very relaxing. And I feel like talking to you for hours and hours."

She turned to the chauffeur and asked: "Is there food at home, Gaafar?"

"Yes, mistress. I prepared a light meal and left it in the refrigerator."

"Good."

151

The car seemed to swallow the distance home. It was like living in a dream. The powerful car flying along with Ruth by my side. I found it difficult to absorb it all. And above all Ruth's attachment to me. Was all this affection and warmth no more than a pretence? But if so why? No, it was not possible that she was merely acting. I was sure of that. And yet I had moments of doubt, felt that I was simply taking my desires for a fact. Love. Before this moment I had never thought of using this word to describe our relationship. And yet, yes, it was love, at least for me. Perhaps I should ask her. My heart leapt every time she was near. I needed her, and above all needed her love. If her feeling for me was real love I would be the happiest man in the world. I put out my hand towards her, she leant over and brushed my cheek with her lips.

Gaafar carried up the baggage. In the flat, I sat watching her as she moved around, looking happy to be home. She left me alone for a while and I filled the moments of waiting with the pleasure of anticipation. When she came back she had slipped on a loose robe. The blue ribbon around her head left her hair to fall freely over her shoulders.

"Now I am all yours. Tell me everything."

I smiled. "I doubt if you can ever give yourself up to anyone."

"That's not completely true. Sometimes I feel like surrendering myself to someone, throwing all my troubles and responsibilities on his shoulders. But then I would have to find a person like you, who can be trusted."

"It's a feeling we all get at times. But as far as I remember you once told me that you have a husband with whom you share your life."

She took some time before replying.

"True I have a husband but we live separately. Don't turn the conversation to me, I asked you what you have been doing during recent weeks."

"Nothing apart from the study I have started working on again."

"What about work?"

"Nothing new."

"Why didn't you call me?"

I hesitated. Should I be frank with her? It was better to say.

"For several reasons. I started to ask myself where this relationship is leading. You must have noticed my feelings for you are growing. Despite moments of hesitation I have let myself be carried along by my emotions. At times I have refrained from calling but that has nothing to do with my feelings. It has to do with the fact that I am a man without work or money. Whereas you are rich, you have a lot of means at your disposal as well as wide relations with people. You don't need anything. The relationship between us is unequal."

A shadow crossed her face.

"There are different needs in life. I need you much more than you think. You cannot see into me, so why not let me decide where I stand with regard to you. I want our friendship to go on, so there is no need to put barriers between us. Material means, pride and many other things don't count. What is important is the feeling between us. Don't you see that?"

It took me some time to sort out what she had said in my mind.

"It's an easy way out."

"For whom? For you? And supposing it is, why not? Do we have to complicate things, to look for ways of being unhappy? I don't see why we should always be victims to some hidden feeling of guilt."

"My position is not easy Ruth. You know I'm in love with you."

"But I love you too Khalil."

Suddenly she was in my arms once more and I was kissing her hair, her eyes, her lips so tenderly soft. She lay beside me and gave herself with the violence of a woman burying the memories, the sorrow, the letters kept at the bottom of a drawer. She closed my eyelids with kisses. I whispered, "I want no one but you." "My darling," she murmured.

We slept as though washed of our sins, born anew. When I woke she was staring at the ceiling. She turned round and said: "You've awakened?"

"Yes."

"I never thought love could be like this. I no longer fear death."

"Why?"

"Because once you've lived, death doesn't matter any more."

"It's the pleasure of a moment; once over, life will impose itself once more."

"Maybe, but that's how I feel now, and to me it's important. Life after all is a series of moments."

I kissed her and started to get up. She looked at me questioningly: "Where are you going Khalil?"

153

"To the bathroom."

She held my hand and said: "Come back quickly."

When I returned, I stood by the door and contemplated her, telling myself that all this beauty was really mine. She seemed preoccupied, and didn't hear my feet on the carpet. I sat by her and she looked round. She spoke with a distant voice as though she was far away.

"Khalil. I want to talk to you about something we discussed before. But first promise that you will listen to me quietly."

There was a short silence before I answered.

"I promise."

"I love you Khalil, and know that you're passing through a difficult period. Nevertheless you are forcing me to sit back and watch."

I asked cautiously, "What do you mean?"

She looked at me uncertainly. "I don't want any conflict between us again. I can help you to find a new job if you like, or to go back to the one you had before. What's wrong with accepting help from a woman who loves you?"

Again the same conflict surfaced. Part of my mind said yes, and another said no. What she had said was reasonable. Nevertheless, I was loath to accept her help, as though the moment I did the freedom I enjoyed in my relations with her would be lost, that I would owe her something and be obliged to pay back. The last time, I had angrily asked "What is the price of your help?" and despite the spontaneous way I had blurted out my question this instinctive feeling lay behind it. I remembered back to the tales of childhood, to the sorcerer weaving a web of fine silk like Ruth's beautiful hair. Her attraction for me was sometimes overpowering, awakened obscure desires, and brought to light hidden corners. There were moments with her when I felt in danger of losing myself. If I accepted her help, her influence on me would be even greater. With her I remained a divided self. Part of me a flowing river, eager to meet with her sea, and part of me the serene bank covered in green. I asked: "How?"

She answered patiently. "I told you last time. By resorting to somebody I know."

"Can you tell me who that person is?"

"If you agree to my intervening on your behalf, I have no objection to telling you who he is."

She was doing her best to convince me, if necessary even by arousing my curiosity. I would have to decide now.

"I agree."

She hugged me enthusiastically. Her face expressed a childlike happiness. She rested her face on my hand and said: "You will not regret the trust you have put in me. No matter what happens I will never do anything to harm you."

The last phrase rang like a bell. It came back so often whenever we talked about matters related to me. Why?

"Who is the person you are expecting will be prepared to help?"

"The President of the Popular Representative Assembly."

I rested my head against the back of the sofa and took a deep breath. She certainly had connections in high places!

"How did you get to know him?"

She laughed. "I hope you're not going to behave like other men, and start jealously investigating my relations with the other sex."

I admired her intelligence, her way of killing several birds with one stone.

"It has nothing to do with jealousy."

"Curiosity then?"

"If you wish."

"Then I'll tell you. My husband introduced him to me. He visited Cairo as a member of a businessmen's delegation."

"Your relations must have become really close for you to be able to raise this matter with him."

"Well, he has already helped us conclude a couple of agreements."

"So that's how things are done!!"

"What's so strange about that? The world of business operates through intermediaries. It's quite normal."

"True. Why should I be surprised? People like me live in an imaginary world."

"As long as you achieve what you want, what difference does it make who intervenes on your behalf."

"The end justifies the means."

She looked at me as though I was an unusual kind of person.

"You must cross over the frontier into the world of reality. Is this the first time you have heard of things being done this way?"

"No. I've known it for a long time, but now I'm having recourse to the same methods myself."

"You mean to say this is the first time in your life?"

I looked at her. Her eyes had narrowed. There was something calculating, even cruel in her expression such as I had not seen before. Maybe it was just my imagination. These days I was moody. Most faces could express cold calculation at one or other time. I was trying to find explanations for some of the things I was noticing in her as we went along. I was beginning to feel disturbed.

"I will get in touch with him tomorrow. But what have you decided to choose? A new job, or the previous one?"

I preferred the post I had occupied before. But I was also trying to test how much influence she had.

"I prefer to go back to Thebes Pharmaceuticals."

"Then you insist on choosing what is more difficult?"

"Why not try? I was dismissed in a humiliating way. I want to be reinstated in my rightful place, to give them a lesson they will not easily forget."

I had no sooner pronounced the last sentence than I felt I was riding the high horse without doing anything myself. She was the one who was going to do everything. I was going downhill all the time. She sat motionless buried in her thoughts. Perhaps it was what I had said. She looked sad, as though I had brought back unpleasant memories. The best thing for me now was to leave. This way I would spare her — and myself.

I went to the bedroom and dressed quickly. When I came back she exclaimed. "Khalil. Where are you going?"

"I have to go home."

"But I haven't told you anything about my trip to Paris."

"I can't stay Ruth."

"I have no right to press you, but you see I suddenly felt depressed."

"Why?"

"I don't know. Maybe I haven't thought of it deeply enough." She stood up throwing her hair back with the characteristic movement of her head. I was becoming familiar with her gestures. She grasped my hand suddenly and put it on the bare flesh of her belly. She said: "If only I could have a child from you." Then she was quiet for a while before asking: "How is Esam? Is he good-looking like you?" She emitted a joyful peal of laughter. "I'll call you tomorrow morning. Maybe I will already have some news."

"As soon as that?"

"You don't realize Khalil how deep are my feelings for you. If things were only different . . ." Her sentence trailed into silence.

I held her close in my arms for a long moment, and then gently let her go. "Good night Ruth. Always remember that I love you."

I was swallowed up by the lift. It shot down to the ground floor and I walked out. The last nights had started to be cold. I turned up my coat collar and hastened my pace. I felt more and more at odds with myself, almost like an internal alienation. It was as though I had become another person. Within the short space of two months my life had been turned upside down.

The following day I was sitting in the garden when I noticed the silver car pull up slowly in front of the house. Gaafar got out and stood on the pavement verifying the number of the house. I walked to the iron gate. He was carrying a white envelope and when he saw me touched his finger to his cap and said: "Good morning Mr Khalil. I have a letter for you."

I opened the envelope and quickly scanned the lines scrawled in English.

My darling,
For the last two hours I have been trying to get in touch with you. I thought you had gone out, but realized it was unlikely. I was afraid the line might be out of order, and as I have important news I sent the car to you. Can we meet on the Nile near the Helwan Rest House. Or if you prefer Gaafar can bring you to me, and then we can go there together.
Kisses, Ruth

My heart beat quickly. She must have news concerning my work. Or maybe it was something else. If it was about the job, she would have told me in her note. Perhaps she wanted to tell me herself. In any case it did not seem that she was the bearer of bad news. I kept turning the matter over in my mind as I changed. I looked out of the window. Gaafar was smoking a cigarette. A strange man. He never said more than two or three words. I had never met a person who said less. When he went around in Ruth's apartment nobody could hear him move; his face was expressionless. Sometimes when I looked at him, a thin shiver would go through me. He was like a machine that did everything with a quiet precision. Even the way he smoked had something mechanical about it. His hand moved up and down at regular intervals and he kept blowing out thin lines and circles of smoke and watching them disperse in the sun. Sometimes I felt he was watching me closely. If he ever hated anybody, he would wait just as patiently for the right moment to finish him off. I shivered.

157

I got in the car and stared out of the window at our garden in bloom. He made me feel I was not welcome to sit by his side. I could see the back of his head and neck in one rigid, straight line that barely bent when the car turned. I could feel him watching me in his mirror with a cold detachment. When he and Ruth spoke together I felt they had a special language, that they understood one another very often without having recourse to words. They gave me the impression that everything concerning them moved in a predestined direction. He was her silent right arm, and I could see that she depended on him absolutely for certain things.

The car reached the entrance of the Cairo Sheraton. He look leave of me explaining that he would inform Mistress Ruth that I was waiting below, and climbed the steps with a rapid effortless movement. With him there was always this feeling of a wild cat but without the fury.

After a while Ruth came running down the steps. She climbed into the driver's seat and said: "Khalil. These telephones are terrible. I lost all hope of getting in touch with you, and sent the car instead. Come and sit in front. We'll leave Gaafar here and go off. I've missed you despite the fact that we were together only a few hours ago. Where would you like to go?"

I could see she was happy and excited. There was an eagerness in the way she talked to me, a desire to be close. I could feel the tips of her fingers move on my palms with a trembling warmth.

"Why not stop the car on the Nile near the Helwan Rest House?"

She drove at a speed unusual even for her, as though in a hurry to get away from the crowded streets to some quiet spot. Her cheeks were flushed, and her eyes shining. She stopped the car just before the Rest House, and she guided me by the hand to the white stone parapet. She lifted herself up on it and sat with her back to the Nile. I sensed the triumph of a woman on top of the world. "Khalil. Congratulations. Tomorrow you will be back in the plant."

I stared at her with a mixture of admiration and incredulity. "Like that, in less than a day and a night. Are we living in the age of miracles."

She laughed happily, a long ecstatic peal of laughter carried by the wind over the wide expanse of flowing water, the still green corn, over the heads of the women washing clothes on a white stone, raising their eyes to the heavens, straining their ears to catch the echoes of joy, on and on to the little hamlets of mud huts and the eucalyptus trees swaying on the other shore. I put my hand on the smooth fabric of her dress, felt her thigh underneath throbbing and warm. My eyes were filled with her image. She had become my whole world and I threw everything else overboard.

Part IV

Khalil Mansour Khalil

The day after we met on the Nile I went to the Company. I felt like a sailor who had left his country in his youth, and returned after a lifetime's wandering. I was no longer the same person who had gone every morning from his house to the plant. I saw everything with different eyes. My return to the plant was no more than an empty victory, an achievement without consequence, perhaps because it was not I who had fought for it. The black-eyed girl in a white gown still watered the flowers on the balcony, and the bakery at the corner still gave out the scent of hot loaves each morning. But my senses took in these details with the detachment of someone who had alighted at the wrong station and was in a hurry to be off.

The chairman welcomed me like a dear brother back from the war. He wanted me to be completely at ease and not to hesitate to ask for anything I might need. He would only be too pleased if there was something he could do for me and so on and so forth. In face of this shameless about turn I hated him even more. When his telephone rang I seized the opportunity to make my escape. Each time I walked along the corridors or entered a room, there were questioning looks if people thought I wouldn't notice, exaggerated expressions of joy at my reinstatement, whispers, or stony silence. Sometimes I even caught a hint of fear quickly disguised by a rapid smile. All day people kept walking into my office to shake hands with me, and mutter a few words of welcome. They reminded me of mourners at an important funeral, lining up to shake hands with the deceased's family.

After a while I discovered a rumour that I had been used to find out who were the strike leaders had preceded me. Also that the Board of Directors had fired me to cover up the role I had played. Now I understood the expression of fear I had read on some faces.

Thus I found myself accused of being in the pay of the SSSPS. It was an unpleasant surprise. And after a while, to my even greater surprise I discovered it was the SSSPS agents themselves who were spreading this rumour. Little by little it dawned on me that the SSSPS was aiming at a double effect. On the one hand my complete isolation by depicting me as an undercover agent, and on the other hand to try and break my back.

I returned home long after the first day back was over. Everything seemed to be turning to ashes, to failure, to a rising bitterness. When I opened the front door I found Amina in front of me on the sofa. I don't know why, but I realized immediately that she had found out about my relations with Ruth. Something in the set of her face, in the expression of angry despair in her eyes. I was overcome by the feeling of being driven inexorably to a fate I had not chosen. I was crushed, helpless, incapable of doing anything to save myself. I sat listening to her describing how she had seen me with Ruth near Helwan Corner. I listened with detachment as though she was talking of someone else, overcome by a terrible exhaustion which left me speechless, devoid of any emotion. I noticed that my shoes were covered in dust, and followed a ray of sunlight as it crept over the floor, then turned my attention to Amina and started to examine her with curiosity. Her hair had grown longer and she had painted her eyelashes with kohl. She looked different, and when she pronounced the word separation my mind kept telling me that it was normal since she was not the woman I had known.

After that I remember Esam watched me as I packed some clothes in a bag. I stood on the threshold of our house looking at the deserted street and a lone dog that gave me a sympathetic look and then walked off. Amina said something. I felt my hand move out towards her with the key, and was unable to tell whether her fingers or the key was cold. After that I came to myself sitting on a wooden bench in the train going down town.

The cutlery neatly arranged on the table next to the window glittered in the sunlight. I stretched my legs over the carpet, yawned and closed my eyes. I felt someone move up close to me, and turned to see Gaafar silently awaiting my orders.

"Good morning Gaafar. Where are today's newspapers?"

He moved with his rapid silent tread to the telephone table and returned carrying the morning papers. I heard him ask: "Shall I prepare breakfast now?"

"Yes please."

After a moment I realized he had gone. He was like a phantom. I felt suddenly cold, gathered the woollen *burnos* around me, and looked out of the window at the Nile shining in the sunlight and reflecting the blue winter sky. I heard her voice near the kitchen door, she came into the room, and everything else seemed to disappear. She filled my world, gave her love to me without reserve. With her I became the romantic youth I had once been, trembling at her touch,

164

living in her eyes. We played no games, maintained no reserves, bared our naked flesh, unafraid. From beneath the ashes we had restored to life the original flame.

The hours I spent in the plant were very different. They dragged endlessly, and aroused a growing feeling that to stay there was not possible. I could no longer tolerate the wall of isolation which had been raised around me, nor the silent accusations I read in people's eyes before they turned away, nor the rumours which subsided for some time only to be revived again. Saïd had disappeared, and in any case I was not keen to meet him during this period. Amina still worked in the furniture factory. I was sometimes afraid that we might meet on the road and wondered what I would do if we did.

But how could I escape from the trap I had set for myself? I couldn't ask Ruth to find something else so soon after my reinstatement. Perhaps I made no effort to overcome my difficulties, because I felt she would willingly help me find another job. Again I was choosing the line of least resistance — gradually becoming an opportunist, taking advantage of her love for me to get what I wanted, losing what little self-respect remained. Now I lived in a flat where she owned everything, and sometimes I read disdain, or perhaps irony in Gaafar's glance. Like a fine silk thread stretched to its limits every vibration in the atmosphere affected my mood. Without Ruth's tact and sensitivity we would never have enjoyed so much happiness. I accepted her generosity because I knew that she loved me. She showed concern, expressed her emotions with total simplicity and relations between us were easy. Once when we were discussing our situation she asked me: "If matters were reversed, would you refuse to share everything you have with me?" It was a logic I found difficult to refute. And yet I could not rid myself of the feeling that after all there was a difference, since I was a man and she a woman. I could not abstract myself completely from what we are told is considered normal. Nor could I completely ignore Gaafar's looks.

So, I decided to say nothing more about my work. But I had overlooked how close we had become, almost like two bodies fused into one. During the day when we were both busy I would wait for the moment when we would be together again. I had lost everything else, and she filled my life. And to my astonishment she seemed to feel the same about me.

I rushed home when the day's work was over, usually to find that she had already arrived. She spent a lot of time reading the books and documents she had collected for her thesis. Sometimes she played back her taped interviews and we listened together. I learnt a lot from the way she worked, and we discussed many things, including the trade union movement in Egypt. She saw things differently, and with a critical sense that made me rethink some of my ideas. All this stimulated me to go back with redoubled energy to the study I had once despaired of ever completing. The only subject on which we continued to disagree was politics and so we avoided it whenever possible.

We were getting ready to sleep. I lay in bed on my back, watching her moving about the room on bare feet, waiting for the moment when I would feel her nestle close to me. I heard her suddenly say: "Khalil. There's something you're hiding, fighting against all the time. Some nights it keeps you awake, or spoils our moments of happiness. I can feel it and there's no sense in trying to hide it from me."

I was surprised and didn't answer immediately. It was useless to protest, she would know I was lying. I decided to be frank.

"The problem is my work. It's becoming almost impossible for me to continue with it. I can't stand it any longer."

She was obviously taken aback, and closing the dressing table drawer, came to sit on the bed, close to me.

"But why? What's happened?"

"Ever since I went back, I have been surrounded by an atmosphere of suspicion. People affect to be pleased to see me, but I know it's only pretence. I hate meeting people now. I run away from them and close the door on myself, so that they leave me alone."

"They pretend to be pleased because they've probably guessed someone higher up must have intervened to have you reinstated. Why bother yourself? If people are hypocrites, they deserve only to be despised."

"I don't like it. But that's not what's most important. Most people in the company think I'm an SSSPS agent, a spy."

She was suddenly deathly pale. Once again I felt her slipping away, following a path which only she knew. I had become a stranger. I lay wondering how she managed to be several personalities simultaneously. Then lost in my thoughts, I felt her return. She looked at me tenderly.

"Perhaps you are imagining things again?"

"No. I am sure. The rumours have not stopped since I returned. People say different things about me all the time. That I'm a relative of a high National Security official, or an undercover agent of the SSSPS who denounced his colleagues in a well-known political trial and was released from prison before he had completed his term, or that I agreed to co-operate with security in return for my job, or that I established relations with it recently because of the constant pressures they exerted on me. It's an organized campaign maintained by the company's security unit, although the directive itself has probably come from higher up. How can I work in an atmosphere like that?"

She looked profoundly disturbed; I noticed lines in her face for the first time. She put her hand on my shoulder, and pressed it as though consoling me. I turned and brushed her fingers with my lips.

"I didn't want to upset you. I had decided to say nothing but you asked me. And since we've opened the subject let me say that I feel you, too, are hiding something from me."

She compressed her lips and was silent. I patted her cheek gently and said: "Ruth. I'm sorry if I have made you worry again. I didn't realize it would affect you so much. Perhaps it's not as bad as I've made it sound. You know where feelings are concerned I tend to exaggerate. Let's talk of something else."

She abandoned herself to my arms like an unhappy child. We said nothing for some time, occupied with our thoughts. Then she murmured in my ear.

"Don't worry too much my darling. There are some things to which I am very sensitive, and one of them is you. I hate to see you suffering or unhappy. You're so careful and attentive to me, despite all your problems. I see now, that we must look for something else. But this time we must think things over carefully. And please leave emotional considerations aside. I have an idea. Are you ready to hear it now?"

"Yes, of course."

"Must you work with an Egyptian company? Why not try to get away from a situation which will always cause you problems because of your political past. There is growing co-operation here with foreign concerns, and in this area it is much easier for me to find work to suit you."

I was perplexed. The idea of working for a foreign company did not appeal to me. It had so many overtones for a person like myself. We had become prey to foreign companies recently. Like locusts they ate up everything for almost nothing in return. But I needed work. I also needed money. I wanted to travel, to see the world. These foreign companies had immense means at their disposal, and I could benefit from that. In an Egyptian company I would always be pushed into a corner, constantly harassed. Why not listen to her? After all, she could be right.

"What do you propose exactly?"

"My husband is the representative of a number of export-import pharmaceutical companies. You can work with him."

I looked at her speechless. How could I work with her husband? How could such an idea ever occur to her?

"Your husband?"

She laughed lightly at the look in my face.

"Oh . . . At heart you are still an oriental. Why not?"

"It's not a question of being Western or Oriental. How can I work with your husband while we are living together?"

"Are you against working with him, or is it our relationship which you do not approve of?"

I remained mute. I could see what she was driving at. She wanted to expose the contradiction, the hypocrisy of my position.

I heard her say: "If our relationship is immoral, then it remains so whether you work with my husband or not."

"But how can I face him, work with him, build up a relationship with him and then go to bed with you at night?!"

"What's the problem if he has no objection?"

"No objection?! Are you making fun of me Ruth, or are you serious? How could he not object to our being lovers?"

I felt a growing bewilderment. What was wrong with her? I'd never seen this side of her before. Her smile had been replaced by an expression of almost furious determination, as though confronted by something or somebody she hated.

"Don't worry about yourself." Her tone was ironical, even scornful. I felt a wave of dislike for her. Her voice was harsh, bitter, as though she had decided to wade to the end of something distasteful. "I have told him nothing about us so you're quite safe. You see, for years now, he and I have been living in a way which it is perhaps difficult for you to understand. Each of us has an independent life, despite the fact that we are married. I do what I please without telling him, and he does the same."

"But then why remain married?"

"That's a long story which I don't feel like telling you now. The time will come."

She wanted to remain his wife and enjoy herself with me!! Everything started to crumble again, to become meaningless. Rot was creeping into our lives. In what way did I differ from other people? I had abandoned my wife and son and spent my nights in the arms of this foreign woman. The corruption I saw everywhere had engulfed me. My conscience only stirred when I began to have pangs of jealousy. I remembered Amina. With her I had no doubts. She was upright and faithful. But this American woman — did she really love me, or was I just another conquest?

"You're beginning to doubt me aren't you? That's what happens. A woman is always suspect. I never interfered in your relationship with Amina. When you separated from her we started to live together. I hid nothing. I cried out from the rooftops 'here is the man I love'. I never asked you to hide, to come to me only after dark, and to slip away before daybreak. I decided to do everything to help us to be happy together, and to think of your needs before mine. And now you are jealous. Jealous of another man with whom I shared my bed. But your jealousy shows that you understand nothing; you don't understand that I love you, I no longer notice other men. The most beautiful thing that has ever happened to me is our relationship."

My heart was filled with regret. I put out my hand to her, but she sat like a stone, as if no longer capable of feeling. But a moment later she patted my hand.

"I can arrange the question of your work in a couple of weeks. I'll send a letter to Paris. If he answers positively, we can go there together. So . . . what do you say?"

I stared at her in wonder. Everything for her was so easy. With her I would go far. I saw myself flying high up in the plane, walking with her along the banks of the Seine, buying books, and flowers, and records, having lunch at a small café — wild duck, and cherries and pink champagne — then we'd make love!

I looked at her with admiration. My eyes said "Yes, yes Ruth, with you I'll go to the end of the world." Her face was once more that of the romantic young woman. She slipped under the sheets and murmured, "Khalil. Make love to me now, quickly."

We spent ten days in Paris and met Mr Harrison four times. A blonde man, very tall, very handsome. His white teeth shone in a frequent smile. His straight nose, his lips, his chin, his ears were all carved in perfect masculine lines, as though they had been programmed well in advance. His clothes bore the marks of a man whose favourite sport was horse-riding, with just that hint of negligence which is supposed to be a mark of real taste. While we talked he made notes with a fine silver pencil in a brown pocket notebook, and was accompanied by a secretary whom I surmised was his female counterpart, although she looked younger. Between them there was a silent language — a gesture of the hand, or a look, or a movement of the head — which she clearly understood. He invited us to dinner in a small restaurant on the East Bank facing the Notre Dame. When he entered, the head waiter rushed towards him, bowing and smiling and throughout the dinner discreetly hovered around. We said very little at first. Ruth answered his questions in monosyllables, and I contemplated the people sitting at the candle-lit tables, the movement of a hand, the flash of a bracelet or a tall stemmed glass, full of champagne. After the second course Mr Harrison started to ask me a series of questions which I couldn't avoid answering without being rude. His eyes were in shadow but when I answered, I could feel them weighing me up.

After dinner we went to a night club. I sat in silence with the secretary, and watched him dancing with Ruth. Their bodies moved with a smooth frenzy in the flicker of the coloured lights. He seemed to have an endless vitality prancing alternately with Ruth and his secretary while I sat there, feeling that compared to this man I had been badly prepared for life. He was so full of vitality, so tall, so confident, whereas I sat there on my chair barely of medium height, wearing spectacles with thick lenses and an old suit, carefully cleaned and pressed. I felt inadequate, unprepared to cope with this new life. The world to which I belonged was very different. But when we returned to our hotel and closed the door of our room, Ruth threw herself into my arms, saying "Together at last." I felt my confidence returning. With her arms around me she looked at me with a radiant face as though she had recovered someone infinitely precious. And suddenly I had an intuition that this new life would destroy what remained of me.

We spent the hours until dawn talking, isolated in a world of our own. She told me that her mother had given her the name, Ruth Artaja Gonzales. That she had never seen, or tried to find her father. Brought up in one of the Latin American emigrant districts of New York her mother did odd jobs, washing clothes, or helping in restaurants and bars — she had tried everything except prostitution.

She was deeply affected by this account of her life, which I guessed she had never told to anyone before. She went on, "And so, very early

I knew what it meant to be the illegitimate daughter of an emigrant mother in New York. Before I grew up all childish illusions were lost and I saw crude reality. My teeth and nails very soon grew sharp, but more important I understood that if I wanted to be independent I needed money, and that I must hide myself with armour so impenetrable that nothing could pierce it.

"In many ways we are similar. You want nothing but genuine emotion, a woman who will love you as you are. And I want a man who will love me as I am, who doesn't want to rule or simply take what he can."

At dawn she fell asleep, and I lay beside her wide awake, stroking her hair when she seemed disturbed, or took shelter in my arms from something in her dream.

I saw the sun rise between the buildings on the other side of the street, shining on the autumn leaves. Disengaging myself gently, I went to the bathroom and took a long, hot shower, watching the warm rivulets flow over my skin, wondering about the turn my life had taken, about the hotel room, and Paris, and the sleeping woman Ruth. When I returned to the bedroom she was lying on her back, looking at me. She smiled, and kissed my wet head, and the water that flowed down my neck, and I was lost in the world she offered.

We walked for hours in the gardens along the broad avenues and the banks of the Seine, wandering under the autumn trees, listening to the street musicians, to voices singing in a café, sat on the white cane chairs, drank red wine, gorged ourselves with snails, oysters, frogs' legs, and mountains of ice-cream. We danced in one another's arms as though alone in the world, yet filled with love for all creatures.

Before leaving Paris I settled the details of my future work with Mr Harrison. I became the sole commercial representative for the Arab countries in the export-import business which he largely controlled. My annual salary was to be $36,000, plus a car and running expenses, and a housing subsidy. If sales were above $2 million I would get a bonus which escalated with the increase in sales. The contract was for three years, with the first year probational. My main function was to market drug specialities produced by four American companies in the Arab countries of the Middle East "using all suitable means". I had $300,000 to establish an office, and $10,000 a year for "expenses". Any expenditure in excess would have to be sanctioned by Mr Harrison personally.

At first I did not fully realize the extent of the change in my life

which would result from my new functions, nor fully grasp the significance of the sums of money I would be handling. To me they were
figures and became concrete facts only later. Initially I had a feeling of
freedom, of being more master of my own situation than ever before, of
new possibilities, and too, a feeling of greater equality with Ruth. But
as time went by, other aspects began to strike me: it was difficult to
forget how I had got my new job. But for my relationship with Ruth
none of this would have happened. Her husband paid my salary. And
little by little I became aware that I was less free than it seemed. It was
clear that now there was no room for anything but a careful calculation
of expenditure and profits. Feelings, whims, principles, everything
had to be abandoned in an endeavour to capture the market; and Mr
Harrison would be monitoring how I acquitted myself. When I signed
the contract I realized that the large hands lying flat on the table were
ready to reach at my throat, and squeeze if necessary. Had such
reflections not occurred to Ruth? I wondered. Knowing Mr Harrison
so well such thoughts must have crossed her mind many times, but
perhaps it seemed to her that she could protect me from the more
unpleasant consequences. Having seen them together I wondered how
she had brought herself to marry him.

So the ten days in Paris were a time of great happiness, even though
sometimes marred by contradictory feelings. But it became clear that
Ruth shared few of her husband's attitudes; that she valued money
only for what it could buy and for the freedom it provided.

Time went quickly because we were so happy, and slowly because
so much was happening. We tried to forget that the day of departure
was approaching — but it caught up with us at last.

The taxi sped along the left bank of the Seine, we held hands and
watched bridges, trees, flower markets and book stalls fly past. Then
factories, fields, coloured hoardings, arrows, signs, doors with
numbers like a stadium. We stopped at the kerb, pulled out bags,
pushed trolleys, walked. Tickets, boarding cards, glass tunnels,
leather seats, passport control, a tunnel of steel and plastic, a clean
shaven man in uniform, an open bag-rack closing, a belt around the
waist, two seats, and her hand groping for mine.

I sat at the round breakfast table watching the river flowing below. The
silver cutlery glittered in the sunlight through the open window. I could
hear Ruth's voice wafted along the corridor. On a silver tray lay an
envelope, white, oblong, unstamped, I looked at the handwriting,

turned it over in my hands, opened it with a bronze paper knife, pulled out a single sheet of paper and read the few lines. Then folding the sheet of paper, put it back in the envelope, slipped it into my pocket, and leaning my head on the high back of the chair closed my eyes. The clock on the wall ticked out the seconds — like footsteps approaching.

Saïd Abou Karam

When I heard that, along with my three colleagues Mostapha Ramadan, Ali El Sharkawi and Hassan Eid, I had been dismissed, I was angry and depressed, for clearly the authorities had discovered what we had tried so hard to conceal. When the President of the Federation told me the news, Khalil's image, as he sat with us in the coffee house, flashed through my mind. I remembered his pallor and his silence. Was Khalil an informer? He had seemed uneasy, as if dogged by some inner conflict. Later I learned he had been absent during the strike — and after. Was this just a coincidence? Yet this seemed to confirm my doubts. But he and Amina had been such good friends. Worse still my three colleagues had to leave Helwan because they were unable to find work anywhere in the district. What we had built up together was so quickly destroyed, it would not be easy to develop a new leadership.

My spirits rose when I heard that Khalil had also been fired, because this confirmed that my suspicions about his loyalty were unfounded.

It soon became clear that I would not find work around Helwan so I decided to go to Aswan to look for work.

The day before leaving for Aswan I went to visit Khalil. As I walked up their street it seemed a long time since I had last traversed this familiar route.

They received me with open arms and we were soon talking away at a tremendous rate, interrupting each other, jumping from one thing to the other like excited children, joking and laughing with the warmth of old friends meeting after a long time. I held Esam in my arms and walked around remembering the happy moments spent in these rooms.

I lifted him in the air and he gurgled and chuckled with delight, and Khalil and Amina gazed at him as if he was the most marvellous creature in the world!

We sat around the kitchen table and I told them what had happened to me after the strike, books I had read and the vain quest for work.

I continued to talk of the lessons we had learnt from the strike, and how the success we had achieved was mainly because the workers had participated right from the beginning. How perhaps the only negative aspect had been our failure to protect the leadership before and after the strike, since nobody had stirred to defend those who had been fired. Khalil's expression suddenly changed and I realized that he had been struggling to hide how badly shaken he was by all that had happened. It was terrible, and I began to feel really guilty, for deep inside he could easily think I was, to a large extent, responsible for the serious harm he had suffered. I had encouraged him to step out of his corner and join in our struggle. Yet after all he was a mature man with long experience, and was fully responsible for the decisions he took concerning his life. There was no need for me to shoulder the blame because he was not strong enough to support the consequences of his actions. Life was like that. And yet somehow I could not completely absolve myself from the responsibility for what had happened. I had exerted some pressure on him and since he was sensitive he might have agreed to go along with what I suggested to avoid being thought a coward. For me the most important thing was the struggle and our interests as workers, and my zeal might have blinded me to the fact that he was in no condition to stand any more setbacks. But even if that were so, was it not true that in every struggle there were victims? But sacrifice was not necessarily an inseparable part of involvement in the trade union movement. When there were losses and penalties to be paid it was wrong simply to shrug. Amina's eyes rested on my face for a moment as though she had divined what was passing through my mind. Perhaps she too had been assailed by similar thoughts. She lived with him, and was aware of things nobody else would notice.

We talked of this and that for a while longer, and then it was time to leave. They accompanied me to the gate and I walked briskly down the street. At a bend in the road I stopped and turned round for a moment. They still stood in the garden. He had his arm round her shoulders and when I waved, they lifted Esam high up in the air so that I could see him, and waved back. I felt a catch in my throat, and a feeling that I and Khalil would never meet again.

174

I stayed some time in Aswan, delighting in the warmth of my family. My mother prepared my favourite foods, I ate fresh dates warm from the tree, talked with childhood friends. It was a wonderful oasis of peace for me but there was no work to be had there and my meagre savings were almost gone. Then one day the brother of a friend came to visit and talked of needing help in a workshop he had set up in Helwan. I eagerly asked him if he would accept me and his eyes lit up at the prospect of having someone from home working with him; and so it was agreed and I returned with him a few days later.

One day I wondered how Khalil and Amina and little Esam were keeping and decided to see for myself. And so the next evening I found myself walking out of Dar El Salam station. When I reached the beginning of the street, I glimpsed their house at a distance. Lights were shining into the night from the window, and I could hear strains of music. I approached and stood in front of the door. The noise inside was very loud, as though lots of people were running around. I could hear the sound of laughter, and the ringing voices of children. I pressed the door bell twice but nobody answered. So I held my finger on the bell. I heard Amina's voice call out on the inside. "Mahassin, Mahassin, the door bell's ringing. Please go and see who it is." After an instant it swung open, and I found myself staring at a middle aged, robust woman, who stared back at me with large brown eyes. She asked: "Who do you want?"

"Mr Khalil Mansour Khalil."

She looked flustered for a moment, then her features settled down as though she had found a solution.

"He's not here. Would you like me to call his wife? Who are you please?"

"I am Saïd Abou Karam, a friend of the family."

She disappeared inside. Through the open door I could see coloured paper decorations and balloons with "Happy Birthday" written on them. I could hear music, the sound of many feet running over the floor, chairs being moved, children shrieking and laughing. At last Amina came to the door; she was wearing a brightly coloured dress, and a garland of jasmine, and her face was flushed and her eyes shining. She exclaimed quickly: "Saïd, how nice to see you. Where have you been all this time? I'm so happy you came today. It's Esam's birthday." She dragged me in gently. "Some friends with their children are inside."

175

In the living room all the furniture had been taken out except for a long table against the wall, covered with plates of food and jugs of fruit juice. A group of men and women were talking and eating at the same time. Through the open windows I could see small children playing in the garden, chasing a shiny red ball and laughing. Esam, seated in a low chair, was waving his arms and following the game with obvious joy. I felt a hand on my arm and turned to find Amina, "Mango, guava, or orange juice?" she asked.

"Orange juice please."

She fetched me a glass of iced orange juice, and I said: "Where is Khalil?"

"He's not here at the moment."

"But it's Esam's birthday."

Her look clearly indicated that I shouldn't pursue my questions further. She said, "Are you in a hurry Saïd? I have to look after my guests, and the children haven't eaten yet. Why not wait until everybody has left, then maybe we can talk?"

I nodded in assent, so she left me to attend to her guests and I went into the garden, stepping carefully to avoid colliding with one of the children running around. I stood near Esam for a while before he noticed me and looked up with a smile. I squatted down beside him and talked to him, while he followed me with his eyes as if he understood what I was saying.

Around half past nine the last guest left the house and Amina dropped on the couch and said: "An exhausting, but wonderful day. I'll just take a quick look at Esam and come back."

She disappeared into the bedroom for a moment then returned and said "Do you want a cup of coffee?"

"No. Thanks. You must be dead tired. Perhaps it's better if I come another day."

"No, not at all. I am tired of standing all day. But now I can sit back and enjoy the calm." She smiled, "Did you notice how Esam has grown?"

"Yes. What a marvellous child. I sat with him in the garden. He followed what went on around him, smiling and waving his hands. Now and then he looked at me as though to say, "Do you see how I can enjoy myself on my own?"

She beamed with happiness, and sat silent for a long moment then turned to me and asked, "And you Saïd. How are things these days?"

"Not bad. But tell me. Where is Khalil?"

"He no longer lives here."

I looked at her in amazement and waited for her to continue.

"We've had a disagreement, and have separated. In fact we are divorced."

"Divorced! I can't believe what you are saying. You and Khalil divorced?"

"Yes."

I stared at her in disbelief.

"And if I ask you why, would you consider that poking my nose into what does not concern me?"

"No, Saïd. You have always been our friend."

"Then tell me what happened. I'm all mixed up, My head's going round and I doubt if it will stop until I understand what happened. But I don't want to cause you any pain. So if you prefer we can talk of something else . . ."

She cut me off.

"Why. I don't want to run away from things. We separated because Khalil is in love with another woman. I had felt a change in him for some time. Then one day I saw them together. When I asked him he didn't deny it."

"Khalil! In love with another woman! But what of the love between the two of you?"

She fell silent as though struggling for control and then looked at me with calm determination, but her voice shook a little when she spoke.

"Our love? I don't know Saïd. Sometimes I think it never existed, on his side at least. But when I think things over I say to myself that one shouldn't destroy everything. Our love did exist. Maybe a man can love two women, and perhaps women are the same. My reason tells me that I am not the only woman in the world who deserves to be loved by him, and that he's not necessarily the only man. But my emotions say no. It's not possible. I still love him. And love does not submit to reason."

I kept looking at her with amazement. I had never heard anyone say the things she was saying to me. Never had it occured to me that people could think this way. Now life had become so complicated that even the ground on which I stood seemed to be giving way.

"But you Amina how can you live like that without Khalil?"

"How can I live without Khalil? Do you think that all I care for is having a husband by my side. I'm still breathing you know, my body still moves, my mind still works. I still watch the sun set, and the blue sky from my roof. I still lose myself in painting. I loved Khalil but my love goes beyond him to other things, to Esam, my friends, my brushes and colours and frames. And maybe one day I'll meet another man. Of course I suffer, but that does not mean that life for me is over."

She fell silent, her eyes staring at something in the corner of the room, then turned to me and smiled, and I saw the Amina I had always known.

"My friend I don't think you came here expecting to be plunged into our family problems. The matter for me is settled, and there is nothing more I can say, or do. In time I will remember the good times and forget the bitterness. But now the bitterness is still here and prevents me sometimes from seeing things as I should." She stood up and went into the bedroom as though she had heard something, then came back. "I thought Esam had awakened. But tell me Saïd. You haven't said anything about yourself."

"I'm fine Amina. Everything's all right. I'll come and talk about me another day."

There were tears in her eyes, and I too felt like weeping. I took her hands in mine. We stood up and she accompanied me to the door. I walked out into the street and when I looked back I could see her tall silhouette against the lighted doorway. At the bend in the road I turned and waved, and somehow in the dark she saw me and waved back.

Khalil Mansour Khalil

I opened the folded letter and read it again.

> Dear Khalil,
> Perhaps you will be surprised to receive these lines from me, long years after circumstances separated us. But there is a matter of importance to you about which I would like to have an exchange of views. Please get in touch with me as soon as you get this note. A delay could lead to unpleasant consequences. I prefer that you contact me in the office.

178

My personal telephone number is 299731. I am always there from eight in the morning until four in the afternoon, and from eight to ten each evening.

Greetings till we meet,

Yehia El Saadani

I turned the sheet of paper face downwards. My heart thumped heavily. Yehia El Saadani. I had not seen him for over twenty years. The first time we met was in the Council of the Student's Union to which we had both been elected. We struck up a friendship very quickly. He was fond of the theatre and music, and played the lute beautifully. We were like twins, always together. Our interest in politics began when we were university students and we joined the left-wing party a short time later. But subsequently life took us along different ways and from the day of my arrest I had never seen him. I heard he had left to study in the States, and had specialized in criminal research. When he returned to Egypt he became one of the few experts in this field, and offered his services to several institutes. He had built up close relations with various United Nations organizations, and international institutes, as well as with the highest levels in the Ministry of National Security and the SSSPS. While in the States he married a young Boston girl, and they worked together now.

From the tenor of his note it was clear the matter was very important. "Please get in touch with me as soon as you get my note. Any delay could lead to unpleasant consequences." But for whom? He had not said. Maybe the matter concerned me less than it did other people? However, obviously I was involved. Perhaps he wanted to impress me with its urgency, and yet avoid causing me anxiety? He could have said: "Any delay could lead to unpleasant consequences for you." Why did he prefer that I meet him in the office? Was he trying to emphasize the official nature of this contact and avoid the implications of our old friendship. It was said that he now headed the planning and control unit of the SSSPS; that he had been promoted to the rank of Minister. Why would a man like that contact me?

I was filled with anxiety. Always I lived on the borderline between security and fear. But I shouldn't have anything to fear from Yehia El Saadani. He could not forget that once I saved him from certain catastrophe. Some months before my arrest I went to visit one of my party comrades. As I turned into the narrow lane where he lived, I saw him — handcuffed — surrounded by a group of secret police agents; a

179

grey van and three uniformed policemen stood by. His brief, impersonal glance in my direction signalled a warning. I turned casually into the nearest doorway, ran up the stairs to the second floor, pressed the bell and asked the pale faced, frightened girl who opened the door for a person I had hurriedly invented. She shook her head, said I must have the wrong address then quickly shut the door.

I descended the stairs slowly, paused in the doorway to light a cigarette and walked unhurriedly away. Once out of sight I began to run in the direction of the station, as though late for my train. Then I remembered that Yehia El Saadani kept a small printing press in his basement. I quickened my pace, ignoring cries of protest as I collided with pedestrians, or narrowly avoided a car. He was at home. We packed the press into two boxes, rushed out for a taxi and loaded both boxes on the luggage rack. I went in the taxi to my farm about thirty miles away, and helped by an old and trusted servant, buried the boxes behind the cattle sheds.

When we met in a coffee house a few days later he told me that the police had been and searched his house at dawn. But finding no evidence against him went away. We laughed until the tears streamed from our eyes. When we parted we embraced, and Yehia said, "I will never forget what you did for me Khalil."

I folded the letter and put it away, picked up the phone and dialled 299731, spoke briefly to Yehia and arranged to meet him the following day.

Everything in his office was new, modern, Western. The coloured telephones recorded messages, and functioned with a memory. There was an internal audiovisual circuit, and sound-proofed windows, doors and walls; the lighting was restful and carefully arranged. Behind his desk an electronically operated panel provided him with figures, bar charts and other information at the flick of a button.

He was sitting in a blue leather armchair reading a book, when I walked in. He rose to greet me and I noticed that he was now almost completely bald. He moved ponderously and looked at the world through gold rimmed spectacles; he had grown flabby. I tried to find something of my old friend in his face. The lines were familiar but the expression had gone. His voice alone had not lost its warmth.

He pressed a bell by his side, asked the young man in shirt sleeves and a tie over his open collar to bring us fruit juice and coffee.

We exchanged casual pleasantries until the refreshments arrived,

then he said, "Now, I think you know the lady called Ruth Harrison?"
For a moment I thought of denying what he had said, then realized that
I would only look ridiculous. He probably knew everything; besides, I
was living with her.

"Yes, I know her very well. Why?"

"Be patient my friend. Let me say right away that my aim in
meeting you is to pay back an old debt, or have you forgotten?"

"No. I haven't forgotten."

He paused momentarily as if remembering those early days, then
went on: "So you know Ruth Harrison and your relations with her are
close, very close?" He threw me a quick, ironic glance, and added. "Is
that not so?"

"Yes."

"And before you committed yourself to such a relationship did you
ask yourself who is this Ruth Harrison?"

"To tell the truth I didn't."

"Despite your experience? Love must really be blind!" He laughed
shortly and humourlessly.

I began to feel irritated; what right had he to speak to me like
this?

"No, it's not a matter of blindness. It's a question of feeling."

"In the age of electronics you still go by your feelings?"

"Yes. I still do."

He shrugged. "So be it. But I don't want to discuss your philosophy
of life, but to warn you about Ruth Harrison."

"Warn me?"

He looked at me straight in the face and said: "She works with an
intelligence agency."

My heart lurched, for a moment I could hardly breathe. I ran a
finger under my collar, easing it from my throat. He watched me
steadily. I said: "And what has that got to do with me?"

"What has that got to do with you? She's the woman you're in love
with, for whom you abandoned your wife and newly born child. You
live with her and then you ask me what this has to do with you?!"

Why was I saying such stupid things!

"I mean, I know nothing about it."

"But appearances are not on your side. In official circles people are
saying that she has recruited you."

The blood rushed to my head and then seemed to drain away; I
almost fainted. I sat without movement.

He gave me another searching look.

"Don't be so worried. With things as they are now, people at high levels will not be displeased by your position, quite the contrary. You are in perfect accord with present requirements, and are rendering signal services to a friendly country."

My voice emerged with difficulty.

"I am rendering services to no one; I have no inclination for roles of that kind. But are you sure of your information? Why are you telling me all this?"

He looked at me with an expression of long-suffering, like someone dealing with a dullard.

"My relations with you Khalil were cut short long ago, otherwise you would not ask such questions. My work gives me access to such information, and I am certain of its accuracy. As regards your second question my motives are clear. I think that this woman's behaviour will lead to catastrophe, that the relationship between you is becoming an increasing menace to a lot of very important things. A crucial factor that convinces me that the menace is real is certain aspects of your personality I know very well — especially your rashness, your readiness to do things before which other people would hesitate a long time. When we started receiving information about your relationship with her I knew that you probably had nothing to do with her undercover activities. You live openly with her, and have not tried to hide it. We kept a close watch on all your movements, and discovered the only activity with which you have any connection is the import and sale of pharmaceuticals. I realized you were unaware of what was going on around you, of the dangers lurking a few steps away. I said to myself: 'He doesn't know where he is being led. Once he saved me from arrest and perhaps many years of prison. It's time I repaid that debt'."

I stared at him. The memory of what I had done for him that day seemed to displease him. I suddenly felt that he hated me, that he wanted to humiliate me.

"I have been trying to persuade those responsible for Ruth Harrison's activities to move her elsewhere, but in vain. I do not understand why they are so insistent on her remaining in Egypt. Perhaps she is doing a particularly good job, or maybe it's her husband's influence. Of course everybody knows of your relationship with her. And yet they have systematically refused to take any action against her. Sometimes they are so conceited! Like little gods they cannot tolerate being told they are wrong." A note of hatred crept into his voice. "Perhaps her desire to remain in Cairo has something to do with you, although I doubt if a woman like her is capable of emotion." I felt sick inside. "So I thought that if what exists between you is ended, she might change her mind."

Ruth Harrison — how could she be part of this world? How could she sleep in my arms, give me her love? Could a person live two such completely different lives? Or was all the feeling she had shown me merely role-playing? How was it possible to believe in anything any more, to feel any future waiting for me once I stepped out of this room? I was seized with an overwhelming desire to escape from this man. But a moment later I was overcome by a terrible weariness, deprived of my will to live, ready to face death with indifference.

I walked out through the iron gate into the street watched by the eyes of security guards and secret police pretending to stare into space. I walked with slow steps over the pavement. What was I going to do now? I threaded my way through the crowds of people, the continuous flow of cars, buses and trams, my feet finding their way like those of a blind man.

I crossed Lazoughly Circle and walked down National Assembly Street. On either side, rows of trees, government buildings, police at every corner, crossing or gate, cold-eyed men in civilian clothes idled with apparent aimlessness. On the pavement, surrounded by small piles of printed papers squatted a young woman dressed in black, selling forms which could no longer be found on the post office racks. The black market extending its tentacles everywhere, greedily squeezing the arteries of life; underground forces operating all the time, harassing me at every step with short bayonets fixed to automatic rifles, with imported goods and foreign banks, with disco music and the call to prayer, veiled faces and naked breasts, police, spies, secret agents and traitors.

I walked along with a heart full of hate for the shining cars, the stupid children gazing from doorways, the women with white shoulders and flowing hair, the blue eyes which stared. I hated all complacent faces, people with bank deposits, smooth skins and red lips which lied. I hated treason spinning its webs around me, and above all I hated myself.

I walked along unseeing, harassed by the fences stretched along the Nile, the barriers around the President's house, the Israeli flag flying at full mast. My steps guided me to the terrace overlooking the expanses of sunlit water, to the easy chairs, and the rose-coloured wine. The porter greeted me with smiles. The watch dog eager for his pound of flesh. A cog in the system, a pimp and a spy and a thief like the rest of his kind. I put my key in the door, swung it open and walked in. Now it was Gaafar's turn to stare. Their eyes were everywhere. He was wearing his white jacket and black tie. Another of their men, smooth, efficient, well paid. My illusions were gone. Gone were the fumes in my head, the whisky, the dollars, the lust for white flesh.

Everything was clear. The observant eyes, and the elastic tread, another link in the chain, another thread in the web. As close to her as her shadow. Who knew what was their relationship? In my body burnt repulsion and desire, hatred and love, jealousy and vengeance and lust, things innocent and foul. Something awoke inside me like a giant or a devil, like a cunning animal waiting to pounce, endowed with a terrible strength, a capacity to face any danger, to manoeuvre, to be treacherous and cowardly. Now I was sure of everything, full of an awful certainty and now I doubted everything, was full of a terrible doubt. I was a man walking a familiar path at one moment, lost in the dark the next. I loved and trusted this woman completely, and I hated and doubted this female devil with each throb of my pulse. I was a drunken old man staggering up the stairs to die, and a daring hunter slipping barefooted through the forest with a knife. I was nothing and everything.

I knew she was sitting on the balcony waiting for me. Gaafar stood like a shadow. I looked at the furniture, the pictures, the sofa and armchairs where we had sat talking so often. A beautiful trap. I had walked into it with wide open eyes and willing feet. I could feel Gaafar's eyes watching me. Why had I come back? Why did I want to relive my own hell? Would it have not been better to run, to put the greatest distance possible between me and this place? I couldn't face her now, look into her eyes, and talk as if nothing had changed. The best thing was to take a hot bath. That would give me time to collect my thoughts, regain my composure.

"Gaafar, please inform Mistress Ruth I'm going to take a bath."

I went to the bathroom, locked the door behind me, filled the tub with hot water and slipped into it. After a while my body relaxed and the throbbing in my head gradually subsided. I gave myself time; I needed to confront her with a clear mind. I put on a cotton gallabeya and soft leather slippers. I felt like someone preparing for a duel,

184

walking with slow steps to the venue of encounter, out on to the terrace. She was leaning over the stone parapet absorbed in something on the other side of the river. It would be better not to mention my meeting with Yehia El Saadani. She had a sharp mind and would not be easily cornered. I needed to collect evidence she could not deny. My presence in the house with her would permit me to do that, if I watched carefully. This idea made me feel better. It postponed an immediate confrontation, and gave me more time to think and prepare for what was coming. She turned round. The tones of her beautiful voice rang out.

"Khalil, are you trying to make me miss you by keeping me waiting?! I sat here imagining you wallowing in the bath and was in half a mind to join you!" She laughed happily. I looked at her. It was as though I was seeing her for the first time. My body refused to respond to her and my mind kept its distance. A spy! I had been sleeping in the arms of a spy whispering to her that I loved her. I saw her honey-coloured eyes watching me tenderly.

"What's wrong Khalil? You seem strange. Has anything happened?" She eyed me anxiously.

"No, nothing has happened. It's just that I feel very tired, I don't know why, and I have a terrible headache."

She moved over to me. I felt her body touch me for a quick moment, put my hand on her shoulder and pushed her away gently. Her eyes seemed to cloud for a moment then clear. She returned slowly to lean over the stone parapet. Gaafar brought the coffee tray, put it on a small table and withdrew.

She came over and poured coffee and carried a cup to me. She asked quietly: "Where were you today?"

I was not prepared for her question, and didn't answer immediately.

"Visiting a friend in the High Council of Industrialization. I wanted to pick up some information about new government policies in pharmaceutical production."

She gave me an obscure smile. I continued to stare in front of me and sip my coffee.

"Did you get the information you were looking for?"

"Yes, but it's rather a long and boring story; I'm sure you wouldn't be interested."

She gave me a rapid glance and said: "Khalil, if you don't want to tell me what happened this morning, it's better to say nothing."

This woman was not going to be easy to manage. But now I knew where I stood. I no longer believed her. I had to be patient, move step by step, remove one mask after the other until she stood completely exposed. I wanted to put my fingers around her smooth neck and squeeze, to throw her to the ground and trample on her. I could imagine her crying out as I beat her. I fought hard to control my private turmoil.

Her eyes narrowed. Unless I was careful she would build up her defences, and I would never find out. The. game had to be played differently. I moved close to where she stood, and rested my lips on her bare shoulder for a long moment. She slipped into my arms with a quick movement.

I felt her body tremble, she whispered urgently, "Khalil, Khalil" and led me gently to the couch. Her body was at once burning and icy cold. She carried me away to a strange world of passion and despair.

After that night, our eyes met with a new understanding, as though each knew what the other was hiding. Her look seemed to say: "Now you know. Inside I am empty. So thrust in your fingers, I can no longer feel them tear. The rare relationship we had is over."

Yet still there were moments when I weakened, for I loved this woman, so versatile, so clever, full of limitless energy. I loved her honey-coloured eyes, and the proud way she carried her head.

I started searching for the evidence I needed. Something told me she knew, that deep down she wanted me to find what I was looking for. She used to leave me for long hours in the flat alone. She would send Gaafar home, then invent some excuse and go out. I wondered why she didn't hand over the evidence herself or discuss the matter openly, instead of prolonging this cruel game, which neither could win. Perhaps it was her training, or her pride that prevented her revealing her real activities. Or maybe a desperate clinging to the love that must die.

I began to comb patiently through everything in the flat. I searched with a kind of feverish calm. Nothing escaped me: chairs, tables, cupboards, beds; tablecloths, towels, carpets, mattresses, pillows, curtains. Everything was opened, examined, palpated, smelt, and replaced. I searched her clothes, underwear, bags, shoes; a piece of orange peel, a refuse bin, a cake of soap, a tube of cream, a jug of milk, a piece of cheese — nothing was innocent. I became a schizophrenic. Half my mind was working normally, and the other half never stopped its feverish search. I had to find what I sought, nothing could stop me now.

186

One evening I was sitting in the living room, Ruth was out, Gaafar had been sent home. The wide windows looked out on to the terrace. There was no movement in the air. All around a deep silence and the scent of jasmine. I was listening to a tape of Chopin's studies played by Artur Rubinstein in an attempt to calm myself. As one piece ended and, half under the spell of music, I waited for the next I heard, not the liquid silver of Chopin but a man's voice asking:

"What time is it now?"

A woman answered, "It's half past eleven."

"I'm tired. But you're leaving tomorrow, and we have to go over a few things."

"As you wish."

"Have you sent the latest report about the construction of nuclear power stations?"

"Yes, three weeks ago, through MWK 20."

"Good. What about the study concerning distribution of the Nile waters?"

"It's almost ready. I think it will reach you by 15 February."

"Don't go through the same intermediary. It's important to follow separate channels. Use ST 4531, and change codes."

"Will you send a copy to Axis Centre or do we just send one to you?"

It was Ruth and Mr Edward G. Harrison — her husband. Yehia El Saadani was right. But how had she forgotten to erase this tape? Recently her vitality had faded, she had become negligent about a lot of things, as though nothing mattered any more. She would sit for hours drinking whisky and staring at nothing. When I spoke to her it was as if I had called her back from far away, and she would focus her eyes on me like someone slowly waking from a deep sleep.

There was a long silence on the tape before the man answered.

"No, just send me a copy. I don't want it to go to Axis Centre without my comments. Keep a second copy until I send a cable to Ajax Cairo saying that I have received it, then destroy all copies. Meanwhile keep the original in the dead store. Give it to intermediary Star X."

"Is there anything else?"

"Yes. This question of Khalil."

There was another long silence, then he continued.

"You promised that by the time you came to Paris again the matter would have been settled. It's taken much too long. I've helped you to the best of my ability. I found him a job in my company as you requested.

He's still running about free as a bird. When will he be part of the set up?"

"Isn't it enough that sales have gone above two millions within the space of one year, since he has taken over the Arab market?"

"I'm not talking about that. You know what I'm driving at. He must be involved in our other business, so that we can make full use of him, and protect ourselves at the same time. And I suspect that you are delaying it as much as possible. In fact, I'm sure you are."

"You're mistaken. I don't have enough confidence in him to attempt such a step. He's changed a lot since his young days, but he still has an unsuitable temperament for this kind of work. Do you want us to face another catastrophe? Have you forgotten what happened with that professor in Turkey?"

"You're too unrealistic. I think he would make an excellent operator and do very good work. He's intelligent, attractive to both men and women," he emitted a short laugh, "and has a lot of information. His new work has widened the scope of his contacts. He has old friends with whom he can renew relations. The question is, how do we tackle him? And you, honey, have a rich experience in this area," he laughed again.

She said nothing; then he went on again.

"Look, let me be absolutely frank with you. I can't continue to defend you indefinitely. It's true you're one of our trusted people, and that you're doing what is perhaps the best job anybody has done so far in your post. I am sure that as far as you are concerned the problem is no more than a kind of naive romanticism. You still behave in these things like a young girl. You want to protect him, and keep him away from our kind of business. I've always found it difficult to understand you. We're living on top of the world. We have money, and are actively helping to shape events. But none of this moves you. What do you want? There's no way of leaving the business. Like all important but dangerous things in life — it's double-edged. Usually the edge is directed against others, but under certain circumstances it can turn. The Axis Centre has raised the matter with me again. They're beginning to accuse me of using my influence to shield you."

She answered almost tonelessly: "I promise that next time I will have settled the matter."

"All right, but this is your last chance. We are on the threshold of important events in Egypt and anything could happen. We must concentrate on the left, and here Khalil can play an important role."

There was a click, then silence followed by a whistling noise, and the music resumed. I waited until the tape ended, extracted it, put it in the inner pocket of my jacket, replaced its box, and then slipped a blank tape on to the machine. I felt strangely calm, as though I had arrived after a long and arduous race. Everything was now clear. The moment had come when we would have to face each other.

My mind now functioned with a cold hatred. With nothing more to lose, there was nothing more to fear. This woman had cheated me. And yet she had tried to shield me. Why? To protect the organization to which she belonged, or to save me from sharing her fate? To serve her interests and maintain the life she was leading, with its money and excitement, or to protect me from the dangers she knew so well? Her feeling for me could not have been only deceit, her words to me could not have been only lies. Surely I could not have been as mistaken as that? When I took her in my arms, and heard her say "I love you. You are my friend, my dear one, the only true love I have ever known," was she lying? Like a condemned man I clutched at shadows. There must be something I didn't yet know; I couldn't doubt everything. But how had she become a spy? I shivered at the word — I, Khalil Mansour Khalil was living with a spy! Her husband paid my salary and they had sat late into the night discussing my role. A wave of fury sent the blood to my head. I would kill her! Why not? Was it not she who had dragged me down? No, that was not true. I had walked into her flat with open eyes. Except for her maybe I would have become a spy myself. She had fought to keep me away. Like a whore protects her child. She was like us all, capable of touching the heights and grovelling in the depths.

I sat waiting for her. I heard her muffled steps on the carpet. She stopped in the doorway for a moment. Her face was drained of colour. She came closer, suddenly moving with assurance, sat down in the armchair, and flicked back her hair with a quick movement. Our eyes avoided each other, then slowly met.

I heard her say: "So now you know?"

"Yes."

She sighed, "Who told you?"

"Yehia El Saadani."

"He's been trying for a long time."

"Trying what?"

"To become my lover, and convince me that I should operate for him also."

I felt I was wading through a cesspool.

She asked: "Only Yehia El Saadani?"

"And from a tape I found here."

She frowned as though trying to remember. I said: "A taped conversation with your husband in Paris. You should have destroyed it."

She smiled. "When one is being destroyed oneself, the recording no longer matters."

I sat up straighter as though I wanted to be in a position where it would be easier to pass judgement on her.

"But I'm amazed. You admit everything so easily. During the last few weeks I felt that you were hoping I would find out."

She seemed to be thinking over what I had said. All this was unreal; here we sat talking about these things calmly as though it was the most natural thing in the world.

"It never occurred to me that way. But sometimes everything weighed on me so heavily I would say to myself 'If Khalil discovers it will be a relief'."

"And do you think that was a normal feeling?"

"Normal? Sometimes anything becomes normal."

"What do you mean?"

"I mean that I can no longer stand living this way." She stared out of the window then said dully, "It's better to die."

"You were the one who chose it."

"Yes."

"Then I don't understand."

She looked at me as though disappointed at what I had said.

"It's one of the times when I find things difficult to explain."

"Why?"

"Because this time you won't believe me although I have never been so truthful."

"I promise to believe you."

"You see, I love you Khalil."

Was she playing a game with me again? I hesitated.

"Ruth, I love you too. But in the last months I learnt to hate you."

"Why not? I hate myself. Have you never hated yourself?"

"Yes."

"When?"

"When I felt that I was no longer myself."

"Then you have had that experience?"

"Of course. I'm living it now."

190

"Why? Because you fell in love with me?"

I searched for a way to evade her question but she insisted.

"Say it Khalil, because you fell in love with me?"

"Perhaps. And for other reasons."

"What other reasons?"

"Everything. I have abandoned everything I believed in."

"And yet I would say that the greatest thing that happened to us is this love. Do you know what it may cost me?"

I was silent. She looked at me steadily and said: "They'll never forgive me. And yet I don't regret it. With you I knew what it is to be happy, and so I have to pay the price. Happiness is forbidden for people like me."

She stared at me unseeing.

"I grew up with the street urchins. Learnt how to fight the males with teeth, nails and even a knife. I became a commodity which could fetch a high price, a female for sale, an object of pleasure. White breasts, hips and belly. But my mind and heart were valueless — useless accessories. I soon learnt that I had been born a victim and that my only protection was money, because money rules over women and men. I used my beauty and sold myself to the highest bidder; the price was marriage. I used the means at my disposal to arm myself with new weapons, with education to get into the brain market. I gloried in the power of knowledge, independence, and a chance to give myself to what interested me. But of course I could not take all the time without giving in return. I thought my husband was just a business man, but after a year or two, he had to tell me that he was involved in high level intelligence work. And so suddenly I found myself transported to a very different world. When he suggested that I should work with him I didn't object. This was a new source of money and influence — a new and exciting life. I didn't stop to think that I would lose the independence I had fought for; that I should refuse to go along with him. On the contrary I threw myself enthusiastically into my new job. Looking back I find it difficult to understand myself . . ."

She shrugged and was silent, brooding. There was nothing I could say. I could only sit and watch. She knew she was surrounded on all sides. Even the love which had bound us was condemned. She had come full circle, and returned to where she had started; an illegitimate child caught in a net from which there was no escape. She had tried to cut a way for herself only to become more firmly entangled.

I could see she had taken a decision, I knew what it was, and that I

191

would try to dissuade her. But I also knew the battle was lost, and she would not retreat.

She looked at me and said: "Khalil. This is the last night before we part. I want you to do something for me, I will never ask you for anything again." She hesitated and her voice dropped. "I want you to hold me in your arms until morning. I will go to bed now and wait for you. But if you don't come I will never blame you."

After she had left I sat staring at nothing. I heard a slight scratch like the sound of someone softly striking a match. I looked around; the tape had come to an end. I took it out and put it with the first one in the inner pocket of my coat. I got up and went to undress, hung my coat in the wardrobe, put on a gallabeya, and went into the bathroom. I brushed my teeth, washed my face and hands and walked into her room. I stood for a moment watching her as she lay in bed with her eyes wide open, then I took off my slippers and stretched my body beside her. She didn't move. I put my arms around her and laid her head on my shoulder. Her hair smelt faintly of jasmine. I heard the sound of a car passing down the street.

There was a long silence before she asked "Tell me what will you do after we part?"

"I don't quite know yet. I have a friend who runs a private research laboratory. Maybe I'll work with him. Or I may go abroad."

"Where to?"

"To Morocco."

"Why Morocco?"

She went on asking me questions and I answered, our voices murmuring softly. Her hand rested quietly in mine, and her eyes looked at me in the dark. The night was clear and the stars glittered in the sky. After a time I heard her regular breathing close to my ear. Every now and then she would move restlessly and mutter a few words like a child. My eyes remained wide open. The hands of my watch pointed to three o'clock. My arm had become numb so I moved it gently from under her head. She nestled close up to me as though afraid I would slip away in the dark. The hours passed as we lay in one another's arms and the daylight started to creep through the open window.

Amina Tewfik

I sat in the garden breathing in the fresh morning air. Esam was making mud pies, and putting them in the sun to dry. Although he filled my life, sometimes I was lonely. I hadn't thought of marrying again but I needed someone to talk to, with whom I could exchange my feelings and thoughts. Khalil had become a bitter-sweet memory. But as the days went by I realized that despite the loneliness I was much better off than my married friends. I was free to do as I pleased, to have friends, to go out, and to do the things I liked. During this period I had a group of women friends and we would often meet in my house and talk about our lives and problems.

When the newspapers published the story of Khalil and Ruth Harrison it was a great shock. I never imagined that things would go that far, it brought back all the painful memories I thought I had forgotten. Some of the women in our little suburb would look at me with sympathy and understanding. But it seemed to me that the quick, side-long glances of the men were full of accusation — as though I was the cause of it all because I had insisted on severing our relations. I began to hate the atmosphere that seemed to surround me in the small suburb, and my resentment towards Khalil multiplied. But when the trial began, and week after week went by, I began to see things differently. I realized that a campaign of slander had been launched against him from the start; most of what they said was a tissue of lies. I could see that they were weaving a net around him. Despite all the evidence they tried to build up I was certain he had not committed any crime. I knew his weaknesses well, and that like all of us he could kill. But deep down I was convinced that Ruth Harrison had taken her own life. When I reached this conclusion I realized that my place was by his side, and that I must forget the past, at least until his trial was over.

So I started to attend the trial. Sometimes alone, sometimes I took Esam, because although Khalil had not asked me to take him I realized he longed to see him. Some time later when I asked why he had never said he would like to see the child he looked at me quietly and answered, "I don't know. Maybe because I feel I no longer have the right to ask you for anything or . . ." he hesitated for a long while "because I'm like a straw carried by the wind, bereft of my own will. And this prevents me from taking a position on anything, including asking for the simplest things. Perhaps it's despair, or the sensation of looking down on what's happening with indifference. And as you know," he smiled faintly, "extremes often meet."

When I try to remember details of the trial, or the people involved or even about Khalil himself, my memory fails. Like a half-remembered dream, its outlines dim, flickering, obscure. But like a half-remembered dream too, certain images emerge with startling clarity. Khalil, sitting on a wooden bench between two uniformed policemen, his shoulders drooping. Khalil, standing straight as an arrow, like someone freed of all hesitation, defying his fate. His words fell like hammer blows on the heads of the judges where they sat high up; their faces paled, the General National Prosecutor shrank in his seat and he wiped the sweat off his brow with a white handkerchief extracted from beneath his black robe. At times the silence was palpable.

It seemed that for Khalil what mattered was not Ruth Harrison, Yehia El Saadani, the police, and the judges and the General National Prosecutor, but a whole corrupt system that had to be exposed. Then I recognized the old Khalil whom I had known so well, and loved. He insisted on his innocence, repeated again and again that Ruth Harrison had put an end to her life in an act of desperation, and that at the time of his arrest, he was carrying two tapes in the inner pocket of his coat which would prove his innocence. He accused the SSSPS of hiding the tapes so that it would appear that he had shot Ruth Harrison. And when they asked what motive the SSSPS had for committing such a grave offence he said "to protect the intelligence network to which the deceased belonged, as well as her husband Edward G. Harrison, and the chauffeur Gaafar El Nimr."

I went to Esam where he squatted on the ground playing and put out my hand; he staggered up to me holding on to my finger. He looked up at me and smiled, and his smile reminded me of Khalil. I lifted him up and held him close as though protecting him from some hidden danger.

He stood in the box and lifted his arm above his head, but they pretended not to see. He shouted out loud. "I have something to say. The General National Prosecutor is asking for my head. Why has he abstained systematically from calling on Mr Edward G. Harrison, the husband of Ruth Harrison and the man who employed me in his company, to give evidence?" The Prosecutor crouched in his seat, eyed the accused almost with fear, then stood up, and with a voice which was barely audible said: "We asked the witness to appear before the court when he last came to Egypt, but he left the country without responding to our request. We sent a letter to his Embassy explaining the urgent need for his testimony, but so far we have received no answer."

"And Doctor Yehia El Saadani, head of the Special Unit in the Ministry of National Security? Why has he not attended as a witness for the defence?"

I heard voices in the hall shouting "Yes, Yes." The President of the court hit the rostrum with his hammer and threatened the audience that he would evacuate the hall if there were any further interruptions, then waited until there was complete silence before saying:

"The court has already refused the request of the accused that Doctor Yehia El Saadani, Chief Counsellor in the Ministry of National Security be called upon as a witness for the defence. The accused insists on portraying this whole trial as an attempt by the SSSPS to frame him in the murder of Ruth Harrison in order to protect a spy network operating in the country. He also accuses Doctor Yehia El Saadani of being fully aware of what is going on and conspiring to prevent it from coming to light during the trial. And since he has not been able to produce any evidence at all to prove the veracity of these serious accusations, we must insist on refusing such requests once more, and on his complying with the decision of the court."

On the day the court had fixed for pronouncing sentence Saïd and I went together. I remember Khalil entering, surrounded by policemen, then looking out through the iron bars of the witness box. I tried to pass him a cup of iced coffee but an officer curtly rebuffed me — contact with the prisoner was forbidden. Sometimes Khalil smiled at us and we cautiously smiled back.

When the judges had assembled and the Prosecutor taken his seat the court President put a file in front of him, opened it and started to read in a monotonous voice. He read on for a long time then suddenly stopped. He stood up and quickly went out followed by the judges and the Prosecutor. I looked around trying to find out what had happened. An officer went to the accused's box, Khalil stood up, his face pale in the midst of the black uniforms. The next moment he had disappeared, as though they had spirited him away. Saïd's dark complexion was ashen grey. I saw his lips moving but no sound came out. I asked him, "What did they say?" He spoke in a low whisper. I couldn't hear what he said. I leaned close to him, "What did you say Saïd for God's sake?" He looked at me in despair, "The bastards! They've condemned

195

him to death." Black clouds rushed up behind me and the world went black.

Esam stood staring at me with wide open eyes. I saw him drop his hand to the wet patch on the front of his pants. He smiled happily as though he had performed a feat. I lifted him up in the air over my head and heard him burst into gurgles of laughter. Mahassin leaned out of the window and I heard her call out with her strong voice.

Several months passed while his appeal was being examined. Now and again I visited him, and took him a home cooked meal. Sometimes Saïd accompanied me. We would talk quietly of different things and I'd remember the evenings we spent together at home. The newspapers wrote that his appeal had been refused and that his papers had been referred to the Mufti for final ratification. One of the weekly magazines reported that when the prison Director suggested he appeal to the President, he simply smiled and asked whether he could be allowed a parcel of books. After that when I visited him they allowed me to stay longer than usual, and the officer treated me with gentleness. I realized that the end was drawing near. When they shaved off his hair, my heart contracted and I struggled hard to keep back the tears. His eyes this time were very sad, and the sadness lingered even when we laughed at a joke. He spoke to me about his trial, told me everything that happened after we divorced. I listened without interrupting as though in a dream. I shall never forget his words and one day I will shout them from the roof tops, from the highest point of the city for everyone to hear.

I can see him now as he said, "Amina please forgive me for everything. In my heart I have nothing for you but respect and love. I do not want to say that all this was fate. For each of us is responsible for his actions. But in a land where oppression is the rule there is no escape. All that worries me now is how to face death. At times I feel strong, prepared to meet anything. But sometimes I feel panic clutch at my throat. I see the ropes curling around me like snakes, and I feel like shrieking at the top of my voice. 'I am innocent. I have committed no crime. Those who are hanging an innocent man should die'."

His eyes were dark and clouded. I shivered suddenly. Esam put out his hand to the box of sweets, took one out, undid the coloured wrapping, looked up with serious eyes and held it out to Khalil. When I looked into his eyes this time they were gentle and clear.

My eyes travelled round the garden. The flowers were in full bloom.

Sweet peas on the fence, jasmine climbing over the iron railing of the terrace. He was fond of the scent of flowers on a summer night. I stretched out my hand to Esam and just at that moment I heard someone call out "Amina", "Amina". Saïd was standing at the gate. I walked up to him.

"Saïd. Tell me . . ."

He held out a newspaper. On the front page, splashed in red it said:

"The Case of Ruth Harrison closed today. Khalil Mansour Khalil executed at dawn. The killer continued to say 'I am innocent'."

I let the paper fall at my feet. I stood as though I had lost my way then suddenly I started to weep, silently.

Epilogue

The Prosecutor

I stood looking in the mirror. There was a layer of dust on its surface. I told the servant girl repeatedly that there must not be a single speck of dust on this mirror, but it was like talking to the deaf. She used to treat me with respect — until the day she caught me eyeing her thighs when she was bending to wash the floor. As for my wife, the change in her attitude was even worse. When we first married she was an innocent girl, with powerful buttocks and a submissive voice. She never looked me in the face but kept her eyes to the ground. After years of marriage her voice never rose above a weak cry of protest when I was a bit rough. I never saw her undress, nor glimpsed her naked body even once. But recently she had changed. She had started to read the papers and magazines I brought to the house, and I had caught her with a book. I pretended not to notice but when she left the room I picked it up and found it was about the relations between men and women! I felt that some hidden danger had suddenly descended upon us, that the tranquillity of our home had been shattered. I cursed everything that brought the outside world into our lives, including Hamida El Shati, the woman who lived next door and worked in the Ministry of Social Affairs. Several times I had come upon her and my wife talking together — what about? Then there were these women's television series, and Women's Corner and probably many other things I hadn't even noticed. It's true these TV and radio programmes insist that a woman's place lies in the home, and on the importance of our traditional values but sometimes I think they draw women's attention to things they have never thought about before.

All these worries on top of everything else! Why? Why all these catastrophes at the same time? But perhaps what was happening in my home was quite common. Perhaps the only difference was that I kept my eyes open and let nothing escape my attention; otherwise things might break down, like everything else these days. I am often astonished how things are deteriorating despite all our rulers' efforts to bolster morale, and defend the values of our society. Only last week I was searching my son's pockets and found a packet of condoms — "Tops" — and a tube of sleeping pills! It wasn't the condoms — after all they were a protection against VD. I felt proud of the boy in a way, it was a proof of his virility. Besides it was part of the government's family planning programme, the mark of a good citizen. But those pills . . . What should I do? Speak to him? But I never spoke to him about anything except the need to attend to his studies, and spend less money. Now this mirror! Every morning before going to the Prosecutor's office or to court I stood and carefully examined myself in this mirror. My appearance was most important. I was the General National Prosecutor representing the government in one of the most important cases in Egypt's juridical history — the trial of Khalil Mansour Khalil for the murder of an American woman, Ruth Harrison. And there were finger marks as well as dust on the mirror! The world I had known seemed to be collapsing! The bald patch on my head was growing, and my lips were coarser than they should be . . . and there was my short stature . . . But these were minor problems, compared with the situation I was facing in this court case. I often remembered the proverb: "If man could tell the future, he might choose the present." For the truth is that I had left no stone unturned to be nominated for this case — little knowing what I was in for.

When the case was transferred to our office it sparked off a hidden struggle for the appointment of Chief Prosecutor, for it was considered the open door to a brilliant juridical career. The mass media's attention made it an event which captured the public's imagination. Even the international press reported the proceedings extensively. A beautiful American woman had been found dead in bed in her luxurious flat overlooking the Nile, with a bullet hole in her head. When the police arrived, they found an Egyptian man, Khalil Mansour Khalil, sitting near the bed with his eyes fixed on her as though she was the only thing in the world. The woman's black servant stood in the hall watching the policemen, secret agents, and first aid nurses who had burst into the flat after his telephone call. He refused to answer any questions, saying he would speak only in front of a magistrate.

I was determined to be appointed to this case. I ran around talking to people I thought would be useful. I searched my memory for all the connections I might use. Then one morning I suddenly remembered Yehia El Saadani. We had been colleagues during our postgraduate studies and later met in Paris where he was working for UNESCO. After I returned to Egypt we did not meet again for many years. But when he was appointed Chief Counsellor in the Ministry of National Security and head of the Planning and Control Unit of the SSSPS I was one of the first people to visit him in his new office and congratulate him. And when there was a festival or a religious occasion I always paid him a courtesy visit, for he had become the second man after the Minister, and had connections at the highest levels. I decided to go and see him.

Despite his busy schedule he accorded me half an hour of his time to discuss the matter I had come for. When he eventually said, "I think you are the man we need in this trial." I nodded gratefully. "But as we are friends, I feel I should draw your attention to some of its aspects with which I am familiar as the head of the ministerial SSSPS unit."

Was he looking for excuses to refuse my request? But he went on, "I know your capabilities and consider you as particularly well fitted to assume this responsibility." I nodded again, but he ignored me. "As long as you are prepared to accept all the consequences, and conduct the case along the lines laid down by government policies, there should be no problem."

"But of course. That is my duty. And I have never failed in my duties as a government official."

"Good. Then we are in agreement. I will speak to the Minister about you today. However, as you know, the final decision rests with the Minister of Justice and Public Morals, and perhaps even with a higher authority than him," his lips twisted into a smile, "but there should be no problem where you are concerned."

Four days later he telephoned me and said that I had been chosen as Prosecutor in the case of Ruth Harrison as it had come to be known. I was overwhelmed with delight. On my way home I bought five of the best Chilian Black water melons, seven kilos of veal, and four kilos of lamb, then I bought two bottles of Remy Martin and drove back with the feeling that I was about to achieve great things.

But as the case proceeded my euphoria evaporated. I was afraid and felt inexplicably . . . guilty! Sometimes my mind became confused and it seemed that it was I who sat in the prisoner's dock. I even started to dream about it, and would waken bathed in sweat, shrieking soundlessly. My hands had started to tremble, and this morning I had cut myself badly while shaving.

I looked at my wristwatch: only nine o'clock; the sessions started at half past ten so I had plenty of time. I sat down in the armchair. I felt exhausted already. If I could only tell someone about the things I was carrying inside me. Even my wife. But that was impossible. They had to remain secret; not only because they were dangerous, Leila could not be trusted. But the real problem was that I had become involved in a horrible crime, and the criminal was not Khalil Mansour Khalil, but me myself. Even those closest to me would turn against me if I told them the details of this case. Never, even in a nightmare, did I think that one day I would fall into a trap like this. I am an ordinary man, even good-hearted in a way. I made my way up by hard work and sweat, and a total obedience to my superiors. I never wanted to harm anybody. On the contrary, sometimes if I felt that a person I was prosecuting might be innocent, I would intentionally leave gaps so that the judges could find a way out. Of course, in a political case I always fought to get a condemnation. Deep in my heart I was sorry for people who went to jail. And when I had to ask for capital punishment, I'd spend one or two sleepless nights.

I remembered the first day of this case, Khalil Mansour Khalil was sitting in the box, waiting. I started to examine him, partly out of curiosity, but also in an attempt to feel what kind of a person he was, since a prosecutor must understand those he has to deal with. I had met him several times during the inquest, and now I wanted to assess how he would behave during the trial, for court proceedings are very much like a duel, with the accused or his defence as the antagonists. Once our eyes met, and for a long moment I held his gaze. His look was so tranquil, it seemed to say: "I have paid my debts to all parties. I have settled accounts with my conscience and with God. And now I owe nothing. So you can do whatever you like. Nothing will touch me any more. I am out of your grasp."

I looked away and felt suddenly depressed. All that night, I kept turning over in bed unable to sleep; strange thoughts ran through my head. This man was innocent and I had accepted the role of the instrument which would take his life. The big question in this trial right from the start was: "Did Ruth Harrison commit suicide or did Khalil Mansour Khalil shoot her in the head with her own revolver?" At that time I had not yet made up my mind, but a number of things began to disturb me. There was the SSSPS's attitude of open bias; they had made unusual efforts to mobilise as many witnesses against him as possible. They investigated his past with an admirable thoroughness and discovered that he had once been in love with a young woman called Tahani Rashid. They put her name on the list, but on the day she was to be questioned she didn't turn up. Some days later the Director General informed me that she had left for Kuwait to join her husband. He sounded very annoyed as though he attached a lot of importance to her testimony and felt that she had managed to escape. I knew the case was important, but the extraordinary zeal with which they went about trying to prove his guilt caught my attention. I said to myself that after all it was natural in view of the victim. She was American, and seemed to have relations with important circles. She was also a woman and her death had been publicised very widely. For a moment I wondered if she had been a part of an intelligence network, for these days such things were quite plausible. But I immediately brushed this aside; the case was complicated enough already. Besides, it could be highly dangerous to start poking my nose in these areas. In any case it would have no bearing on the way I was conducting the investigation. At least that's how it seemed to me.

I spent most of the time in court carrying out a detailed interrogation of the accused. I tried to understand the way his mind worked, but failed. All his answers were extremely simple. He told me the whole story from the moment he met Ruth Harrison until he opened the door of her room and found her dead, in a straightforward way free of irrelevancies. He didn't seem to be hiding anything and spoke quite openly of their relationship. He described how they travelled to Paris together to meet Mr Harrison, the contract he signed and his functions. He also explained the circumstances under which he lost his previous post in the Thebes Pharmaceutical Company. He answered all my questions without hesitation and never said anything contradictory, so that at the beginning I thought that this structure must be prefabricated. But as the days went by and he came and went I realized that such a thought was absurd. He could not possibly tell his story with such clarity unless it was truthful.

Sometimes I questioned him until very late at night; I'd shoot a series of questions at him one after the other, try to make him lose his calm or contradict himself, but nothing shook the assurance with which he answered. Not only did he seem to have infinite patience, but an unlimited capacity to withstand strain. I wondered how he made what seemed to me a superhuman effort to answer all my questions, say the same things over and over again, parry the blows I aimed at him without once showing signs of fatigue or irritation. I myself would return home drained of energy, my legs almost giving way and my head like an empty shell. I realized that his stamina wasn't simply a matter of inheritance or training, but mainly the result of his psychological state. He seemed to have reached such an extreme of suffering that he no longer cared what happened. The supreme indifference of a person who has touched the nadir of human experience. But sometimes all this seemed pure nonsense, and he seemed just a hardened criminal able to exercise complete control over his reactions and emotions. Then I felt better, more easy with the role I was playing, and my questions would follow one another like the lashes of a whip. And yet his steadfast gaze never faltered. He seemed to be telling me, "All your attempts will fail. I have transcended the areas of feeling and pain. You can no longer reach me, so don't try."

Yes, he was in love with Ruth and she had loved him. The night preceding her death they had decided to part. They spent the night together in her room, and in the morning he woke before her, packed his bags and put them in the hall. He had finished his breakfast when suddenly he heard what sounded like a muffled shot. He rushed to the bedroom, opened the door to find her lying on the bed. Over her ear was a hole oozing blood and in her hand a revolver. He took hold of her wrist but could feel no pulse. When he turned round he found the servant Gaafar standing in the doorway. He asked him to call the emergency police. After a little while the police force arrived. They arrested him and Gaafar. He heard nothing about Gaafar after that. I asked him if the cause of her suicide could have been their decision to separate. He said it might be one factor, but the most important motive lay elsewhere, and would be clarified probably at some later stage. In this connection he mentioned two tapes he had in his coat pocket when the secret police arrested him; they had searched him and taken them away. He asked me to request their inclusion in the material evidence. He added that Gaafar would probably corroborate his version of what had happened. I asked him how it was that they had slept the night together despite their decision to separate the next day. He looked at me with surprise and asked: "Why not? We still loved one another." How could a man and a woman quarrel, decide to separate and then sleep in one another's arms? I didn't quite understand him. He seemed a strange man. I have never met anyone like him. Sometimes I felt he was trying to lead me astray, or pretend to be noble and high-minded whereas he was no more than a criminal. There had always been some woman in his life. Tahani Rashid, Amina Tewfik his wife, then this American woman . . . maybe there were others. Why was he so attractive to women? He looked quite ordinary, neither short nor tall, rather thin, and wearing glasses. I don't need glasses, my eyesight is perfect. And yet there was always some woman who fell for him, and they were all attractive and that despite his years in prison, and his difficult circumstances. There was a secret behind this, something abnormal in his sexual life. Women, especially foreign women, like

206

men who are not normal. They have strange appetites. I hated him! his composure, and the steadfast look in his eyes. His type should be eradicated. Besides, he was a communist and even an agent, engaged in subversive activities. He wanted to destroy everything we believed in, sap the morality on which we based our society.

Yet sometimes, that he was a criminal seemed absurd. I should remember to find out what had happened to the tapes he kept talking about, which he said would prove his innocence. And Gaafar . . . I would send for him tomorrow. The tapes were probably in the SSSPS's possession — if they existed. Yet why should he invent this story, since if the tapes did not exist it wouldn't help him?

Khalil Mansour Khalil's insistence that at the time of his arrest he was carrying two tapes was one of the main things which drew my attention to some of the abnormal aspects in this case. I remember writing "Ask about the tapes after questioning the witnesses" in my notebook. Then I phoned the liaison officer appointed by the SSSPS and asked him to bring Gaafar for questioning on Saturday morning. It was a Thursday around one o'clock. I was preparing to relax over the weekend, but by then I had begun to feel nervous, and found it increasingly difficult to put the case out of my mind. They seemed so keen on maintaining an undivided control on everything. Hardly a legal way of doing things! I was beginning to ask myself more and more questions. I had no objection to co-operating with them. What really annoyed me was that they had not confided in me, nor sought my advice, as though they considered certain aspects of the case outside my area of competence. After all, I was the General National Prosecutor and this way of dealing with things was deeply humiliating, and made me feel that those at the top didn't trust me.

But perhaps I was exaggerating. This wasn't the first time the SSSPS had exerted pressures, or interfered directly in juridical matters. I had worked with them for years and we always co-operated closely. There was no sense in being too much of a stickler. The important thing was to arrive at the truth. One had to be realistic! Nevertheless there were times when I felt deeply humiliated, they seemed to consider me of no consequence. And then where was the sanctity of the law? Where was the traditional independence of our magistrature, and the role of the General National Prosecutor?

They made their presence felt all the time; moving in and out of my office, lurking around the witnesses and the accused. When I suggested that Khalil be moved from the Citadel to another prison, they refused, saying it was important to keep him under constant supervision, because they were afraid something might happen to him. From the way they answered me it was clear they considered the matter closed. Whenever they spoke about Ruth Harrison it was always as the victim. This surprised me, since the evidence seemed to indicate suicide. But they were apparently in no doubt that she had been murdered. They kept doing it all the time, and soon, unconsciously, I found myself using the same term. When I realized my mistake, I corrected it immediately, for it is inadmissible for a member of the magistrature to assume the culpability of the accused before this has been proved. True, the Prosecutor's role makes it difficult for him to be neutral, but he should always try to arrive at the truth, without prejudice. This is very difficult, especially for the General National Prosecutor, as usually he is involved in cases of social or political significance. The state expects him to defend the system against its adversaries, and against any criticism against it. So how can one be neutral? I began to suspect that the authorities were keen on proving that Khalil Mansour Khalil had murdered Ruth Harrison and were doing all they could to ensure that the court would arrive at this conclusion. I know that anyone who belongs to the left is a dangerous enemy of Islam, of the family, and of the moral values on which our society is built. This is not the first time that I have had to deal with such people. Yet I have often had mixed feelings where they are concerned. I'don't like them, but they are quite unlike seasoned criminals. They tend to defend their ideas with an almost naive enthusiasm, and as a result end up with a heavy sentence, but they stand hardship with amazing fortitude.

Anyhow, I never let myself be carried away by such considerations — they are really no concern of mine. Nevertheless I feel that the law should be respected, and it bothers me to see how it is treated. Systems and rulers can survive only if there is a minimum respect for legality, and legal provisions. But what is happening to the laws these days? Sometimes I feel I am participating in crude farce, or a dream from which I will soon awake. Throughout my life, even in my student days, I kept away from politics. Of course I have my views, which I sometimes express to an intimate few, or discuss with my parents-in-law. They hold me in high esteem, and treat me with the respect due to a highly placed government official. What they don't know is that these days no one has any real standing, not even a minister. Ministers are appointed and dismissed with a snap of the fingers. My in-laws put me in my rightful place, but when I enter the Minister's room I feel totally insignificant and overcome by depression.

But left wing politics — all this talk about equality, and the rights of workers and peasants doesn't impress me. I am of the right wing, but I believe in a legitimate right wing, and the first condition for this is respect for the constitution and the law, and for freedom of speech and thought. That's what the government professes too, but what's happening? We are living in the twentieth century and yet our rulers still think it necessary to promulgate laws which limit the right to form parties, and pursue people for their opinions in the name of morality, and concentrate power in the hands of one man to use as he sees fit. Of course I never say this to anyone, but there are days when I wonder where we're going. Sometimes I think to own a sandwich barrow is better than to be a Prosecutor General.

This case harasses me day and night, and the faces of those I have questioned keep flashing through my mind. That man Gaafar . . . I dream of him all the time. The moment he entered my room with his cat-like tread I said to myself, "Here is a man who could kill in cold blood." His face was expressionless, as though carved in black rock; his eyes were unnaturally cold, but wide awake. He thought over my questions carefully before answering. He seemed to feel his way with his body and his senses, wide awake to everything, tense yet relaxed, like a wild cat. His answers were couched in terms that conveyed what he was aiming at, and yet were just sufficiently ambiguous to make it difficult to pin him down. He seemed to be patiently weaving a web around Khalil Mansour Khalil, insinuating that he had murdered Ruth Harrison, but without saying it outright. He had not seen him holding the gun, but had seen him at the moment he walked quickly down the corridor to her room. And when did he hear the sound which resembled a muffled explosion, after Khalil had reached her room, or before he got up from the table? I could see his eyes unblinking and cold, staring into mine. "If I remember well it was after he went to her room." "But his fingerprints were not on the gun." His lips twisted slightly in a smile, "People don't leave their fingerprints on guns these days." Then he added. "I do not want to accuse an innocent man, but is it impossible to think that he might have used her gun?" He lapsed into silence leaving me with the thought. After a little while in answer to other questions he started to enumerate the virtues of his former mistress: "She was wonderful . . . generous, courteous . . . found work for Khalil . . . did her best to make life easy for him . . ." Everything he said appeared quite logical, but what most occupied my thoughts was the cold determination with which he emphasized certain points, which could mean only that the accused was a wilful murderer. He could have expressed himself differently, been a little more hesitant about when he heard the sound of the gunshot. He knew quite well that this was a crucial point. And there was his remark about the absence of fingerprints on the gun. He was no ordinary witness; he seemed to be trying to lead me to a particular conclusion.

The man should have been kept in custody. But I had agreed to his release after a telephone call from the Director of the SSSPS suggesting there was no need to keep him, since it was clear that he had nothing to do with Ruth Harrison's death. This intercession so soon after I had been appointed to the case had struck me at the time as being rather strange. But habit is strong and for years I had been accustomed to receiving different requests from the security people. The Director said he was convinced that Gaafar was not involved in the "murder of this woman" (sic) especially as Khalil himself had dismissed any suggestion of his involvement. Legally speaking I was perfectly authorized to set him free, since there was nothing against him. And yet, when I asked what had happened to the flat he said that Mr Harrison had arrived immediately after his wife's death and proposed to stay until the case was over, and that he, Gaafar, was also there, carrying out his duties. The realisation that this could permit some kind of an agreement between them in preparation for future interrogations left me uneasy. Mr Harrison would hardly be devoid of motives to make things worse for Khalil; jealousy, or a desire to avenge himself for his wife's death. But I could not understand how he could employ a man in his company whom he knew to be his wife's lover. In the West, men seemed to attach little importance to their own dignity and feelings, unlike we men in the East. If Leila behaved like that I would kill her! What was happening to me? I, the General National Prosecutor, thinking of killing my wife!

For several weeks I remained totally absorbed by the case. Yehia El Saadani phoned once and asked how I was faring. He said nothing about the case, nor did he ask any questions. I interrogated all the witnesses produced by the SSSPS very thoroughly. These included the Chairman of the Thebes Pharmaceutical Company, the Director of Administration, the two secretaries who had worked with Khalil, the people working in the plant's security unit and several other employees, his ex-wife Amina Tewfik, his friend Saïd Abou Karam, the porter of the building where Ruth Harrison had lived and a number of SSSPS officers, since one of the matters raised in the inquest was his past political activities. They produced reports indicating that he had belonged to the radical left and was a member of the clandestine party, as well as a dangerous Moscow agent who had been condemned to five years hard labour.

As the case progressed, it began to take on a highly political character, especially as the woman was a citizen of the United States with influential connections in academic and other circles. These aspects did not trouble me unduly but I felt that in their zeal the security authorities were beginning to overstep the limits, and make such a big fuss that people might begin to feel the case had been mounted to serve the aims of certain government policies. There were moments when all these pressures accumulated and I felt on the verge of collapse, my health suffered. But how could I be Prosecutor in a case like this and avoid worrying? If only I didn't have to go to this trial every day. I heard the voice of the radio announcer in the adjoining room, and jumped up. To be late at a time like this could be misconstrued. Leila was standing in the hall, she looked at me out of the corner of her eye and said: "When will you be back?" I answered angrily that I didn't know, it depended on the President of the court not on me.

I walked down the stairs; the lift had been out of order for three days and nobody cared. Why had she asked me what time I was coming home? This was something new. I must remember to buy half a kilo of aniseed, it had a much better effect on my nerves than tea. Life was becoming more and more complicated. How could one be sure of anything?

I climbed into the car and sat in the right-hand corner as usual. A government car was a boon these days, and Hag Amin was an excellent driver. True, he stole a good deal of petrol every week. But who didn't steal? In any case the government paid. Things were no longer under control and everybody was out to make as much as he could. There were rumours about a Cabinet change, and people said my name had been mentioned among others as Vice Minister for Justice and Public Morals. They were probably satisfied with my performance in this case. I only hoped it would be over soon. There were moments when my conscience gave me quite a lot of trouble. But eventually I had suppressed my qualms, and accepted the situation. It had not been easy. The price seemed pretty high. I was involved in what was tantamount to a crime.

A criminal: What could I do? To sacrifice my post after all these years would be stupid. Besides, that man Khalil Mansour Khalil could easily be a murderer. Violence ran in the veins of every communist. By being reasonable I had saved my own skin.

But after finishing with the witnesses I suddenly remembered I had forgotten the most important of all, one who could probably tell us a lot about the relationship between the accused and the woman Ruth, namely her husband Edward G. Harrison. How had this fact escaped my notice? And why had his name been omitted from the SSSPS list, although relatively minor people had been included. Could they too have forgotten to include him? An unlikely coincidence. This omission from the list of witnesses gave me a clue; I realized that the authorities had not included him for their own reasons. I tried to pretend to myself that it was not important. But then, supposing some time later things changed, and an enquiry was opened into the case, the first questions asked might be: Why had Mr Harrison not been asked to give testimony? How had the General Prosecutor omitted to call such a vital witness? What would my answer be? I put out a trembling hand and lifted the phone and spoke to the liaison officer, saying it was absolutely essential to interrogate Mr Harrison. There was a short silence before he explained that in order to do so he must inform his superiors. Then he replaced his receiver. I was furious. How dare an officer of minor rank permit himself to cut short the General Prosecutor! That was what we had come to. People who were just nothing now rode roughshod over those with talent and brains. We lived in a country run by black marketeers, brokers and watch dogs, so such effrontery was quite normal!

I waited several days for an answer. Nobody got in touch with me, and I wasn't sure what to do. I could send a courier directly to the witness and ask him to come to my office. But that would be acting like someone who was living in a world of his own making. I would be defying certain forces that were in control. On the other hand if they left me without an answer it meant I had failed to protect myself against future eventualities. The only solution was to put it down in black and white. That way I would have proof of the action I had taken, if I was ever asked why I had not called upon Mr Harrison to testify.

The following day I send a confidential letter by special courier to the Minister of Justice and Public Morals. Then I began to regret my rashness. Would it not have been better to have spoken to the Minister before making the matter official? This case was making me lose my balance. There were so many undercurrents and secrets, and matters affecting influential circles that it was difficult to chart a way through. The nationality of the woman, and the political past of the accused were further complications. But I had begun to feel that the matter went even beyond all this, that there was something that everybody wanted to keep hidden, and I was becoming aware of a deepening atmosphere of silence and conspiracy.

I spent the whole of Friday at home, alone in my study reading the newspapers and watching television. At rest in this familiar room I felt relaxed and forgot the worry and tension of the past weeks. I had always imagined that once I had reached the higher levels of authority life would become easier, I would reap the fruits of my hard work, and be able to enjoy a period of relative security. But what had happened was just the opposite.

The following day, as soon as I arrived at my office my secretary informed me that Doctor Yehia El Saadani had left a message asking me to call on him in the Ministry at half past three. I suspected that this had something to do with the letter I had sent to the Minister. I also suspected that the courteous terms in which the secretary had couched the message were not those used by Yehia El Saadani, who, under his smooth and polite surface, hid the soul of an executioner.

I hated Yehia El Saadani. My anger kept mounting, but deep fear was gradually taking the upper hand. Why had I run after this case with so much zeal? It had caused me nothing but trouble, right from the beginning. I ordered a glass of hot aniseed and quickly swallowed two Valium tablets. Gradually I was invaded by a pleasant feeling, and life seemed easier. But I was unable to concentrate on anything for the rest of the day, and sat there waiting for my appointment. By the time it was three o'clock the effect of the Valium and aniseed had worn off.

At exactly twenty minutes past three I sat down in an armchair in the outer waiting room. It was almost a quarter to four before the door opened and El Saadani's assistant appeared, dressed as usual in shirt sleeves and a tie. He stood there for a moment examining me with expressionless eyes, then silently gestured me to go in. Yehia El Saadani was sitting at his desk, wearing a pink, open-necked shirt. His powerful arms, covered in black hair, rested on the desk and his stumpy fingers held a pen as he leant over writing on a white sheet of paper in complete absorption. He continued to write rapidly as though he hadn't noticed my entry. His assistant pointed to a corner. I walked over and sat in one of the soft leather chairs. In front of me was a long, low table, with a cigarette box of almond wood ornamented in pearl, a silver platter of sweets, and a small, black tape recorder, all placed together as if in preparation for whoever was coming. I was hungry but refrained from touching the sweets, which seemed to be imported, since I had not seen anything like them in the shops.

At last he lifted his head and looked across the room. His eyes seemed to lie some distance behind his round glasses, like pieces of lead. He stood up, and came over to me. We shook hands and he said: "Please excuse me if I kept you waiting. There were important matters I had to finish first."

I muttered a few words indicating that no apology was needed. We sat down. He sat opposite me examining my face as though trying to discern if any change had occurred there since we had last met. Then suddenly he sprang a question at me.

"When you sent your letter to the Minister of Justice and Public Morals asking that Mr Harrison be interrogated as one of the witnesses in the case of Khalil Mansour Khalil, did you not realise that it could be taken as an indication of your inability to assess the situation appropriately?"

I thought this over for a moment before responding.

"As you know, Excellency, I am a man of law. This case is probably the most important I have had to deal with in all my legal career. How can I overlook essential aspects, and leave gaps which might later place me in a difficult position? I could not omit to send for Mr Harrison. He is not only the husband of the deceased but also knew of Khalil's relationship with his wife, met him in Paris, and appointed him to his company."

"I am not discussing the legal aspects of the case."

"But that is my sole responsibility. I am not involved in any other of its aspects."

"When a man becomes the General National Prosecutor, and enters the higher levels of the magistrature his responsibilities ramify and become much more complicated. Your essential task is to defend and preserve the higher interests of the state, its reputation, and its relationship with friendly nations. And I am sure that you know full well who our friends are these days."

"Yes, of course."

"And know that both Mr Harrison and his deceased wife are not only citizens of the United States but people of uncommonly high

214

standing. He is a business man with influential connections, and she was a brilliant and respected member of her country's academic community and a person with a solid scientific reputation."

"I am of course familiar with these facts. But is it not my duty to find out exactly what happened in this case? For there is a very big difference between concluding that Ruth Harrison ended her life by committing suicide, and considering that she was murdered in cold blood by Khalil Mansour Khalil. If the first assumption proves to be correct he will be set free. But if it is the second, there will be no escape from the gallows for him."

"And do you still think that he did not murder Ruth Harrison?"

I was completely taken aback. How could he be so sure this woman had been murdered? I knew now that this was the conclusion for which the SSSPS had fought right from the beginning. But Yehia El Saadani was quite a different proposition. If that was his view then it meant much more. It meant that the very limited ruling circle right at the top considered Khalil guilty of murder, for Yehia El Saadani was known to reflect its views.

"I did not ask you to come here today to discuss the niceties of the law, or for that matter anything legal. For, as you know, I have no legal background myself, nor have I ever had any relationship with the magistrature. It is also not my intention to tell you what I think you should do. My only desire is to ensure that you are fully informed about all the aspects of this case. Then it is up to you to take any decision you may see fit. You are of course familiar with the fact that Khalil Mansour Khalil, on three different occasions during the interrogation said that at the time of his arrest he was in possession of two recorded tapes which he handed over to one of the responsible officers of the SSSPS, a man by the name of Abdel Hadi Nigm."

How was it possible for him to have such detailed information about what had gone on during the interrogation? It was perfectly true that Khalil had spoken of the tapes on three occasions. I nodded my head silently. He stood up and walked over to a small black safe embedded in the wall. He fiddled with it for a moment before it swung open. He put his hand inside, extracted something, and came back after closing it carefully. He glanced at me and said: "You shall listen to the tapes, if you're interested of course." He smiled faintly, "But since it will take some time, let me first ask what you would like to drink? We have everything including whisky." He smiled again.

"Thank you. A glass of orange juice and a cup of coffee without sugar."

He pressed a bell beside him and a blue uniformed messenger came in. "Ismail. Bring one glass of orange juice, and one glass of Indian mango juice, two cups of coffee without sugar, and a jug of iced water."

I stared at the tapes with the sensation of someone who is about to witness a magic ritual. I realized that soon the secrets hidden in the two tapes would be revealed. He got up from his seat and made a few phone calls, speaking in a voice too low for me to hear. The messenger boy knocked and came in with a tray which he placed on a nearby table and withdrew silently. Yehia El Saadani said: "Now we can begin."

He put a tape on the reel and closed the lid. I heard it go "tic" and jumped in my seat as though somebody had plunged a needle into me. For a moment there was no sound at all, then came a man's voice speaking in English and a woman answering.

He stopped the tape, rewound it, then turned to me: "I want you to follow closely everything that is said on these tapes. The first is the recording of a conversation between Mr Harrison and the deceased in Paris. I know this fact from Mr Harrison himself. He visited my office and listened to it. He wanted to take it with him, and I promised to hand it over when I no longer needed it. The second is a discussion in Arabic between Khalil Mansour Khalil and Ruth Harrison, probably on the eve of her death. It is full of interesting things for a man like you who is enamoured of unusual cases." He pressed the play button again and I leant forward ready to absorb every word.

I don't remember how long it was before we came to the end. I felt myself plunged into a strange dream. The tape recorder went round and round. I was a pair of huge ears sucking up the words and letting them fall into the depths of my mind, then locking them in like the secrets of the dead.

Suddenly there was a silence in the room. I sat on unable to move. I turned to the man who sat a few paces away, looking at me with a cold curiosity.

I stood up unsteadily, holding onto the back of the chair. My steps faltered as I walked. He accompanied me to the door. I felt his icy fingers close around my hand, and then he said: "Ah, there is something I forgot to tell you. Gaafar, the servant, has been working with them in this intelligence net for years, even before Ruth Harrison arrived. They included him in the facilities for work accorded to her when she arrived to take up her post. He had been used before to get inside information from the houses of important people."

As I walked down the long corridor I could still see his grin.

I looked out of the car window. We were approaching the main entrance of the court. The car purred to a stop at the bottom of the marble steps. A porter dashed forward, opened the door, and cried out in a loud voice. "A good morning to you, Your Excellency." I walked up the stairs with a dignified step. I felt people stopping to look at me. My legs seemed to have grown weaker and to bend a little under me. I straightened myself up, and continued to climb. At the top of the steps, a group of journalists were talking and laughing. They gathered around me, and I could see from the way they looked at me that to them I was an important man. I felt stronger, looked at them smilingly and said: "No statements today. The trial is nearing its end and from now on the proceedings must not be the object of comments in the press." There was a chorus of protesting voices. "Anything Your Excellency. Public opinion is merciless and has a right to know. Information is the essence of democracy. After the careful study you have made of this case, would you say that Khalil Mansour Khalil was an agent of Moscow?" I thought for a moment then said. "Without a doubt. There is more than one proof of his intimate relations with the Soviets." They pulled out pads and pens and quickly wrote down what I had said, while I continued on my way.

I liked sitting high up on the rostrum and looking down on the people gathered below. Here I felt above the level of others, in the place I had earned after years of effort. My worries melted away, and I would listen to my voice as it echoed in the hall, see the prisoners in the dock shrink into their clothes. I was a warrior wielding a sword in defence of the law, and everything that upheld society and its moral code. I was a giant among dwarfs.

I remember how, on the first day of the trial, I felt like someone who had reached the top of a high mountain and could see all around him as far as the distant horizon. But as the days went by it was as though I had started to fall. Nobody else realized this, but perhaps Leila sensed a change. Once she looked at me with an expression of fear, but now I noticed a new defiance, even a hint of scorn. And yet there was no reason for this since she knew nothing about the details of the case. However, one evening while we were eating our dinner, in complete silence, as was often the case nowadays, I remained plunged in my thoughts, she suddenly asked: "This man who is being tried, did he

217

really murder that American woman?" I was taken aback by her question and didn't know how to answer, which is unusual, since with her I have always been in the habit of answering whatever she said in a tone that brooks no discussion. I muttered something unintelligible under my breath, and told her that as my wife she was not supposed to interfere in my work, especially as I held responsibilities of a very important and sensitive nature. She lapsed into silence again, but from that day I noticed that the expression in her eyes underwent a change. And shortly after that, when I had complained to her about the dusty mirror — not for the first time — she had simply shrugged and said, "Why don't you get a cloth and polish it yourself?" I was deeply shocked and hurt by this, despite the marks of respect with which I was surrounded elsewhere. I felt I had lost my worth, fallen from my rightful place.

Now when I sit up on the rostrum my body seems to shrink. The eyes of the accused stare at me from the box, and follow me wherever I go. Most of the time when he looks at the three judges sitting in their high-backed chairs, and at me in particular, I read in them a quiet irony. At moments it changes into a sudden anger as though he is saying: "You are hypocrites and liars. You are assassins." Then my eyes look elsewhere, or I begin to doodle meaningless circles, squares and stars, but one day I found myself drawing a gallows. I looked around me quickly to make sure no one had noticed, tore up the paper and put the pieces into my pocket. My fingers touched a small packet. I felt it carefully and realized that it contained small chunks of local chewing gum. I had bought them for Leila and forgotten to give them to her. These days my memory had become bad and my health was getting worse. Last week I had even failed to have an erection when Leila and I embraced. This case was going to be the end of me.

I could see his former wife Amina Tewfik sitting close to the box. Despite the way he had treated her she still attended the sessions regularly. During the recess she would sit talking to him quietly. An unusual woman. I had never met anyone quite like her. He and she were a special kind of people. One day when I interrogated her she looked at me boldly for a long moment and said: "At certain moments anybody can kill, including you yourself Mr Prosecutor. Nevertheless, I know Khalil well and I am sure that he did not kill this woman. She must have committed suicide." I was at a loss how to answer her, and remained silent. This was perhaps the first time during an interrogation that I was not completely in control of the situation. She seemed to be so powerful, so confident of herself. There was a kind of decisiveness about her that disturbed me deeply. There was nothing soft and womanly about her and I wondered how any man in his right senses could accept her as a wife. Perhaps that was why he had run away from her, and thrown himself into another woman's arms. And yet, when she looked at me sometimes I felt a sudden attraction. It would take me unawares and then I would forget the question I was preparing to ask her. I realized she could be extremely feminine. She kept her eyes fixed on me while I busied myself with some papers, then asked the next question, and heard her voice echo with its characteristic richness. "I was in love with Khalil at one time, but that is all over. Nevertheless I cannot let him down, especially now. I also have to consider Esam my son. When he grows up I must be able to help him understand what happened to his father. I don't want him to feel shame, but to be strong and confident."

Saïd Abou Karam, his friend, defended him obstinately throughout my interrogation. Even the Chairman of the company spoke of him as a gifted person, and a man respected by colleagues and subordinates.

I sat watching him. Amina lifted her son high in the air, and I heard the child's laughter as he stretched out his hand and touched his father's face through the iron bars. Something pierced my heart, painful and sharp. How could I face my life after the trial was over? Now that I knew the truth, life would be no more than a nightmare, and each day spent in my office a torture.

He pulled a packet from his pocket and extracted a long cigarette. He sat down on the bench and one of the policemen lit if for him. He blew out a thin cloud of smoke, then turned in my direction. His eyes looked right into mine, carried with them an accusation. "You are an assassin. You know I am innocent. Can you ever be at peace with yourself again? Can you ever face yourself in the mirror again?"